D0281677

Good G

100 240 878 1

Sheffield Hallam
University

WITHDRAWN

To the 'P's in my life

Good Girls Make Good Wives

Guidance for Girls in Victorian Fiction

Judith Rowbotham

Basil Blackwell

WL
823.8
RO
SHEFFIELD CITY POLYTECHNIC LIBRARY
CITY COLLEGIATE CRESCENT

Copyright © Judith Rowbotham 1989

First published 1989

Basil Blackwell Ltd
108 Cowley Road, Oxford, OX4 1JF, UK

Basil Blackwell Inc.
432 Park Avenue South, Suite 1503
New York, NY 10016, USA

All rights reserved. Except for the quotation of short passages for the purposes of criticism and review, no part of this publication may be reproduced, stored in a retrieval system, or transmitted, in any form or by any means, electronic, mechanical, photocopying, recording or otherwise, without the prior permission of the publisher.

Except in the United States of America, this book is sold subject to the condition that it shall not, by way of trade or otherwise, be lent, re-sold, hired out, or otherwise circulated without the publisher's prior consent in any form of binding or cover other than that in which it is published and without a similar condition including this condition being imposed on the subsequent purchaser.

British Library Cataloguing in Publication Data
A CIP record for this book is available from the British Library.

Library of Congress Cataloging in Publication Data

Rowbotham, Judith.
  Good girls make good wives: guidance for girls in Victorian fiction/Judith Rowbotham.
      p.   cm.
  Bibliography: p.
  Includes index.
  ISBN 0–631–16395–6 — ISBN 0–631–16396–4 (pbk.)
  1. English fiction—19th century—History and criticism.
  2. Girls—Great Britain—Books and reading—History—19th century.
  3. Feminism and literature—Great Britain—History—19th century.
  4. Women and Literature—Great Britain—History—19th century.
  5. Young adult fiction, English—History and criticism.
  6. Didactic fiction, English—History and criticism.
  7. Middle classes in literature.
  8. Marriage in literature.
  9. Sexrole in literature.
  I. Title.
PR878.G57R6   1989
823'.8'0992827—dc19   89–30185
                                                                    CIP

Typeset in 11 on 12pt Baskerville by
Wearside Tradespools, Fulwell, Sunderland
Printed in Great Britain by
TJ Press Ltd., Padstow, Cornwall

Contents

Preface

This study is based on a long interest in collecting Victorian fiction and periodicals, which, during the course of research and teaching in other areas of history, I became convinced had a value for the historian. It is not intended primarily as a study of women's history, though I certainly hope it makes a contribution to the work undertaken by so many other notable historians working in this field. Much has had to be omitted, and in particular, consideration of the didactic fiction aimed at the working-class adolescent girl. That is worthy of an entire and separate study in its own right, rather than trying to fit into a study primarily aimed at surveying changing middle-class attitudes through the channel of the fiction aimed at the young girls of their own class. The focus in both cases can be similar, but the class considerations, in particular, and the expectations of what was fitting for a working-class girl are very different, and thus it seemed better to concentrate, this time, on the middle-class fiction.

I am indebted to a large number of people for help and encouragement over the number of years in which this book has been brewing. I must thank the staff of the British Library and the Institute of Historical Research in London for their help. Booksellers throughout Norfolk, including the proprietor of Scientific Anglian and the auctioneers at Nigel Hedges Ltd, have helped me to acquire further volumes, drawn on for this study, and my debt to the Reverend David Hunter for his assiduous work in seeking out fresh tomes for me on the least provocation is also great. I have given preliminary seminars on topics included in the book to seminars at the Institute of Historical Research, and am most grateful to the various members for their helpful comments and criticisms over the years. In addition I must thank my friends and colleages, in the Institute and the School of Oriental and African Studies, for their help and encouragement, particularly Dr Sue Martin, Dr

Gervase Clarence-Smith, Ms Maryjayne Hillman, Mrs Joan Ridgwell, Professor F.M.L. Thompson and his wife, Anne, Amanda Sackur and Jean la Fontaine. It is impossible to list further the other colleagues and friends, in and out of the historical world, who have been of assistance in various ways, but I must mention also my flat-mate Dr Maria Dowling who kindly read and corrected drafts of chapters for me, and has been a constant source of support in the project. Dr Robert Preston listened to me working out my theories during train journeys to and from London, and George Nianias indulged his leanings towards eighteenth-century patronage. Rosemary and Terry Rix have been a fount of invaluable advice and criticism, particularly over the knotty question of title and exclamation marks in my work! Finally my family. My aunts, Sybille Higginson and Pamela Canavan, have given me practical help and moral support, my sisters, their sympathy. My mother and father have put up with me collecting the books in the first place, and then read, corrected and collated my own work, and given me whisky and immoral support. I can only thank them, for without them this book would never have been started, let alone finished.

List of Plates

Acknowledgements

Plates 7 and 9 are reproduced by kind permission of the Bodleian Library, Oxford. All other plates were kindly supplied by the author.

Abbreviations

RTS   Religious Tract Society

SPCK   Society for the Promotion of Christian Knowledge

Introduction
A Good Dose of Jam:
Girls' Fiction, 1840–1905

For he who'd make his fellow, fellow, fellow creatures wise
Must always gild the philosophic pill . . .[1]

The use of literature as an historical source poses considerable problems for the historian. Attempts to approach a particular period through contemporary literature can be superficially attractive in a number of ways. As a number of scholars have pointed out, however, the creation of an essentially fictional world depends on an essentially emotional reaction by the reader channelled through the images and language employed by a particular author.[2] Charles Dickens, for instance, hoped to create a sense of moral indignation in his audience with books like *Our Mutual Friend*, and thus to assume that this tale can be used as a basis for a scholarly assessment of Victorian London is likely to lead to considerable ambiguity.[3]

Yet despite these drawbacks and reservations, it is possible to work out an approach which will permit a constructive use by the historian of certain literary sources. The nineteenth century saw the creation of a tradition that saw childhood, including adolescence, as a state set aside from that of the adult, in important mental as well as physical ways. The child was considered, in particular, to be both initially innocent and far more malleable than the adult. Stemming from this, education of young minds became a matter of increasing concern and

[1] W.S. Gilbert, *The Yeomen of the Guard*, Act I.
[2] See for instance, Mark Naidis, 'G.A. Henty's Ideal of India', *Victorian Studies*, VIII, autumn, 1974, pp. 49–58; Louis James, 'Tom Brown's Imperialist Sons', *Victorian Studies*, XVIII, autumn, 1973, pp. 89–98.
[3] Charles Dickens, *Our Mutual Friend* (Chapman and Hall, London, 1865).

study.[4] The child was the father of the man, and it was important to adults to ensure that children, who represented the next generation, should be properly taught. The question that occupied many minds, however, was of what did a 'proper' education consist? In an England profoundly affected by industrial and social change this was by no means either obvious or universally agreed. By the 1840s, the middle classes had established themselves as a major force both economically and socially, with the power to make their ideas and opinions felt in a variety of ways; and one area in which majority middle-class opinion had a deep interest was that of education. The middle classes believed that education of the young was a significant focus for change, and that therefore, training of English youth was one way in which they could ensure that their supremacy remained.[5]

The middle classes promoted a system of education with a considerable degree of common consent amongst members, based on distinct class and gender divisions. While there was considerable interest in the education of the working masses, there was equal concern to ensure the correct teaching of the children of their own class. Literacy levels were a major concern in working out an educational strategy in the case of the former, but in general it was taken for granted that the offspring of the middle ranks of society would be literate. Thus educational strategies for middle-class children could be based on the printed word to a very considerable extent.[6]

Didactic writing was no new phenomenon. Books, of educational, usually moral, guidance aimed at the young, were a feature also of the eighteenth century.[7] They were, however, intended more for an upper-class market and were frequently written in the form of essays or polemics on a particular moral point rather than as books where morals gave point to a particular storyline. At the start of the nineteenth century Maria Edgeworth achieved considerable popularity and social status through the production of stories for young minds that,

[4] Philippe Ariès, *Centuries of Childhood* (Jonathan Cape, London, 1962).

[5] Ibid., Peter Coveney, *The Image of Childhood* (Penguin, Harmondsworth, 1967).

[6] F.K. Prochaska, Women and Philanthropy in Nineteenth-Century England (Oxford University Press, Oxford, 1980).

[7] Ibid.

while being improving, were also entertaining. By the 1840s such tales were still popular, and much read by middle-class children, along with more recent stories by writers such as Mrs Sherwood and Catherine Sinclair.[8]

The reading matter available to middle-class children was, certainly by careful parents, strictly controlled, especially for girls, in order to ensure that impressionable young minds received only the correct and highest of impressions. Considerable stress was laid on the supposed impact of the printed work, partly due to adult experience of its usefulness and effectiveness. For instance, the notion of using works of fiction as guides to adult behaviour was well-established amongst the aspiring middle classes of early nineteenth-century England. The 'silver fork' novels of the first decades of the century had proved invaluable to the *nouveau riche* as Alison Adburgham has commented:

> The novels were handbooks to the language of the beau monde, to the etiquette of chaperonage, to permissible and impermissible flirtations, to extra-marital affairs, to all modish attitudes and affectations.[9]

It should not thus be seen as surprising it was presumed by adults that carefully written and chosen didactic fiction could be used as a means of social control for children. It was thought that stories could have the effect of painlessly leading the youthful readers to the paths that adult society wished them to follow to ensure that the next generation would maintain the values and traditions of its parents and teachers.

Another factor which encouraged an increasing use of the printed word for didactic purposes was the vast new potential that had opened up by the second half of the century in the field of printing, as a result of technological advances.[10] This

---

[8] For example: *Instructions for a Young Lady in Every Sphere and Period of Life* (A. Donaldson, Edinburgh, 1773); *The Polite Lady; or a Course of Female Education. In a Series of Letters from a Mother to Her Daughter*, 2nd edn (Newberry & Carnan, London, 1769). Also, Maria Edgeworth, *Moral Tales for Young People*, 3 vols (J. Johnson, London, 1802); Mrs Sherwood, *The History of the Fairchild Family* (J. Hatchard, London, 1818–47).

[9] Alison Adburgham, *Silver Fork Society: Fashionable Life and Literature from 1814 to 1840* (Constable, London, 1983), pp. 1–2.

[10] Improvements in printing presses, distribution etc. See R.C. Terry, *Victorian Popular Fiction 1860–1880* (Macmillan, London, 1983), chs 1–3.

began to lead to the production of large numbers of books on cheaper paper at relatively low cost, with a consequent impact on the availability of moderately-priced books after the 1850s. The bulk of it was written for the 'middle classes'; in effect those whose income permitted them to buy books, and whose avocations left time to read them. There was a smaller amount of fiction intended specifically for the 'upper classes', though it is often difficult to identify such works with certainty as they frequently blur with that intended for the middle classes. (One major feature of this upper-class fiction is that it tended to be less overtly didactic and more coded in its language and approach, presuming both a readership 'in the know' and one in less need of reinforcing information.)

The quantity of fiction intended for the 'lower' or 'working classes' increased from the 1840s, being either of the penny-dreadful and penny family magazine character or written by the morally well-intentioned; be they members of a higher social status or merely spiritually superior members of the same orders. The amount of fiction written for the working classes never, however, outstripped the amount produced for the middle ranks, if only because much of that intended for the middle orders was thought to contain messages also suitable for those lower ranks.

These printing developments encouraged in particular the production of increasing numbers of works aimed at the juvenile market. The production of stories for this market became a profitable field economically and, in theory, spiritually. Increasing time was spent by adult society on its merits and demerits. For instance, observers came to believe that works like Miss Edgeworth's *Moral Tales* made the moral object rather too plain both for enjoyable reading and effective assimilation by the young. Realization of this by authors such as Charlotte M. Yonge and by the buyers of books, from parents to teachers, encouraged the development of a new literary style.[11]

A style of fiction was developed where the intention was to give an illusion of reality through the setting of the story in order to give 'verisimilitude to an otherwise bald and unconvincing narrative' – or to put it more bluntly, to coat the powder

[11] Charlotte M. Yonge, 'Children's Literature in the Last Century', *Macmillan's Magazine*, XX, May–Oct. 1869, pp. 448–56.

of the moral in the jam of a good narrative.[12] In order to increase both realism and digestability, these stories were carefully aimed at specific age, class and gender targets. The fiction written for adolescent boys, i.e. those over the ages of 11 or 12 up to manhood, in terms of earning a living, is well-known. Yet in contemporary terms its output was at least matched by the production of novels aimed at an adolescent female market, one covering the years from puberty to marriage or confirmed spinsterhood. While it is rare to find a story that does not to modern eyes, and probably to contemporary juvenile eyes, make its moral or message plain, most authors claimed that they did not write 'goody' books. Instead, they claimed to write stories that would act as guides, influencing children in the ways in which they should think and act for the rest of their lives.[13]

The wide availability and renown of books in this genre, particularly those written for boys, and their reputed influence on readers, have tempted observers to seek ways of using them as historical sources. However, scholars like Josephine Bratton have pointed out the pitfalls and problems of trying to approach this field through an attempt at assessment of the impact of this fictional genre on the minds of the readership. Nor does sufficient good quantitative evidence exist for the size of the readership, though publishers' records and the income of the authors working in this genre does indicate a considerable market for these works.[14] However, approaching certain areas of the genre, at least, from a different viewpoint can, when allied with the work of other social historians, justify the use of this didactic fiction to reach certain conclusions about conventional attitudes during a particular period.

Nineteenth-century society saw itself in gender as well as class terms. Men and women occupied different and separate, if complementary spheres. Men were by nature suited to operate in the public sphere, the active and aggressive world of politics,

[12] W.S. Gilbert, *The Mikado* (1885) Act II; Georgina Battiscombe, *Charlotte Mary Yonge: The Story of an Uneventful Life* (Constable, London, 1943), p. 68.

[13] Authorial prefaces frequently contained this assurance, e.g. L.T. Meade, *Four on an Island: A Story of Adventure* (Chambers, Edinburgh, 1892).

[14] J.S. Bratton, *The Impact of Victorian Children's Fiction* (Croom Helm, London, 1981). pp. 31–62; Agnes Blackie, *Blackie and Son: A Short History of the Firm 1809–1959* (Blackie, Glasgow, 1959).

the military services and commerce, for instance, where they could use their capacity for logical thought to best effect. Women, by contrast, were naturally formed to occupy the more passive, private sphere of the household and home where their inborn emotional talents would serve them best. It was on this basis that the nineteenth century invented the tradition that it was the women who were the 'natural' guardians of morality and standards, and the teachers of these to the next generation. There was an inherent contradiction in this 'traditional' view of women, that while they were the natural upholders of moral standards for society, they could, if not properly guarded by men and protected from the contaminations of the public sphere, also be the frailer sex morally as well as physically. Women were both angels and prostitutes, and any temptation to fall from grace must be prevented.

Those authors writing for the middle-class adolescent girls' market were very consciously using their work to convey messages of contemporary and to some extent, personal concern. Charlotte Yonge, for instance, viewed herself in authoral terms as 'a sort of instrument for popularising church views'. Certainly the writers of this genre of fiction believed that they did have a marked effect on their readership.[15] Moreover, adult contemporaries seem to have accepted this interpretation of their impact. Firms of publishers from Blackie and Sons to James Nisbet and John F. Shaw, as well as the specifically religious houses like the Religious Tract Society and the Society for Christian Knowledge, chose both their books and their authors very carefully. Undoubtedly this was partly in the knowledge or belief that most parents would supervise a girl's reading closely, and thus would be reluctant to purchase novels that did not contain a 'useful' message. It is for this reason that the back of many novels contains lists of other books currently available, together with an indication of the plot and a summary of the message, frequently in extracts taken from reviews of the stories. Works by such women received a surprisingly wide coverage by reviewers in newspapers and periodicals. While it might be expected that the religious press would take an interest in such works, it is an indication of the seriousness

[15] Georgina Battiscombe, *Charlotte Mary Yonge: The Story of an Uneventful Life* (Constable, London, 1943), pp. 60–71.

with which this genre was regarded by contemporaries that these novels were regularly reviewed in newspapers and periodicals from *The Manchester Guardian* to *The Morning Post*, and from *Punch* to *The Saturday Review*. In addition, the authors themselves were featured in interviews in magazines as diverse as *The Strand Magazine* and *Macmillan's Magazine* on the basis of the important contributions they were making to society through their fiction.[16]

Taking this as a starting point, therefore, it becomes possible to examine this genre in order to trace changing contemporary attitudes and opinions, and not just towards women. It is worth noting at this point that the boys' fiction is, overall, less useful to the historian than that written for girls. Stories for boys contain little in the way of information about the lives and expectations of women or girls and no real indication of how these might be changing. It was not considered right or necessary to go into such details. The tales for the embryo adult male throughout the period were generally concerned to reinforce the established and little-questioned manly virtues and to discourage both vice (such as sexual indulgence with either sex, cowardice, cheating, gambling) and too much philosophical thought about the position in which they might find themselves in later life. Consequently, the stories concentrated on tales of adventure and the sound results of patriotism and quick-thinking; and women in such stories are generally simplistic, background stereotypes, with relatively small contributions to make to either plot or character development.[17] It is well-established that girls read the books written for boys.[18] In itself there was usually little in a good boy's book to damage the purity of a girl's mind. Nor would girlish readers be encouraged by them to believe that in comparision with the female characters found

[16] See, for example, 'Portraits of Celebreties at Different Times of Their Lives: Charlotte Mary Yonge', *The Strand Magazine*, VII, July–Dec. 1891, p. 479, which comments: 'Miss Yonge's books have done good ... by their healthy moral teaching'.

[17] For example: G. Arnold, *Held Fast for England: G.A. Henty, Imperialist Boys' Writer* (Hamish Hamilton, London, 1980); Isabel Quigly, *The Heirs of Tom Brown: The English School Story* (Chatto & Windus, London, 1982).

[18] See, for instance, Agnes Blackie, *Blackie and Son*, pp. 39–40, when the author refers to the fan mail received by G.A. Henty from girls who had read his books.

in, say, a G.A. Henty novel, they were being unfairly treated, since the majority of the heroines in such books invariably behaved according to proper, even old-fashioned, standards of female behaviour while transmitting and upholding correct moral standards.[19]

There was an increasing fear that by contrast with boys' books, the options offered to girls both in and out of fiction were less obviously inviting. Yet too much reading of adventure stories could create a spirit of dissatisfaction. This was dangerous, for society as a whole, in view of the pivotal importance laid upon the feminine role in society. In order for the values of middle-class English society to survive, it was seen as essential for middle-class women as well as men to play a central role. There seemed little likelihood of male rebellion against the stereotypical roles marked out for them. There was considerably less complacency about feminine acquiescence in the limited sphere open to their sex.

Thus girls' stories aimed to explain and justify the feminine position in society, both in gender and class terms, as well as making an appeal to the emotional nature of the feminine psyche that would convince her of the need to conform to conventional expectations of her sphere. Generally authors used the device of presenting to their readership by incorporating into their stories a much wider picture of society than was necessary for the more easily satisfied male, so that girls could see the pivotal nature of their role. It is possible to learn almost as much from these books as those for boys about military matters, to say nothing of ideals of masculinity and expectations of male stereotypes. Though concentrating on adolescent fiction written for a feminine market, issues of importance to both sexes, and society as a whole, can be covered in subsequent chapters as a result of this exercise in 'realism'.

The skill of the writer was important here in aiding the acceptability of the message through the quality of the surrounding 'packaging'. It is true that much of this writing is of dubious literary value, a point literary critics of this genre have tended to emphasize, perhaps over-emphasize. However, whatever their literary standing, such works have value for the historian, because of this 'packaging' and because they reveal

---

[19] G. Arnold, *Held Fast for England*, pp. 58–62.

more explicitly than the other forms of genre fiction in this period the traditions and questions that were of importance to contemporary adult society. This is a development of importance to the historian as such works from this period, particularly those written for women, provide a useful and significant insight into the society that produced and approved them.

Fiction of this genre helps to illuminate not just the role of women in society, but also the self-image that society as a whole desired to present to the next generation. The mass invention of traditions in various spheres of life has been recognized as an important feature of the nineteenth century, part of the attempts of the new industrial society to reorientate itself.[20] The 'tradition' of *Home* and *Woman* as the *Angel* in it was one of the earliest 'inventions' of the rising middle classes in this sphere. As the act of writing down a tradition was presumed to help establish its pedigree and its durability, much of popular nineteenth-century fiction forms part of the evidence for the invention of tradition in the period.

Yet paradoxically, it was this genre of popular fiction that also provided a medium for recognizing the growing rebellion of middle-class women against the limiting tradition of the *Angel in the Home*. Indeed the creation of a body of fiction concentrating specifically on an adolescent middle-class female market actually aided the expansion of women's role in society. It gave a considerable boost to the profession of author, markedly increasing the number of women writers. Because most of this didactic fiction concentrated on generally acceptable social behaviour and attitudes, the authors of such works found themselves regarded with favour, even though they received money through their writing. Numbers of single women even began to be able to earn a living by writing while still being accepted as part of established social circles – a privilege not open to working women such as governesses or even nurses until a later period.[21] Certainly this fiction mirrors the evolution of an acceptable role for middle-class women outside marriage and the nuclear family, with new invented 'traditions' of its own.

[20] E.J. Hobsbawm and T. Ranger (eds), *The Invention of Tradition* (Cambridge University Press, Cambridge, 1983), Introduction, pp. 1–5 and p. 912.
[21] See ch. 6.

Far from being immune to the pressures of social change, these novels display, in terms of an evolving body of tradition, the efforts of the conservative majority, especially in the middle classes, to reconcile the necessity for developments in the role of women with the accepted standards of feminine behaviour and aspirations. As will be discussed in subsequent chapters, girls' fiction thus dealt with all aspects of adult life, in an attempt to provide models and standards for later behaviour in all respectable contingencies, including attitudes towards men, and to provide warnings against temptation in times of stress. Indeed the latter became a stronger strand as the century progressed, giving vivid pictures of the problems faced by single working women. At the same time, it maintained an emphasis on the role of the woman in the family, with details of domestic duties, sweetened by the themes of self-sacrifice and love.

In making my choice of books to draw on for quotations in this study I have quite deliberately focused on a relatively limited number of authors. The criteria I have used have been that the works of the authors used should be typical of the writers in the genre at any particular period, or in any particular style, and that they should sum up ideas commonly expressed in works on similar themes as succinctly and comprehensively as possible. For this reason, I have concentrated on writers like Charlotte Yonge, Evelyn Everett Green, L.T. Meade and Mrs George de Horne Vaizey. It is not intended to suggest that they have any greater literary merit than other authors less heavily drawn on, though that can be a matter of opinion in the case of Charlotte Yonge at least. However, these writers were all prolific and all, on the evidence of reviews and 'fan mail' etc., popular exponents of the genre. Evelyn Everett Green has been especially widely quoted, because her books include most of the themes of this book. Her works can be considered typical of those produced in all areas used here to study this genre and the attitudes and opinions it reflected. Her ideas, however, were by no means unique even if she wrote them in what I have found to be a particularly quoteable form.

1

Household Fairy and *Home Goddess*: The Changing Feminine Stereotype

But the best of household fairies,
Is the wife whose golden hair is
Drooping o'er her husband's Chair – his
Little Woman[1]

Golden-haired, brown, black or even white, the *Household Fairy*[2] has been one of the most enduring, if not endearing, modern traditions invented for womanly emulation. While its origins are discernible in earlier periods,[3] it was in the nineteenth century that it developed into the fully-fledged and coherent stereotype. From the start it was promoted in education, in learned essays and in literature, particularly the popular fiction that is the concern of this study. Detailing such a tradition in print in these various texts was presumed not only to help

---

[1] Theo Gift, 'Little Woman', *Cassells Magazine*, 1873, vol. VII (new series), p. 240.

[2] The *Household Fairy* or *Angel in the House* has been recognized as the 'middle-class ideal of Victorian womanhood in and out of fiction by a wide variety of authors'. For a more detailed discussion of this aspect, see F. Basch, *Relative Creatures: Victorian Women in Society and the Novel, 1837–67* (Allen Lane, London, 1974), pp. 3–15. In the context of this book the term *Household Fairy*, like that of its alternatives, including *Home Goddess*, were used to a large extent interchangeably. However, there was a tendency to use the term *Home Goddess* in the post-1880 period, as being more suited to a later development in the feminine stereotype. It is in that sense used here.

[3] The unlovable heroine of Samuel Richardson's novel *Pamela, Or Virtue Rewarded* (C. Rivington, J. Osborn, London, 1741) can be seen as an early prototype.

spread and formalize it but also to give it the authority and pedigree presumed necessary for general acceptance. However, it was also a limited and limiting tradition in its ultimate form, and one that was reacted against by large numbers of women as they sought to redefine the parameters of their sphere for themselves. The *Household Fairy* stereotype was thus under attack from women in particular, and even from some men, from very early in the nineteenth century. Especially after the 1870s, a considerable degree of success was achieved in expanding the sphere of the ideal woman, and this success was equally reflected in print. By the turn of the century the *Home Goddess* modification of the *Household Fairy* as portrayed in various printed sources, including that of popular fiction, was certainly better educated and presumed to be more capable of performing a number of activities outside her immediate household than her earlier counterpart.

Yet this success must not be exaggerated. As popular fiction also makes plain, for the majority of British society, and especially for the middle classes, the domestic core of the stereotype, with the idea that the best place for the majority of women was in the home, remained constant. While a man needed a career to justify and bolster his masculinity, being a woman was a 'career' in itself, and in an age of growing emphasis on professionalism in careers, it became increasingly important for women to be professionals in this gender sense.[4] Thus, the 'highest' ambition for a good girl of any social class was shown as being to become a professional good wife and mother. The stories written for girls throughout the period expose the pivotal importance of that 'traditional' feminine role in contemporary society, by revealing many of the factors and reasoning behind this limited domestic tradition. Didactic fiction was fuelled by the wish to control as far as possible, if not stifle, independent feminine desires to create a role and power base in society for themselves outside the limits prescribed by established society. Such stories also help to illustrate the extent to which the womanly stereotype spread out from the middle classes to become part of the general social mythology of the

[4] For a discussion of professionalism in the nineteenth century see W.J. Reader, *Professional Men: The Rise of the Professional Classes in Nineteenth-Century England* (Weidenfeld & Nicolson, London, 1966).

time. They also expose the various ways in which it became possible for women, particularly middle-class women, to broaden and modify this central element in the feminine tradition in their own interests, without alienating a male-oriented society.

The origins of the change that occurred from the late eighteenth century on in the accepted stereotype of womanhood in England, particularly for members of the middle classes, must be sought largely in the class polarization and urbanization that accompanied the Industrial Revolution, as well as the religious resurgence that characterized the latter years of the eighteenth century. Accompanying the major economic and social changes of this movement were changes also in the size and nature of the household, associated with the rise of the nuclear family with a dwelling place separate from the workplace as the most common domestic unit. These, along with other developments such as the rise of the factory system, had a significant impact on women and the work that they could perform. Many women of the middle classes no longer had a clearly-defined sphere of work in which to operate, so new ones had to be found; and to this end, the 'home' seemed the obvious choice.

To an important extent also the limited role 'traditionally' assigned to respectable women in nineteenth-century England resulted from a misconception by the aspiring middle classes of the role played by women of the upper classes. As it became necessary for those middle classes to develop a new social role for women which no longer entailed direct involvement in modes of production, they looked upward for suitable models to the class to which they aspired. The belief was fostered that 'ladies' lived merely ornamental or 'unproductive' lives, and that it was, therefore, a symbol of gentility for a family or household to maintain 'idle' females, who could then lay claim to the coveted title of 'ladies'. Such a misconception was additionally encouraged by middle-class reading of the 'silver fork' genre of novels from the early nineteenth century, which served to reinforce the ornamental pattern of upper-class femininity.

The 'silver fork' or fashionable novel became popular with the British aristocracy from about 1814. It portrayed the characters and institutions of the *haut ton* in authentic, almost photographic detail. Thriving on the limited nature of fashionable society, this genre began dying out around the 1840s as fashionable society itself began to change its ethos in response to the challenge of the rising middle classes. Ironically, though, it was the 'silver fork' novel which aided this middle-class challenge. Fashionable novels in the early nineteenth century, written for a select social elite, were also closely read by 'manufacturers who made fortunes moving to the capital from the industrial north' and by City bankers and merchants already on the fringes of that elite. For aspiring social entrepreneurs the detailed realism of these books made them 'compulsive reading with their intimate portrayal of the world they hoped to enter'; initially through the marriage of a suitable daughter.[5]

Such novels gave the impression that the ladies of the *haut ton* which they either aimed to join or admired from afar did little beyond marry, flirt, gossip and entertain. They might indulge in fine embroidery, sketch, speak a foreign language, sing or play a musical instrument. They would certainly dance well. Some would even gamble. They were not often seen to supervise their households, or to help their husbands in the running of their estates etc. One useful novel 'guide' was *The Contrast* by Lord Normanby, published in 1832. Though the theme of the novel is the disastrous nature of an 'unequal' marriage, the hero, Lord Castleton, occupies himself with educating his bride (a farmer's daughter called Lucy) in her duties and behaviour in her new sphere in life. The story then develops in an ominous fashion. Despite beauty and aptitude, Lucy fails to become truly cultured and has to be 'killed off' to give the book the required ending of a 'suitable' match for the hero – a form of snobbery later taken up by some middle-class writers. Ignoring the unpropitious theme, however, *The Contrast* provided a comprehensive survey of necessary knowledge for the ambitious mother and daughter.[6]

The morality of most of these writings was objectionable for various reasons to the majority of their increasingly influential

[5] Alison Adburgham, *Silver Fork Society: Fashionable Life and Literature from 1814 to 1840* (Constable, London, 1983), pp. 68–9.
[6] Lord Normanby, *The Contrast* (A. Culburn and R. Bentley, London, 1832).

middle-class readership. In particular, the power of the Evangelical revival and Nonconformity generally was strong in that sphere of society. Consequently the fashionable novel offended their consciences as well as their sense of thrift. Yet despite this the desire to imitate at least some aspects of the behaviour of the 'superior' social class as displayed in these novels was strong. It resulted in a modification of the code they portrayed, with the discarding of the more dubious elements of the behaviour chronicled in them, particularly for women. Gambling, and for the stricter, even such frivolities as dancing could be ignored as patterns for behaviour. Above all, the middle-class 'lady' had to be productive in her hours of ease. Shorn of undesirable aspects, a clear code of behaviour still seemed to remain which could be added to the separate evolution of the tradition of woman as the *Angel in the Home* to provide the middle-class model of a 'lady' – a creature that would not necessarily have been recognized as such by the canons of a previous aristocratic age.

In the middle-class home, the *Household Fairy* was the profes-sional domestic woman, making her household a comfortable, tranquil refuge, where the busy man could relax on returning from his toil. The revised code of social behaviour derived from these fashionable novels combined admirably with this powerful new tradition, providing a more rounded and aesthe-tic aspect to the purely mechanical domestic notion of comfort. The good woman who was also a 'lady' could be trained to provide her husband not just with home and all the physical comforts thereof, but also with a soothing and uncritical mental refreshment within the domestic arena. As a result, from the middle-class standpoint it seemed increasingly a mark of rising social status and undoubted wealth if a man could afford the luxury of supporting the women of his family as 'ladies', without needing their physical contribution to his daily produc-tion. More and more, therefore, successful industrialists, mer-chants and members of the professions limited the active roles hitherto played by the female sector of their families, particu-larly the roles by their daughters, in order to imitate an upper-class elite. This trend even began to spread to the rural farming sector as women lost their traditional working status there. A very narrow conception of the role of a 'good woman' had thus been laid out for girls to follow by the mid-nineteenth century. Only by following such a path, ideally ending in marriage, could they hope to become accepted as 'ladies'. This in turn would both bolster the status of their families and provide an appropriate degree of comfort in life for men.

In the early period, the middle-class maiden was often at a distinct disadvantage when compared to the daughters of the aristocracy. The latter still tended to have wider opportunities outside the social sphere. For example, their range of permitted amusements was often less restricted by the fear of contravening codes of either ladylike conduct or religion. They were already 'ladies' by birth and had no need to strive to achieve either the status or correct behaviour, and most belonged to less strict religious traditions.[7] Also, where a sense of paternalistic social responsibility was still retained, this gave such girls the opportunity to visit the tenantry, for example, for charitable purposes at a time when philanthropy was still not universally accepted as a middle-class girlish pastime. Greater physical activity, in the shape of riding, for instance, was usually more open to girls from these backgrounds than to the largely urban middle-class girl of this period. At the opposite end of the scale, the lot of the working-class girl was much harder than that of the middle-class one, but in many households she retained her role as an essential contributor to the family income. She was not expected to be a lady.

It was only the daughters of the rising and prospering middle orders who were presumed to stand in need of comprehensive, or even intensive, training in all aspects of their life to fit them for their prescribed role in adult society, that of the *Lady* and *Angel of the House*. Thus it was at the circumscribed but aspiring middle-class girl that the majority of the didactic efforts of the nineteenth century was aimed.[8] Early and mid-Victorian middle-class girls who aspired to ladyhood were expected to live carefully circumscribed lives while in training for marriage ideally and if not, a useful old maid-hood. It was their duty to acquire certain essentially ornamental accomplish-

[7] Upper-class girls learned behaviour from birth – 'they hardly knew how', Charlotte M. Yonge, 'Womankind', *Monthly Packet*, Jan.–Jun., vol. 17, p. 122.

[8] Though increasing social pressure led to the production of large numbers of books for a working-class readership, largely by the Religious Tract Society and similar religious publishing houses, but the total never outstripped that destined primarily for the middle-class readership.

ments, and a sound knowledge of household supervision. As Sarah Stickney Ellis, a well-known author of training manuals for women, emphasized, the 'daughters of England' had to know the practical details of how to run the household properly as well as how to adorn it by products of her skill. The model maiden should never be permitted to sit doing nothing in a purely static ornamental capacity. Every hour of the day was to be occupied in some suitable, if as now seems, practically unproductive, manner. Inactivity, characterized as idleness, was a major sin for such creatures, a factor constantly emphasized by parents, teachers and girls' writers such as Elizabeth Wetherell.[9]

The Victorians believed in recreation but not idleness, with the implication that recreation was in some way productive, morally, mentally or physically. The development of the novel by this date encouraged its use as an educational aid for periods of physical inactivity. Didactic novels for young girls were never written to please and pass away an idle hour. Increasingly, adults saw novels as an important aid to the educational process, as is partly indicated by the growing volume of such publications. The habit of using stories to inculcate a lesson was both well-established and well-regarded by this time, as the continuing popularity of Miss Edgeworth's tales proves. The habit was also well-established of driving home a moral message by placing it in as realistic a context as possible, on the 'There but for the Grace of God' combined with the 'How like my life' principles.

Popular novels were thus, in many ways, both a combination and an extension of these trends, providing something sufficiently substantial to occupy a significant time period with contents that were set in familiar and authentic scenes with

---

[9] Sarah Stickney Ellis, *The Daughters of England* (Fisher, Son and Co., London, 1845). One of the most popular of the magazines for the middle-class market prefaced every issue with lines of Cowper's which were much favoured in this respect: 'Behold in these what leisure hours demand,/ Amusement and true knowledge hand in hand.' Perhaps even more to the point here are the then equally popular Cowper lines: 'Absence of occupation is not rest,/ A mind quite vacant is a mind distressed.' (from the poem 'Retirement') W. Cowper, *The Complete Poetical Works* (Henry G. Bohn, London, 1848). Ellen Montgomery is taught to look to Cowper for moral lessons by Alice Humphreys in Elizabeth Wetherell, *The Wide, Wide World* (Bliss, Sands & Co., London, 1896), 1st edn (1852). For example, see pp. 202–5.

'traditional' values approved of by a controlling adult society. Not surprisingly in such fiction the authors were primarily concerned to reproduce in an acceptable and recognizable setting the ideals that they themselves and the parents of these children already possessed; with the aim of passing these ideals on as firm traditions to their young readership. Only through their continuation could the stability of England's civilization be maintained. Literary excellence was merely the tool by which these ideals would be easily and successfully assimilated.

What were these ideals that were presented to girlish readers as traditions? They seem largely to have been based on principles that so many middle-class Victorians believed had brought status, prosperity and respectability both to their class and to Britain. Thus they centred on belief in Queen and Country, Empire, trade and industry, the rule of law, all with a sound moral base and all pursued under the aegis of a reliable and fairly rigid class system. Stability and success were ensured by professionalism, characterized as conformity to the rules and the performance of tasks to the best of one's ability, that ability having been cultivated by careful training to maximize talent. But the most important element in this equation for social stability and individual success was the Family – the most universally admired and respected social unit of the century, and the context in which the feminine stereotype throughout this period was both evolved and presented to girls for their admiration and emulation.

In any family, it was presumed to be the females that provided the cement which held the home together. Throughout the century, a home with no female old enough or good enough or of the right rank to conduct its domestic affairs was seen to be a cheerless place. Class considerations insisted that working-class servants had neither the refinement nor taste to replace the middle-class mistress. In May Baldwin's *A Plucky Girl*, the death of Mrs Paul left 'A desolate house, a helpless man', and nor could matters be remedied by the Reverend Paul until his sister-in-law came to take over the running of his household and the upbringing of his children for him. Yet the Reverend Paul was no weakling: he was just a normal man and thus without the God-given ability to create domestic comfort. Eleanor Lestrange could only help her brother-in-law at the temporary sacrifice of her own happiness, but being a right-minded and 'plucky girl', she did not hesitate or repine. She recognized the inevitability and the positive benefits of self-sacrifice for a woman, unlike her faulty fiancé who wished to protect women from their duty. She was freed by Reverend Paul's remarriage, and her delayed marital happiness was all the sweeter for her 'conscientious discharge of uncongenial duty'.[10]

The family was viewed as more than an economic unit: divinely organized, it was held together most strongly by emotional bonds. The masculine capacity was for reason and logic, while woman was 'the legitimate muse of emotion'. To hold a family together on a daily basis was an enormous emotional task, and one that could only be achieved at the cost of denying individual desires, in itself an issue of emotion. Women were seen as more able than men to practise self-sacrifice on a regular, consistent basis in daily life. Didactic fiction for girls demonstrated the belief that men were also capable of self-denial, and on a grand scale, but that logic usually led them to take such action rather than pure emotion. Men were, for instance, able to combine physical courage with moral cowardice, as in the case of Dick Blunt in Emma Marshall's *Laurel Crowns*. In the few books for girls where men make an essentially emotional or moral sacrifice, it has to be said that their masculinity does not come over. For example, in Evelyn Everett Green's *Temple's Trial*, Temple ruins his reputation for probity by taking the blame for his brother's wrongdoing: but instead of joining the Foreign Legion he stays at home and heaps coals of fire on Percy's head by nearly dying. Even the author describes Temple as looking rather feminine, with delicate features and a tendency to migraine. He is, moreover, a 'high-minded Christian gentleman' of great moral stature. One is left with the irresistible feeling that she dressed up one of her feminine stereotypes in trousers in order to create a 'powerful' fictional situation, which could not have been done without a hero instead of a heroine. It is thus also an

[10] Sarah Stickney Ellis, *The Education of Character, with Hints on Moral Training* (John Murray, London, 1856), p. 128; May Baldwin, *A Plucky Girl, or The Adventures of 'Miss Nell'* (Chambers, Edinburgh, 1902, p. 162; p. 171; p. 314. The theory that men could not cope without wives or womenfolk of their own rank was the continuation of a long-standing tradition in English society.

PLATE 1   THE HAPPY FAMILY

Household fairies and home goddesses. From *Mattie's Home, or The Little Match-Girl and her Friends*, Anon.

indication of the still-limited nature of the feminine world.[11]

The message of didactic fiction throughout the nineteenth century was that feminine influence was more essential to the daily moral health and strength of the family unit and of the nation than that of a man. It was a woman's first duty in life, therefore, to become as professional in her sphere as a man in his; to cultivate her feminine talents in the emotional realm so as to maximize their usefulness within the domestic orbit. Any woman who wilfully eschewed conformity to the rules necessary for family survival by opting out of a plain duty towards her family for the sake of indulging personal ambitions or a selfish desire for independence was betraying what Mrs Dinah Mulock Craik coyly called her 'womanhede'.[12] Self-sacrifice, not self-sufficiency was the mark of professionalism for women. Fictional tradition was concerned to show that this not only pre-empted any personal desires, but also that its disregard led to general and individual unhappiness, as Charlotte Yonge emphasized in *The Clever Woman of the Family*.

The heroine, Rachel Curtis, accords herself this accolade. She is fascinated by knowledge for its own sake, and is determined to acquire as much of it as possible. Her vanity about her mental powers leads her to despise the idea of marriage and the other accoutrements of femininity which she dubs 'young ladyisms'. Above all she rejects the notion of an essential need for feminine self-sacrifice to complain:

> here I sit with health, strength and knowledge, and able to do nothing, *nothing* – at the risk of breaking my mother's heart! . . . here am I, able and willing, only longing to task myself to the uttermost, yet tethered down to the merest mockery of usefulness by conventionalities. I am a young lady forsooth! – . . . I must not put forth my views. . . .

Though she has been restrained to some extent by duty to her mother, she decides that her age, 25, permits her for the future largely to ignore that convention to concentrate on aspects of

[11] Mrs Emma Marshall, *Laurel Crowns, or Griselda's Aim: A Story for Brothers and Sisters* (Nisbet, Welwyn, 1889), p. 176; Evelyn Everett Green, *Temple's Trial, or For Life or Death* (Nelson, Walton-on-Thames, 1887), p. 383.

[12] Mrs Dinah Mulock Craik, *A Woman's Thoughts About Women* (Hurst & Blackett, London, 1858), p. 35.

life that please her personal tastes better.[13] This wilful determination to focus on her own wishes at the expense of her family leads her to take actions on her own initiative, refusing the advice of either an older womanly woman or any available men. Inevitably this leads to tragedy for Rachel and those she genuinely tried to help.

Miss Yonge was not unaware of the strength of many girls' desires to be independent, and Rachel was meant as a demonstration to such girls of the trouble they were storing up. Moreover, Rachel was contrasted with Ermine Williams, also intelligent and educated, but with a 'real' sense of her position and powers in life. Her conformity leads her to a truer understanding of life and ultimately, to a greater happiness. Rachel's happiness comes only at the expense of her own humiliation, damage to her family's reputation and the death of an innocent. From this she is redeemed by a brave soldier, Captain Alick Keith, who is willing to take the risk of marrying her because he is convinced that beneath her folly, there is a womanly woman. As Rachel finally learns to rely on his powers of interpretation for her view of the world and not her own she comes to happiness in her womanly heritage as a wife and mother.[14]

Rachel Curtis, therefore, was a carefully constructed warning rather than a role model for girlish readers, for all the conventional 'happy' ending. But authors in the genre of girls' didactic fiction generally spent rather more time and care on the building up of fictional images which provided models for emulation. Would-be good girls with hopes of becoming good women were encouraged to look to fictional heroines as well as real 'good women' for guidance. It was thus important to established opinion that those images reflected standard opinion as far as the limits of fiction permitted. As the century progressed, however, the fictional stereotypes underwent significant modifications in certain respects, indicating the progress made in conventional acceptance of expansions in the feminine sphere. Yet these modifications did not yet affect the basic core of what constituted a good woman.

[13] Charlotte M. Yonge, *The Clever Woman of the Family* (Virago Press, London, 1983), 1st edn (1865) p. 3.
[14] Ibid., p. 95; pp. 227–8; pp. 366–7.

Fiction reveals the importance of outward appearance as an indication of inner nature in the basic feminine stereotype that dominated didactic fiction in the period up to the 1870s. It was, in many ways, very much a male-oriented stereotype, though even here there were indications of women modifying the ideal to take account of reality. For instance, obvious physical beauty was of itself not necessarily held to be an indication of a good spirit within, though many fictional heroines were lovely to look on. It was, however, more a question of expression than feature that was seen to make a girl 'good-looking' in all respects. Less than perfect lineaments could be overcome by a happy, heavenly expression, and by a pleasing neatness in appearance. This outward physical aspect was further reinforced by demeanour. A good girl's behaviour was always modest, indicative of unselfish submission to those in due authority over her, such as her parents. It was also nicely calculated to be appropriate to her station in life, making it necessary that she should have an acute consciousness of her own relative situation in the class hierarchy. Additionally, it was desirable that she should be educated as fitting for her station and abilities. A good girl should be able to make a contribution to household affairs, and be able to add materially in a variety of ways to the comfort of the males in her life, be they fathers, brothers or husbands. Finally, the model damsel should find the inspiration and justification for her actions and her thoughts in sound, orthodox Christian doctrine.

This essentially middle-class vision had the advantage, in the eyes of contemporary observers, of being readily modified to take account of family rank and financial means, making it universally appropriate to a wide range of status within the middle orders of society. Elizabeth Wetherell was an early provider of the stereotype of a good girl on the most ideal lines. She made few compromises for her heroines, most notably in her classic of didactic fiction *The Wide, Wide World*, first published in Britain in 1852 and constantly in demand by generations of readers throughout the Victorian period. With all her paragon qualities, its heroine, Ellen Montgomery, was approved of by both adults and children, and it is consequently worth examining it in some detail as an early popular model for girls in their formative 'teenage' years that retained its power to please.

Parents and teachers liked the way that the story illustrated the happy results of an early affinity for lady-like behaviour, religion, cheerfulness under adversity and obedience to those set in familial authority over children. Girls enjoyed the careful details of life in early nineteenth-century New York State and Scotland, and the eventful storyline into which religion and moral messages were woven. Moreover, in order to provide a credible context for her model maiden, the author drew on her personal knowledge and childhood background to a considerable degree, a literary habit followed by the majority of authors in this genre. Though set largely in America, the heroes and heroines in *The Wide, Wide World* are of well-born English or Scottish stock, and they act accordingly. This meant that the stereotype of a good girl growing up with the promise of becoming a good woman given in the novel was considered perfectly applicable to an English reader, while the model was enhanced by placing it in a romantic but believable setting for much of the novel. In addition, it was an image that was, to a very great extent, dateless. Into the twentieth century there were writers such as Amy Le Feuvre who continued the pattern of the ideal apprentice *Household Fairy* as encapsulated in Ellen Montgomery.

The Wide, Wide World is intended as the description of a feminine odyssey to near perfection. Ellen Montgomery's mother is forced by her consumption to go on a sea voyage, and fearing she will never see her daugher this side of heaven, makes suitable preparations, material and spiritual, to ensure a meeting there. Great detail is gone into in this respect, to establish the suitable belongings of a 'nice' young girl, who though not vain, takes appropriate ladylike pains with her appearance. The descriptions of the dressing case, workbox and even writing desk with which Ellen was provided must have roused envy in the hearts of many young readers.[15] It is made plain, though, that Ellen has earned them because she is already trying to be a good girl in all respects. Her behaviour, even under stress, is satisfactorily innocent yet ladylike and it promises to become even better because she is genuinely trying to become perfect in spirit as well as outward behaviour, the only secure foundation for continued improvement. Indeed

[15] Elizabeth Wetherell, *The Wide, Wide World*, pp. 25–6.

one of the important messages of didactic fiction is that genuine effort will be rewarded.

The point is made from the start that unless Ellen's behaviour is based on family duty combined with Christian principles she cannot truly be a good girl or a lady. Thus before purchasing the delights above, Ellen is taken to choose her own Bible. Suitably, she takes almost more delight in this indication of family thought and Christian love than in her other material treasures. She is, however, human enough not to go quite so far. The author's moral is plain as Ellen thanks her mother and promises to take 'the greatest possible care of my new treasures'. In reply, Mrs Montgomery says:

> 'I know you will. If I had doubted it, Ellen, most assuredly I should not have given them to you, sorry as I should have been to leave you without them. So you see you have not established a character for carefulness in vain.'
> 'And, mama, I hope you have not given them to me in vain, either. I will try to use them in the way that I know you wish me to; that will be the best way I can thank you.'
> 'Well I have left you no excuse, Ellen ... my gifts will serve as reminders for you if you are ever tempted to forget my lessons.'[16]

This episode serves also to emphasize the importance that society placed on the maternal role. It was essential for apprentice good girls to have an image constantly before them on which to model themselves, and the best image they could have was presumed to be their mother. Such an interpretation of the maternal role makes it particularly understandable why a motherless family, especially if there were girls, was an object of concern as well as pity. Facing death, Mrs Montgomery acted nobly by providing her daughter with objects and memories which Ellen can use to keep alive her mother's image as a standard for emulation. Her success in teaching her daughter the essentials of being an apprentice good woman can be gauged by the assessment of Ellen given later in the book:

> I thought your mother was a lady from the honourable notions she had given you; and from your ready obedience to her, which

[16] Ibid., pp. 23–7.

was evidently the obedience of love, I judged she had been a good mother in the true sense of the term. I thought she must be a refined and cultivated person, from the manner of your speech and behaviour: and I was sure that she was a Christian, because she had taught you the truth and evidently had tried to lead you in it.[17]

Throughout the book, Ellen's character is tried and tested in a number of ways. In new surroundings after her mother's departure, Ellen is obviously a superior being. Her aunt, Fortune Emerson, is neither a lady nor a Christian, and she does not behave as family duty demands towards Ellen. Though it is true that modern adult readers might well sympathize with the aunt rather than the niece, this is distinctly not the intention of the author. It is made plain to the reader that it is good training and an exercise in sound spiritual discipline when Fortune Emerson sets Ellen to learn how to perform the domestic chores on her farm. However, in trying to deny Ellen the further education that her mother desired, the aunt is clearly at fault. Luckily, Alice Humphreys, daughter of the local minister and a lady of birth and breeding stumbles across Ellen. An ideal role model, she is able to mount a rescue mission and take over Mrs Montgomery's duties. However, Alice Humphreys is such a perfect *Angel in the House* that it is not surprising that Death had already marked her for his own. Before she dies, Ellen learns from her how best to combine education, accomplishments and domesticity, taking over Alice's place as daughter and provider of comfort in the Humphrey's household after Alice's death, also from consumption.[18]

After various storms and trials the reader is shown that Ellen begins to reap the rewards of her efforts to carry out her mother's wishes. She is described by friends (though not in her hearing) in glowing terms:

'She is a most extraordinary child!' said Mrs. Gillespie.
'She is a *good* child', said Mrs. Chauncey.
'Yes mamma . . . I don't think she could *help* being polite.'

[17] Ibid., p. 179.
[18] Ibid., p. 123 and pp. 342–3.

'It is not that', said Mrs. Gillespie; 'mere sweetness and politeness would never give so much elegance of manner. As far as I have seen, Ellen Montgomery is a *perfectly* well-behaved child.

'That she is' said Mrs. Chauncey; 'but neither would any cultivation or example be sufficient for it without Ellen's thorough good principle and great sweetness of temper.'

The extent to which Ellen has succeeded in her mission to be a family blessing is also pointed up by the blank she leaves in the Humphreys' household after going to her uncle in Scotland – but a blank only realized once she had gone. Ellen had imbibed the lesson that a professional *Household Fairy* ministered to domestic comfort unobtrusively.[19]

It is an interesting pointer to the role of class in acceptable contemporary social attitudes that this little piece of perfection is never once chided by the author for neglecting to maintain contact with her aunt or her good and aged grandmother once she has been temporarily adopted by the Humphreys. This contrasts with the determination with which Ellen, once she has returned to her own relatives in Scotland, refuses to abandon thought of or contact with the Humphreys. The unspoken element, of course, is that neither Aunt Fortune nor the grandmother are well-bred, while the Humphreys are Ellen's social equals, if not superiors. In pursuit of achieving the necessary behavioural standards Ellen needs to leave her farming relatives behind, to continue in the path laid out for her by her mother. Both her Scottish relatives and the Humphreys can provide this, and the Humphreys score because her Scottish relatives are not full of Christian principle and they do not have the nice discrimination in their behaviour that the Humphreys have, and have taught to Ellen. In particular, they do not appreciate Ellen's religion (especially her habit of singing hymns), and try to make her forget it as well as the Humphreys. Family duty, especially the remembrance of her dead mother and Alice, as well as the ever-present thought of Mr John Humphreys keeps Ellen rigid in her religious observance and she warns Mr Lindsay of the importance of this: 'do not let me be hindered in that! forbid me anything you please, but not

---

[19] Ibid., p. 314; and p. 428.

that! the better I learn to please my best Friend, the better I shall please you'.[20]

As a reward for Ellen's resolution and consistent attempts (marked by frequent prayer and copious tears) to be a good girl, John Humphreys re-enters the scene in person in the final chapters of the book. Ellen's happiness, earthly as well as heavenly is thus assured:

> The seed so early sown in little Ellen's mind, and so carefully tended by sundry hands, grew in course of time to all the fair stature and comely perfection it had bid fair to reach; storms and winds that had visited it did but cause the root to take deeper hold; . . . Three or four more years of Scottish discipline wrought her no ill; they did but serve to temper and beautify her Christian character; and then, to her unspeakable joy, she went back to spend her life with the friends and guardians she best loved, and to be to them, still more than she had been to her Scottish relations, the 'light of the eyes'.[21]

It was the Humphreys who were best able to appreciate Ellen for what she had finally become, the archetypal good maiden or apprentice *Angel in the House*. It was thus fitting that they should end up with her.

So popular with parents and children was Ellen Montgomery that an aid for girls aspiring to imitate her was swiftly produced in the shape of *Ellen Montgomery's Bookcase*, a further guide to suitable didactic reading for her would-be emulaters.[22] The stereotype of perfection that Ellen aimed for was not unique: though her standard of success in achieving it was somewhat unusual in the reading provided for the English market. Popular authors like Elizabeth Missing Sewell, Mrs Emma Marshall and Charlotte Yonge, provided the earliest comprehensive, purely British stereotypes of good girls as *Household Fairies* in training. While a number of Emma Marshall's heroines, such as Grace Buxton, did rival Ellen Montgomery, the majority of Charlotte Yonge and Mrs Marshall's heroines tempered the ideal with pragmatism. Most girls remain humanly imperfect to the end in some respects, for all that they retain

[20] Ibid., p. 411.
[21] Ibid., p. 428.
[22] Elizabeth Wetherell, *Ellen Montgomery's Bookshelf* (Nisbet, Welwyn, 1853).

an image of perfection before them.[23]

Miss Yonge's goals closely resemble those presented by Elizabeth Wetherell in most essentials, though the religion in her books is depicted in more orthodox Anglican terms, and the English gentry/middle-class emphasis is more often on household supervision than practical experience. In *The Daisy Chain*, her most often quoted work, the heroine, Ethel May, ultimately accepts the parameters of the sphere open to her and is typical of Miss Yonge's characters in that respect. Yet Ethel has had to fight hard to reach acceptance, and is not without understandable human regret over the limited earthly prospects before her. In some ways, though, Ethel is not typical of this earlier specimen of aspiring womanhood, since she accepts that she will remain the unmarried daughter and aunt. Consequently, she can never achieve more than a secondary importance and she does not represent the most typical, acceptable or empathetic model for English girls found in fiction of this period.[24] No doubt many good girls did have to face such a fate; but as even the spinster Miss Yonge most frequently indicates in her books, marriage leading to motherhood was the most desirable and productive end for the majority of readers to imitate, and it was better to enlist hope on the side of conformity.

Another work, *Scenes and Characters*, is more useful in depicting aspects of the most 'typical' English fictional model of this era. The 'characters' consist of the Mohuns of Beechcroft, a family featured in the other Yonge novels such as *The Two Sides of the Shield*. The domestic duties and supervision of the motherless Beechcroft household devolve onto two young sisters, Emily and Lilias, deliciously described as being 'tall graceful girls with soft hazel eyes, clear dark complexions, and a quantity of long brown curls'. The eldest, Emily, relies on her looks and sweet temper to carry her easily through life. Instead, she succeeds only in making life for her father and brothers uncomfortable, the major crime for an apprentice *Household Fairy*. Even when reproached by the elder brother because

[23] Mrs Emma Marshall, *Grace Buxton, or the Light of Home* (Nisbet, Welwyn, 1869). Grace ends up a model of saintly blind domesticity.
[24] Charlotte M. Yonge, *The Daisy Chain* (Macmillan, London, 1856), pp. 593–4.

'There is no activity, nor regularity, nor method, about this household', she cannot rise above her 'long cherished habits of selfish apathy'.[25] Charlotte Yonge's portrayal of Emily emphasizes the hard work that is required of girls with aspirations to become noble and useful women:

> Of Emily there is little to say. She ate, drank and slept, talked agreeably, read idle books and looked nice in the drawing room, wasting time, throwing away talents, weakening the powers of her mind, and laying up a store of sad reflections for herself against the time when she must awake from her selfish apathy.[26]

It is always an important element in this genre that fictional girls are very rarely presented as being so bad that they cannot make some improvements.

Though younger, Lily is the stronger character, and the eventual heroine of the piece. In marked contrast to Emily, she shows herself ultimately ready to work hard at her feminine role. The development of Lily into a fine example of good girlhood emphasizes that necessary element in the basic professional *Household Fairy* – the possession of a strong sense of duty founded on orthodox religion. This was a pre-requisite for developing the stamina necessary to cope with the demands made of the fully-fledged *Angel in the House*. Lily is good-natured, pretty and energetic, but this cannot compensate those around her for her failure to comprehend the role of duty in the life of a good woman and potential mother. In the subtle process of warning the youthful reader not to fall into the same trap it is revealed that Lily sees professionalism in the shape of duty as a cold substitute for love and feeling, instead of the only effective sustainer of it in a woman's sphere.[27]

It is swiftly shown by the author that Lily is initially a failure in her apprenticeship because she is 'neither patient nor humble enough',[28] or more bluntly because for a woman, unrestrained feeling and energy alone are not strong enough to cope with the trials of running a household. Love needs to be

[25] Charlotte M. Yonge, *Scenes and Characters, or Eighteen Months at Beechcroft* (Macmillan, London, 1886), p. 173.
[26] Ibid., p. 315.
[27] Ibid., p. 18.
[28] Ibid., p. 33.

sustained, and energy directed, by a strong sense of self-denying Christian duty, if disaster is not to follow, which in this case it soon does. Lily's actions lead to the unbaptized death of a village child and the corruption of one of her sisters by a servant. The arrival on the scene of Miss Weston provides Lily with a role model who is a professional at being a good girl. Though a secondary character, Alethea Weston is all the things that the Mohun girls (and by implication, the less-than-perfect young reader) have yet to become – if they can. She is good-looking, accomplished, sweet-mannered and affectionate; full of a profound sense of duty towards both family and parish. Her wisdom and tact are early displayed when Alethea tries to enlighten Lily as to the true role of duty in a good girl's life:

> 'Have you not overlooked one thing which may be the truth', said Alethea, as if she was asking for information, 'that duty and love may be identical? . . . what is called duty, seems to me to be love doing unpleasant work . . . love disguised under another name . . .'[29]

Unlike secondary characters like both Alethea Weston and Ermine Williams in *The Clever Woman of the Family* who come very near perfection, Miss Yonge never makes the heroines of her books such ideal stereotypes. Her popular and loved heroines remain instead closer to the experience of her readership. Like her faithful readers, they are all faulty to some extent, but are, or become, very conscious of their personal responsibility for their actions in life and try valiantly to overcome their flaws. Rachel Curtis becomes a good woman, but she retains her old impulse to act without thought of possible consequence. It is kept down only, not totally uprooted, by the training she has had at the hands of experience. Nor does Lily become a perfect damsel, though she does win the approbation of her father and brother for her efforts to ensure their comfort. For Lily, 'the memory of her faults and her sorrows did not fleet away', but were kept in mind to guide her future actions.[30] Though Miss Yonge keeps romantic

29 Ibid., p. 60.
30 Ibid., p. 315.

speculation out of the novel (believing it to encourage an unmaidenly spirit in her readers)[31] there is equally no hint of a spinster future for her. In fact, in the sequel to *Scenes and Characters*, Lily returns in the shape of Lady Merrifield, wife of a brave and noble general, and mother of a family that is 11 strong, ranging from 19 to 5 years of age. Lily is the type of girl growing up into fulfilled womanhood that is most constantly presented by Miss Yonge as an attainable model for her readers.[32]

Charlotte Yonge was not alone in her efforts to produce a feminine stereotype with a tendency to human frailty. The cause of fictional realism meant that others such as Mrs Emma Marshall were, with varying amounts of literary skill, interested in producing heroines on the above model in novels like *Violet Douglas*, another tale of a would-be-good girl whose endeavours lead to happiness as well as a consciousness of sin.[33] The central elements in such versions of the good girl in training for adult life were a talent for self-sacrifice developed by religion, combined with a talent for the traditional feminine pursuits in the domestic setting. In other words, depite essentially minor transgressions, Yonge- or Marshall-style heroines were archetypal *Household Fairies* in training. The reader could be confident that such well-intentioned girls would make conscientious mothers in due course, if granted the opportunity. 'Wholesome' was a term that reviewers particularly liked applying to such heroines, referring more to their spiritual than their bodily health or appearance. But these stereotypes did not really reflect the changing role of women as time passed. Despite their enduring popularity with readers, perhaps more a tribute to their skill in story-telling rather than their educational effect, fresher versions of the womanly stereotype appeared with motives and abilities more relevant to the later years of the century.

However, from the mid-1870s, a new element appeared

[31] Charlotte M. Yonge, 'Children's Literature in the Last Century', *Macmillans Magazine*, XX, May–Oct. 1869, pp. 448–9.

[32] Charlotte M. Yonge, *The Two Sides of the Shield* (Macmillan, London, 1885). In this sequel, it turns out that Lilias has married General Sir Jasper Merrifield, a brave soldier, p. 22.

[33] Mrs Emma Marshall, *Violet Douglas, or The Problems of Life* (Seeley, London, 1868).

which eventually came to dominate the fictional feminine stereotype. This development, or evolution, was the product of changes in society, particularly from the female standpoint. The 1851 census had first showed a surplus of women over men, and that surplus was increasing due to factors like the growing demands of overseas responsibilities. At the same time, economic factors meant that for many families the burdens of maintaining unproductive, surplus women in a household was a great strain on the domestic budget, particularly as the likelihood of lifelong spinsterhood had become greater for middle-class daughters. Equally, a growing number of women were actively protesting against the limitations of the traditional role assigned to them.[34] It became necessary for didactic fiction for girls, if it was to maintain its basis in perceived realism, to reflect at least some of these developments.

Surprisingly swiftly, an expanded version of the feminine stereotype, one much more able to cope with the changing realities of life towards the end of the nineteenth century began to appear. A whole new generation of writers, still mainly women, emerged and from the 1880s, their stories and their ideas dominated the genre. These authors had a fresh outlook on what society found acceptable in the model maiden: one that increasingly made gestures towards the aspirations of girls and women to a wider sphere in which they could, respectably in the view of society, find fulfilment. Consequently, a wider scope of self-reliance, talents and work became encompassed in the stereotype of a good girl in training to be a 'good woman'.

The changes in the physical descriptions of the heroines are the most obvious indication of this. While quite a number of them are beautiful facially, this is even less important than in the earlier period. Mere prettiness tended to be despised. With some exceptions, these later writers from L.T. Meade and Mrs George de Horne Vaizey rarely depict heroines with any outstanding degree of physical beauty. L.T. Meade's Bel-Marjory had 'heavy, rather plain features'. Mrs George de

---

[34] See, for example, John Burnett, *A History of the Cost of Living* (Penguin, Harmondsworth, 1969); Lee Holcombe, *Victorian Ladies at Work: Middle-Class Working Women in England and Wales 1850–1914* (David & Charles, Newton Abbot, 1973); Angela V. John (ed.), *Unequal Opportunities: Women's Employment in England 1800–1918* (Basil Blackwell, Oxford, 1987).

Horne Vaizey's Betty Trevor had a disappointing head of hair (too thin and short) and a large mouth, to say nothing of a rather prettier younger sister. When a heroine was beautiful authors felt it necessary to qualify their descriptions, as did Evelyn Everett Green in describing the ravishing Gwendolyn Maltby. Gwendolyn is 'tall and stately': along with her fair complexion she has 'masses of soft, rippling hair of a deep gold colour'. More important, her excessive dark eyes and 'indications of power and will in the moulding of mouth and chin' give the face character and interest. She thus avoids 'the charge of insipidity' that beauty often invited.[35] The face of the good girl at the end of the century displayed resilience and resource: for her, character is more important than well-arranged features in producing genuine and lasting beauty.

This emphasis on an increased feminine capacity had a wider effect than facial description. Terms such as tall, well-grown, sturdy and resilient begin to be applied to the physical stature of model maidens. Florence Rivers in Evelyn Everett Green's *Bruce Heriot* provides a good example. She is enthusiastically described as reminding the hero of a 'saint in a stained glass window' but she is a remarkably robust one, being tall and strongly-built. This physical strength was matched by mental resource. She proves herself capable of retaining an admirably cool head in the face of a runaway horse and later, a dangerous storm. It is indicated that her strength of body and mind enable her to cope with perils without the least hint of upset, while they would have crushed earlier heroines like Ellen Montgomery.[36]

This increased acceptance of feminine ability went still further. Florence Rivers displays considerable capacity for helping her father, the Squire, run his estate. Indeed, she has far more idea of business than the hero himself, who has an independent fortune from unspecified sources, and thus can afford to buy a neighbouring estate that does not need to be run at a profit,

[35] L.T. Meade, *Bel-Marjory: A Story of Conquest* (Shaw, London, 1878), p. 64; Mrs George de Horne Vaizey, *Betty Trevor* (Religious Tract Society – henceforth RTS, 1907), 1st edn (1905), p. 13; Evelyn Everett Green, *The Heiress of Wylmington* (Nelson, Walton-on-Thames, 1886), pp. 31–2.

[36] Evelyn Everett Green, *The Jilting of Bruce Heriot* (RTS, London, 1904), pp. 110–12.

unlike his bride's inheritance. Floy Rivers additionally finds energy to restore faith in women and in God not only to her lover but also to a number of other itinerant disenchanted males who happen to end up in her remote village.[37]

Nor was this type of resource confined to the wealthier, rural girls. L.T. Meade's Bel-Marjory is a poor Londoner. Philip Edgar, the strong hero whom she eventually marries, falls in love with her because of her matching strength. Bel-Marjory gives no indication of 'womanly' physical breakdown when under very considerable stress. If anything, it is Philip Edgar who comes nearer breaking point. Nor is Bel-Marjory's fortitude seen by the author as a failing or an indication of unfeminine insensitivity. The presentation of a strong-minded ideal as being the most appropriate helpmeet for a good man was quite a radical departure. Bel-Marjory has founded her faith on God, 'Whom have I in heaven but Thee?', and it is this that has made her what she is; a girl who is, at times, stronger than her lover. For her there is a better prospect than an earthly Paradise. Philip Edgar will be a weaker man without her to remind him of his duty. It is a matter of praise that Bel-Marjory keeps going and even sustains her hero, and she reaps her reward in the enduring tradition by gaining the love of a good man. Yet even here the mark of a new fashion comes out for it is emphasized that Bel-Marjory will support and help her husband in more than a purely domestic sense in their married life. She will be associated with him in his missionary work in the London slums, for instance.[38]

L.T. Meade's novel is an interesting indication of the way in which acceptable standards of femininity had evolved outside fiction that rather than sinking without trace, this capability and resilience of spirit and body became a ritualized feature of heroines in the later novels in this genre; as much of a stereotype as the earlier helpless brand of fragility. It can in many ways be seen as an attempt at the working out by these later writers of the contradictions involved in earlier didactic fiction. It is also very much a sign of the increased demands made on women as the century progressed.

Moral strength was well-established as being a traditional

[37] Evelyn Everett Green, *Bruce Heriot*, p. 256; p. 270.
[38] L.T. Meade, *Bel-Marjory*, pp. 312–13.

female prerogative, being in the emotional realm and it remained an essential element for the new-style *Home Goddess*. The new factor is the growing acceptance of an element largely glossed over earlier: that physical robustness was also necessary to perform the duties required of a *Household Fairy*. Previously, tradition associated feminine fortitude, the moral variety particularly, with a tendency to various malaises such as sick headaches and fainting. Even Miss Yonge's more vigorous heroines are prone to collapse, needing sheer male strength in times of stress.[39] By the 1880s, such behaviour was seen in fictional terms as unprofessional. Authors indicated that an 'early Victorian invalidishness' was neither attractive nor desirable nor even Christian in women. Any girl with a tendency to it should work hard to overcome it.

It was no longer acceptable to lie meekly on a sofa, accepting ill-health and taking an active role in life at a remove as a number of earlier heroines did. Margaret May would have emerged from her bedchamber under the new dispensation, and even if still couch-bound, have taken a far more active role in running the household if she wished to retain the title 'good girl'.[40] As many women in this later period still had sound reasons for ill-health, the difference lay in the attitude that it was no longer acceptable to give way to it without fighting to maximize remaining vigour. Mysie, the delicate sister in Evelyn Everett Green's *Half-A-Dozen Sisters*, is described as being 'poor-spirited'. One sister tells her, 'I do think you would be much better if you would make up your mind to try, and would resolve to go through a little discomfort and fatigue for the sake of strengthening your muscles, and getting out of your invalid ways'. Mysie at least is genuinely delicate. Much shorter shrift is given to the girls who with no such excuse, wilfully

[39] Elizabeth Wetherell's heroines provide a fine example of this. Ellen in *The Wide, Wide World* and Fleda in *Queechy* (Warne, London, 1887) succumb to what are obviously severe migraines after spiritual or physical exertion, needing male strength and comfort to recover. Even Rachel Curtis in Charlotte M. Yonge's *The Clever Woman of the Family* collapses under the strains imposed by the revelation of her foolish behaviour, pp. 266–75.

[40] Charlotte Yonge, *The Daisy Chain* (Macmillan, London, 1956). Margaret May's supervision of the household exerted via moral influence over the practical executors. Later-style invalids give orders directly to the servants from their couches.

betray their God-given femininity by retreating into invalidism.[41]

However, this should not be taken to mean that the earlier concepts of what comprised a feminine ideal had disappeared. The multitude of fictional girls, from heiresses who display a capacity to run an estate with only background male help to girls of slender means who manage their lives on limited resources so brilliantly yet in such a ladylike fashion that they make a lasting impression on a desirable hero, certainly emphasize the extent to which the 'little' woman model had become superseded in this fiction.[42] These later heroines have far more than mere physical and spiritual beauty to offer a fortunate hero, and that includes an ability to act the resourceful *Home Goddess*.

Women like Florence Rivers or Bel-Marjory Fraser may appear to run the danger of self-sufficiency, such as brought Rachel Curtis to disaster. These women were undoubtedly better equipped than any of, say, Charlotte Yonge's heroines to exist on their own; yet they are shown as realizing that their greatest happiness and self-fulfilment would come within the limits of a happy marriage and traditional domesticity. As Alice Stronach's brilliant Newnham girl Olive Carew comments, marriage and motherhood bring 'the highest happiness that life can give a woman'.[43] Even if such women do not marry, they still see domesticity in some form as providing the happiest state for women. Certain fundamental elements of the archetypal *Household Fairy* remained integral parts of the new *Home*

[41] Evelyn Everett Green, *Half-A-Dozen Sisters* (RTS, London, 1910), 1st edn (1905), pp. 4–5; pp. 216–18. See also Evelyn Everett Green, *The Cossart Cousins* (Leisure Hour Monthly Library, London, 1908), 1st edn (1903), for a heroine who retreats into invalidism without need, and loses the love and respect of her desirable aristocratic lover thereby. See Jane Lewis (ed.), *Labour and Love: Women's Experience of Home and Family, 1850–1940* (Basil Blackwell, Oxford, 1987) for a discussion of factors in feminine ill-health, such as frequent pregnancy.

[42] It is worth noting that while the epithets 'little woman' still appear in fiction, the more advanced authors in the didactic genre reserve such descriptions for faulty characters. Where men use such terms, they are seen to be somewhat fatuous.

[43] Evelyn Everett Green, *Bruce Heriot*, p. 230; Alice Stronach, *A Newnham Friendship* (Blackie, Glasgow, 1901), p. 286.

Goddess stereotype: particularly the family context, with the need for domestic talents and accomplishments such as music or art. In other words, this broadening of the womanly stereotype was still very much part of an exercise that envisaged women as having a sphere separate and ultimately physically subordinate to that of men despite acceptance of greater feminine capacity. An acknowledgement of women's resilience merely made it possible for women to fulfil their duty to their families via the domestic role better and even more professionally.

The emphasis on strength, resource and character does not mean that the domestic or maternal side of a woman's role had in any way been superseded. Instead, the new-style *Household Angel* demonstrated a capacity to deal with outside or wider interests at the same time as maintaining her full range of primary home and family responsibilities to a high standard. It remained as axiomatic as it had in previous centuries that only a woman could run a household properly, creating in nineteenth-century terms that emotionally derived atmosphere of home that was considered essential to a family's comfort. Throughout the period none of the novels, even those depicting the more advanced feminine stereotype, ever examine the idea that anyone apart from women as wives, daughters or sisters or occasionally, brought-in ladies to act as superior housekeepers, could possibly perform the household tasks traditionally allotted to them. The fictional tradition that most women found lasting satisfaction in household duties also continued largely unmodified.

This traditional domestic core to the genuine good girl is emphasized by those same writers who so determinedly developed the wider aspects of a woman's role in the newer feminine stereotype. The possession of the household keys was shown to remain a proud ornament, rather than a badge of servitude, for a woman of any rank in society. It is bitter humiliation to Charlotte Yonge's Emily Mohun and Mrs George de Horne Vaizey's Peggy Saville when they fail in what they see as their essential sphere. The difference is that after Emily's father requests her to yield up her keys she sinks further into apathy, while the resourceful Peggy sets to work to learn how to cope – and succeeds in both creating comfort for her father and convincing a good man that she would make a

wife who could maintain and not destroy domestic harmony.[44]
Hints continued to be given to the girl reader, by way of
fictional precept, on how they can organize their time and the
type of domestic chores that are within their sphere, as well as
how to deal with servants, both daily and living-in.

The latter concern is not surprising: the servant question,
after all, was a problem that was a major source of harrassment
for middle-class women throughout the period, whether the
household was wealthy enough to support large numbers of
living-in staff, or could merely afford a daily woman 'to do the
rough work'. The authors of these novels were no exception.
Successive generations of writers looked back with nostalgia to
a supposed earlier 'golden age' of service, when servants were
well-trained and 'knew their place'. Cissy Wyverne, heroine of
Evelyn Everett Green's *Sister*, comes to grief over her first
attempts to train a young girl. Cissy finds she 'did not always
know where I should encourage and where check her'. Left to
tidy her mistress's room, the girl tried on her hats instead: 'It is
horrid — it is disgusting'. Cissy was only consoled by the
reflection that Janet was clean 'in her person'. It is 'no excuse
for her', however, and Janet is to be punished by being
confined to kitchen duty.[45]

It remained well-established also that the domestic role went
beyond mere household management. Accomplishments were
still an essential attribute in the good girl or woman, as writers
throughout the period reiterate. The increased duties of the
Home Goddess did not excuse her from the need to spend a
considerable number of her 'leisure hours', those not taken up
by household or community duties, in practising her drawing-
room accomplishments in order to reach the maximum standard her abilities allowed. Earlier, it is part of that 'Clever
Woman', Rachel Curtis's womanly reform that she revives her
piano playing in order to give pleasure to her husband's blind
uncle in *his* hours of leisure. Later, clever heroines, specialized
in by Mrs George de Horne Vaizey, practised for hours to rid
themselves of any taint of amateurism. Those who were musi-

[44] Charlotte M. Yonge, *Scenes and Characters*, p. 390; Mrs George de Horne
Vaizey, *More About Peggy* (RTS, London, 1901), pp. 211–12; p. 286.
[45] Evelyn Everett Green, *Sister: A Chronicle of Fair Haven* (Nelson, Walton-
on-Thames, 1898), pp. 242–3; pp. 246–7.

cally untalented and artistically undistinguished like the Rendell girls were still nimble-fingered and deft enough to be able
to decorate areas of the house with specimens of their 'fancy
work', with sufficient left over to furnish material for bazaar
stalls in aid of charitable causes. By comparison, Evelyn Everett
Green's Jessy Overton is seen to be foolish and 'perfectly
intolerable' by her brothers because she never knew how to
entertain anybody but herself.[46]

However, the work of acquiring accomplishments to as
professional a standard as possible was never a matter of
self-glorification. The good girl or woman remained possessed
of an essential modesty of demeanour throughout this period
which made public display personally painful. This feminine
modesty was one reason why all authors throughout the period
also concerned themselves to some extent with dress. The
message here remained constant, only the fashion outlines
changed. As Evelyn Everett Green commented, 'to dress themselves with dainty finish' was 'almost a necessity to a refined
gentlewoman'. Outward appearance was the first key to judg-
ing character. For a woman to stand out from the crowd by
means of dress was thus both vulgar and an indication of the
lack of that instinctive refinement which was considered to be
part of a modest damsel of good class.[47]

Few authors writing for this middle-class market seem to
have approved, for example, of Paris fashions, especially for
unmarried girls because of their showy nature. Elizabeth Sewell
abhorred them as did Evelyn Everett Green. In *Bruce Heriot*,
Floy Rivers dresses for dinner in 'pure white satin, cut square
back and front, softly finished off with some exquisite old
family lace, and with sleeves to the elbow.' Ella May, the badly
brought up and unrefined flirt, is dressed in a shimmering
Paris creation where 'The glitter of some trimming [that] ...
looked like the sparkle of diamonds' emphasized her movements. Side by side, Ella (who is not beyond redemption) sees

---

[46] Charlotte M. Yonge, *The Clever Woman of the Family*, p. 292; Mrs George
de Horne Vaizey, *A Houseful of Girls* (RTS, London, 1902), pp. 14–15; Evelyn
Everett Green, *Greyfriars: A Story for Girls* (Leisure Hour Monthly Library,
London, 1905, 1st edn (1891), pp. 142–3.

[47] Evelyn Everett Green, *The Percivals, or A Houseful of Girls* (RTS, London,
1903), 1st edn (1890), p. 3; Charlotte M. Yonge, *The Daisy Chain*, pp. 370–1;
Charlotte M. Yonge, *Scenes and Characters*, p. 186.

that Floy's appearance makes her, Ella, look 'tawdry and vulgar'. A good woman looked best when her own natural charms were complemented, not overpowered, by overbright colouring. No woman could go wrong in either black or white, and failing that, delicate or dark colours were preferred to flashy reds or greens which fictionally indicated vulgarity of mind and birth. Nor should a model maiden's dress reveal too much in the way of bare flesh or be too figure-hugging, whatever the dictates of high fashion. Evelyn Everett Green's best heroines all resolutely eschewed garments that revealed their arms above the elbow. As Elizabeth Sewell commented 'it does not follow that to be a lady it is necessary to be fashionable'.[48]

There was another important reason why dress was important. While personal vanity was always reprehensible, it was, however, necessary to be dressed appropriately to one's social station to retain the title of 'lady' and to bolster family credit. Well and appropriately dressed womenfolk were considered a major element in procuring male comfort and pride, both in and out of the home. Yet this might involve wearing clothing not entirely to a girl or woman's personal taste: as Elizabeth M. Sewell's Amy Herbert was reminded, 'a splendid dress is very proper for a queen and very vulgar for the wife of a trades-man'. It was equally as improper to neglect to spend money on dress if wealth was available: 'it is almost incumbent' for the women of such families to dress richly. Thus a proper sense of social as well as family obligation required a woman to assess her relative rank and dress accordingly. Calculations of age and marital status were obviously also necessary, as well as the setting in which the dresses might appear. Equally essential to all this was an assessment of available income, since middle-class social standing depended as much on that as on breeding. A good woman or girl had to 'look well to the ways of her household', which meant that amongst all her other duties she had to manage her physical appearance on a precise calculation of how much or how little it was right for her to spend on bodily adornment, as both Charlotte Yonge's Mohun sisters found to their cost. Emily spent too much, but Lily too little, and even

[48] Evelyn Everett Green, *Bruce Heriot*, pp. 201–2; Elizabeth M. Sewell, *Amy Herbert*, 2 vols (Longman, London, 1844), p. 42.

though she did manage to look well-turned out she is re-proached for spending only 'half her proper income'.[49]

Greater scope was clearly granted to the female model in later novels, but the same fiction continually emphasized that that scope could never be at the expense of the domestic role. Instead, the model presented for emulation, of a good girl in training for adult status as a *Household Treasure* was, throughout this period, both comprehensive and increasingly exacting. Inevitably didactic fiction set itself to counteract the perceived threat of nineteenth-century feminism (though never mentioned by name) to established values, particularly with respect to the family. The accolade of good woman was thus accorded throughout to those who remained first and foremost a *Home Goddess* so long as there was domestic duty to be performed. Increasingly this meant that a good woman was one who stuck to her traditional role in the face of temptations to waste her talents in spheres less worthy of or less appropriate to her. Self-sacrifice was still the key to perfection for a woman. But it was feared that this alone could not solve the fundamental problem of how to reconcile less ideal human girls to the necessity of putting family interests and the domestic sphere before any more personal aspirations.

To some extent this was where the moral warning theme of such novels came in. Authors showed that they 'understood' the temptation felt by such girls to move outside their prescribed role, but showed (as realistically and graphically as possible) the dire consequences that were bound to result if a girl failed to heed the warnings and selfishly departed from the home circle to follow an 'unwomanly' path. Mrs Molesworth's *White Turrets* concerns the desire of the heroine to abandon 'plain home duties and responsibilities' and eschew self-denial for selfish independence. Mrs Molesworth has to call on the supernatural in the shape of the family ghost before Winifred Maryon is returned to her senses and an appreciation of her God-given duties. Other authors dwelt on more down-to-earth fates such as life-long remorse and loneliness. The latter fate was that of Lilias Rendell in *A Houseful of Girls*, who learned the hard way that 'It is impossible to live a selfish, self-engrossed life without

[49] Elizabeth M. Sewell, *Amy Herbert*, p. 41; pp. 188–9; Charlotte M. Yonge, *Scenes and Characters*, p. 266.

suffering for it in hours of loneliness'.[50]

The assumption of innocence in middle-class girls meant that, unlike working-class girls, it was neither useful nor desirable to display to them in fictional form the seamier side of life to be met should they stray from the paths of righteousness. Innocence was both an essential commodity amongst good girls that should not be lightly damaged and in itself, a barrier that worked against a true understanding of such sordid consequences of lapsing from grace. It was more effective to dwell on the positive aspects of feminine conformity by looking at the rewards that might accrue over time to the good girl. It might be expected that romance would figure largely in this respect. It was, after all, firmly established in the minds of most Englishmen and women that women were the emotional sex, just as men were the logical sex and romance could easily be presented as the most fulfilling reward for women in view of this essential aspect of their nature. Certainly, many of the stories, particularly those for girls on the brink of womanhood, had a love interest with a 'happy ending'.

In addition, romance was plainly a useful tool in the armoury of social control for good girls, given convictions about the emotional nature of women. It was seen as both natural and inevitable that for a woman, falling genuinely in love evoked feelings of cheerful self-sacrifice. It was, after all, a tradition long established in fiction and drama and even real life, that a girl in love would happily surrender her person and possessions to her lover. Love was in Byron's words, 'woman's whole existence', while Tennyson's noble woman followed her lover 'Beyond the night, across the day/ Thro' all the world'.[51] It was thus easy for interested authors to develop a more sophisticated extension to this tradition merging it with the necessary new one covering the yielding up of any independent personal ambitions outside the household sphere by women in love. It was hoped that the demands of women for a responsible role in society could to some extent be met by plugging the line that finding a lover with ambitions to become a husband and bestow a suitable household on the object of their affections was the

[50] Mrs Mary Molesworth, *White Turrets* (Chambers, Edinburgh, 1896), p. 168; p. 227; Mrs George de Horne Vaizey, *A Houseful of Girls*, p. 253.
[51] Byron, *Don Juan*, i. 194; Tennyson, *The Departure*.

PLATE 2   IT WAS A VERY CHARMING WEDDING

The Good Girls' Reward. From *Miss Greyshott's Girls*
by Evelyn Everett Green (1905)

real way for a woman to be successful, while at the same time it encouraged the spirit of unhesitating self-denial which was a woman's great talent.

There is a tendency in modern examinations of the genre to dismiss any such romantic element as being merely social control of this nature: and it can seem in badly written books a superficial, unintelligently sentimental and unrealistic ornamentation intended to sweeten an unpalatable moral and attract the immature and inexperienced. Yet this interpretation overlooks the stand from which most of these authors approached their work. To suggest that romance was an unmixed blessing and a sweet reward for girls was to introduce an element of that unreality which women authors wanted to avoid. Married or not most of them viewed the love stories they presented to readers as being very different to 'fairy-tale love'. That kind of emotional outpouring was a thing against which all writers within this genre warned their readers. There was for them no question that a girl could just fall in love and then live happily ever after with a Mr Right. After all, the marriages of even the happiest of these women, such as Mrs Emma Marshall and L.T. Meade (married to Toulmin Smith) were not without problem and general experience (or observation in the case of spinsters) led to the conclusion that the best of unions was bound to bring many trials, including monotony, suffering and disappointment, and all a woman's powers of self-denial would be needed to cope with them.[52]

Moreover, this fiction retained the view that the man was the head of the household, even though the woman was the effective manager thereof. As Emma Marshall commented 'that the wife should be in subjection is an old, old law, and like others from the same unerring [divine] code, cannot be broken with impunity'. For this, it was necessary to be able to look up to

---

[52] See Charlotte M. Yonge, 'Children's Literature in the Last Century', p. 449, where she warned against the kind of unrealistic romance she even felt that Elizabeth Wetherall promoted. Miss Wetherell certainly comes the nearest of these authors to 'happy ever after' love affairs, but the happiness is totally dependent on a mutual Christian feeling storing up goods in heaven. Mrs Molesworth had a rather difficult, if not downright unhappy marriage, but even though she entered into a legal separation from her husband, she remained firmly of the opinion that marriage was a good thing when wisely entered into.

one's husband as well as love him if this balance was to be retained. Love thus could not honestly be peddled by authors within the middle-class didactic genre as some kind of panacea that would soothe all a girl's frustrations with the limitations of their sphere, and to do them justice, most of these women were fuelled by an honest belief in the messages they passed to their readers.[53]

This understanding of the reality of marriage meant that love was placed before girlish readers in an essentially pragmatic way. Like everything else in a woman's sphere a professional approach was necessary. Essentially, true love was shown to be inextricably linked with genuine respect. Both were necessary if a marriage was to have a chance of being happy and successful. Since the ideal marriage was 'made in heaven' it was a sin for a woman to go into a marriage without love for very practical long-term reasons. It was 'impossible for happiness to exist without love' within the married context. Thus a 'loveless marriage was a catastrophe for any girl', one which would lead to 'moral suicide', a 'deliberate settling down into a selfish, self-seeking life' which would lead to misery for all concerned whatever the initial motive. While any specific reference to the physical side of marriage was avoided, apart from hints by later authors at the pleasant nature of a kiss between two lovers, the nature of the relationship between men and women would arouse a sense 'almost of disgust' when love was not present in the relationship, sure death to selflessness.[54]

Respect was equally, if not more essential. Respect might engender love in due course, as it does in the case of Hyacynth Allardice, who respects and reveres her husband, and grows to love him devotedly. The greatest danger came where there was affection without respect. Authors were perfectly aware that it was possible to feel an emotional attachment where there was no respect, but argued that such an emotion was unlikely to be lasting: nor could it induce a woman to look up to her husband. As Mrs Graham warns Aveline Armitage in Jennie Chappell's *Too Dearly Bought*: 'It is a dreadful mistake to marry anybody whom one cannot both respect and love', for the sake of both

[53] Mrs Emma Marshall, *Violet Douglas*, pp. 208–9.
[54] Evelyn Everett Green, *The Heiress of Wylmington*, p. 403; p. 383; p. 202; Mrs George de Horne Vaizey, *A Houseful of Girls*, p. 228.

parties.[55] Evelyn Everett Green's Mrs Warburton is 'a desperate and most miserable woman' because her husband 'had deceived, ruined, betrayed [her]', and her respect for him as well as her affection had gone. Still worse was the fate of the woman who married for material reasons only, regarding her husband with a condescending fondness or even contempt, as does Constance Hastings in *Violet Douglas*. She is shown to have forfeited 'her grace and dignity' in the eyes of right-minded society, as well as any peace of mind within the confines of her relationship.[56]

Such horrors could only be avoided by treating romance in a serious, professional manner. Love and respect were founded on thorough knowledge and understanding of the character and position, ambitions and abilities, of the other party and in this respect, it was women who bore the ultimate responsibility in romance. This genre of fiction emphasized that much of the responsibility for the successful conclusion of a romance and thus the continuance of the next generation was placed upon the woman's shoulders. There was no question of offending feminine modesty by suggesting that women should take the initiative by making advances to a man. Instead authors operated on the assumption which must, quite intentionally, have been flattering to girls looking for ways to express themselves that women were generally best equipped to act as arbiter in the relationship; to judge the quality of men and the love they offered.

Men were, after all, undiscriminating about the opposite sex. Unlike women, even a good man was too easily fooled by a lovely exterior and until awakened by contradictory behaviour, would work on the assumption that face and nature matched. In *A Houseful of Girls* 'like most young men, Ned was convinced that a lovely body must needs be an index to a lovely mind, and that beauty of face was but a reflection from the soul within'. But as one sister says of Ned Talbot, 'for a clever man who has taken degrees and scholarships and appointments above every-

[55] Evelyn Everett Green, *The Heiress of Wylmington*, p. 325; Jennie Chappell, *Too Dearly Bought* (Partridge, London, 1901), p. 254.
[56] Evelyn Everett Green, *Dare Lorimer's Heritage* (Hutchinson, London, 1891), pp. 228–9; Mrs Emma Marshall, *Violet Douglas*, pp. 208–9.

body else, you wouldn't believe how stupid and blundering he is'.[57]

It was clearly necessary for women to be made aware, as young as possible, of the elements that went to form a good man. Unlike the feminine counterpart, stereotypes of masculinity were essentially relatively static between 1840 and 1905, particularly from the feminine standpoint.[58] A good man, aiming for the title of gentleman, honoured and respected women, and treated them with gentle courtesy. Like girls, boys were expected to acquire a devotion to truth. Unlike girls, in this early period at least, that truthfulness needed to be linked to a physical fearlessness which did not necessarily go hand-in-hand with a highly-developed moral sense. Possession by boys or men of such a moral sense in this fictional genre tends to mean either a career in the Church or an early and noble death. Henry Mohun was a fine example of a noble early death, while the more robust Claude Mohun, destined for an active sphere in life, though a good boy, simply cannot attain his dead brother's level of perfection.[59] It is made plain to girl readers that the necessity for participation in an active life, in business, property management or the armed forces, made it impractical for men to develop that pure moral tone that was so important for women. (It was in this respect, of course, that women were presumed to be complementary to men.)

The most obvious and desirable method for girls to learn the essential outlines of the masculine stereotype was through the sibling relationship, one reason why such emphasis was placed on this aspect by thinkers and authors throughout the period. As 'One who Knows them' commented, 'There is something especially tender and truthful and pure in the relationship between brother and sister and where a strong affection and entire confidence subsist between them the happiness of the home circle is generally ensured', because 'In the hour of temptation, a sister's warning will move a young man's heart more than reproach or entreaty from father, mother or

[57] Mrs George de Horne Vaizey, *A Houseful of Girls*, p. 107; pp. 154–5.

[58] See for example, Carol Christ, 'Victorian Masculinity and the Angel in the House', in Martha Vicinus (ed.), *A Widening Sphere: Changing Roles of Victorian Women* (Methuen, London, 1980), pp. 146–62.

[59] Charlotte M. Yonge, *Scenes and Characters*, p. 95.

brother' – an early indication of popular acceptance of the generation gap.[60] Or in other words, the brother–sister relationship provided an opportunity for apprentice *Household Angels* to acquire the experience in their relations with the opposite sex in preparation for adult life, including assessing the amount of self-sacrifice that would be involved in any such relationship.

The good sister, in training to be a good wife or even a mature spinster had a greater mental and spiritual responsibility towards a brother than any brother had towards a sister. In fiction, if there was a poor relationship between such siblings the male half was usually either irredeemably bad or it was the fault of the sister. In the eyes of established society, the good sister had to be prepared to yield up her own preference to cater for those of a brother. In *Constantia Carew*, for example, the brother, Awdry, was a thoroughly unsatisfactory character with a taste for idleness, money and low life in general. Though spoilt by his mother, he and Constantia had never particularly agreed or had tastes in common. When Constantia appeals to Awdry as a sister to change his ways, he rebuffs her with the words:

> You have been no sister to me – shut up with your books, setting yourself up to be clever and superior, and all the rest of it. It is too late now for me to care for anything *you* may say.

Her failure brings 'tears of self-reproach' to Constantia's eyes as she prays for forgiveness because if she had 'done my part as an elder sister years before' things might well have been different.[61]

In view of this responsibility authors throughout the period were also unequivocal in warning girls against the most obvious ways for girls to make themselves unworthy of their powers. In a view of romance that emphasized the wider implications of that emotion, particularly for women, all transactions connected with it had to be treated seriously. An engagement was a

---

[60] *Girls and Their Ways, by One Who Knows Them: A Book for and about Girls* (John Hogg, London, 1881), pp. 6–7.
[61] Mrs Emma Marshall, *Constantia Carew: An Autobiography* (Seeley, London, 1883), pp. 171–4.

serious affair and to be entered into only as a sacred commitment. Mrs George de Horne Vaizey's Hilary Bertrand asserts that a broken engagement was a thing that shamed both a woman and a family: 'I should never, never promise to marry anyone unless I loved him with my whole heart; but when I did, I'd stick to him if the whole world were against us'. It is interesting to note that a woman is always seen at fault in the case of a marriage being cancelled: if the man was a rogue or she had mistaken her heart, or his, she had failed in her womanly responsibilities to judge well before accepting any offer. Equally pity for the unhappy wife of a bad man is tinged by the feeling that usually she bears a considerable responsibility for her fate.[62]

For a pretty and charming girl, it was accepted that there was a great temptation to exercise her feminine influence and wiles by flirting with admirers. Didactic fiction warned against such a pastime in no uncertain terms. No good girl would knowingly indulge in such an unprofessional and distasteful pastime, and needed to be on her guard against slipping into encouraging innocent admiration too far. Flirtation was universally condemned as unfair, deceitful and impious (marriage was, after all, a Christian sacrament) and ultimately, a sure path to misery for the flirt herself, as well as the unfortunates she played with. Basil Roscoe in *Olive Roscoe* summed up general opinion when describing his sister Pearl as a 'pretty and heartless flirt' and warned that 'if there is anything calculated to mar a girl's prospects, and condemn her to the life of an old maid, it is that character deservedly won'.[63] Certainly at the end of the novel, Pearl is the only adult sister left on the shelf.

It was axiomatic in these writings that 'true' and lasting love was unlikely to flourish between two unequally matched people, let that inequality take the shape of class, temperament or religion. It was rare, but not impossible, for marriage to overcome inequalities in social standing, so long as there was equality of merit and compatibility of temperament as there was between John Halifax and Muriel St Clare. It was even

[62] Mrs George de Horne Vaizey, *Sisters Three* (Cassell, London, 1900), p. 261.

[63] Evelyn Everett Green, *Olive Roscoe, or The New Sister* (Nelson, Walton-on-Thames, 1896), p. 296.

more strongly warned that true love could not be founded on fundamental differences in temperament. The 'romantic' ideal that the love of a good woman could redeem a bad man is dismissed with scorn, as in L.T. Meade's *A Sister of the Red Cross* where much emphasis is laid on the misery that any girl stores up for herself by such a foolish and unChristian match. There was divine sanction for a woman not to marry where there was incompatibility of religion, in the shape of the words 'Be ye not unequally yoked with unbelievers'. Earthly as well as heavenly unhappiness lay in not observing that motto. From Elizabeth Wetherell to Evelyn Everett Green, heroines were prepared to refuse lovers who did not share their religious faith. In *Nobody*, Lois resolutely stops herself falling in love until her would-be suitor converts to evangelical Christianity. Ermengarde Challoner in *The Head of the House* refuses to reinstate her fiancé until he professes his belief in God.[64]

There was an additional, very cogent reasoning behind this practical interpretation of romance. It was presumed that by ensuring that the foundation for marriage was love, and not material advantage on either side, it was possible to ensure that the men involved automatically guaranteed the woman supremacy in her own domain. Her importance to the family because of her superiority in the spiritual and moral sphere was acknowledged. Consequently she would be confirmed in lifelong possession of the household sphere and in her ability to control her husband within the confines of that sphere, despite having taken a vow of general obedience. True love on both sides was therefore the best way to real power for women in their own right – indirectly expressed perhaps, but, from the point of view of women in established society, power none the less and therefore desirable. It was also the way to ensure the continuance of the traditions and values that established society believed were rooted in the family unit.

When Philip Dillwyn proposes in Elizabeth Wetherell's *Nobody*, he kneels. Lois, the object of his adoration, begs him to rise, but he replies that their relative position 'becomes me well,

---

[64] Mrs Dinah Mulock Craik, *John Halifax, Gentleman* (Nisbet, Welwyn, 1898), 1st edn (1856), p. 199; p. 217; Evelyn Everett Green, *The Squire's Heir* (Melrose, Ely, 1903), pp. 7–8; Elizabeth Wetherell, *Nobody* (Nisbet, Welwyn, 1882), p. 450; Evelyn Everett Green, *The Head of the House: The Story of a Victory over Passion and Pride* (RTS, London, 1886), pp. 412–14.

and I think it does not become you ill . . . It is the position I mean to keep all my life'. By contrast, the beautiful Guinivere in *Half-A-Dozen Sisters*, who marries a husband who does not love her, finds to her dismay that she has no power over her husband and thus no role in life. He does not respond to her would-be good influence, because he married her for the wrong reasons. Lord Woodvine, her husband has 'no domestic tastes' and without his respect, she cannot create them and so develop her own rightful sphere because she does not have the spiritual and moral control over him that must form the basis for such a development. She ends up as a cypher in the household, without any power of her own. Because of her husband's opposition she cannot even maintain her habits of Christian worship, or bring up her child to it, one of the essential elements in maintaining status as a *Household Angel*.[65]

Thus the later years of the nineteenth century saw the feminine stereotype broaden and increase in capacity, developing from the *Household Fairy* into the *Home Goddess*, largely in response to feminine pressure. Yet the 'true' woman was still presumed to be the professional of emotion. She both justified and fulfilled herself, authors argued, by competent use of her inborn reliance on emotion. In the following chapters, the ways in which the good girl approached the issues of the world outside her immediate domestic sphere, and the ways in which she was trained to use her emotions 'professionally', will be discussed. As will be seen, love in its various forms was the dominant element, being both control and reward.

Women were shown to refine and control those around them, especially men through love, Christian and secular. As one of Mrs George de Horne Vaizey's men commented 'If girls only understood what angels they might be to men', they would realize that their traditional sphere provided them with the route by which women best fulfilled their ambitions of gaining power in their own right without encroaching on male preserves. Yet that same love, particularly in its Christian manifestation, was also seen as a tool by which women could be controlled and contained and justified in their own separate sphere.

[65] Elizabeth Wetherell, *Nobody*, pp. 457–8; Evelyn Everett Green, *Half-A-Dozen Sisters*, p. 286; pp. 315–20.

2

Religion as a Control on Reality

Good wives to snails should be akin
And always their Houses keep within . . .[1]

These lines may have depicted a popular nineteenth-century masculine ideal, but they by no means reflected the full reality of the female situation in this period. The attempts of women to expand this aspect of the womanly stereotype were increasingly successful during the last half of the nineteenth century. Yet there was no serious desire by the vast majority of women to abandon the domestic core of their role, despite increasingly visible moves which did succeed in broadening the parameters of the feminine sphere in certain respects. The effect of such efforts, however, was that more and more space in the stories written for these girls on the brink of adulthood was taken up by impressions of a variety of contemporary issues and movements. In this respect genre fiction was engaged in an exercise to limit the independence of women outside their households, while still setting its ideals and traditions against recognizably realistic backgrounds. Fiction increasingly became an arena where accepted attitudes on correct masculine and feminine reactions towards current issues were collated in what was presumed to be an easily accessible and assimilable form. It was presented in fictional terms as an attempt to guide and safeguard its adolescent readership against the pitfalls of the world where it was feared that the inexperience and innocence

[1] Part of an epigram pasted into a scrapbook of the 1870s, belonging to Miss Caroline Robinson of Portsmouth, in the author's family's possession. Miss Caroline was the daughter of a well-to-do middle-class ship's architect.

of good girls or women would all too easily lead them astray.

This fiction can thus be taken as an indicator of the growing concern with which established middle-class society viewed this broadening role of women. It can also reveal the tools that that society hoped and believed would be successful in controlling these expansionist tendencies. Orthodox religion had a wide usefulness here. It acted to reinforce the conventional secular values and traditions of the middle-class. It also provided the focus for most of the ways in which established society wished girls approaching womanhood to view the world outside the family community. Much time and paper was spent on sermons and texts for such an audience, delineating the variety of orthodox denominational religious attitudes towards various situations.[2] However, the majority of adult society realized that to most young readers, moral exhortations and allegories of this nature lacked reality and entertainment value, and therefore, impact. The weaving of current religious positions and ideas into the genre of fiction that went to considerable lengths both to entertain and create a credible atmosphere was considered to be a particularly good way of reinforcing the Christian and the social message.

Religion played a central role in placing the ideal of family, and the hierarchical order of authority within it, at the centre of society. Didactic fiction aimed to show that for both sexes, filial obedience was the first foundation for a good and happy life. It was also a way of ensuring conformity to the religion and values of a previous generation, including a continuing tradition of obedience to parents and others set in lawful authority for succeeding generations. To modify slightly the words of the fifth commandment, it was a case of 'honour thy father and thy mother that thy days may be long (and thy status assured) in the land which the Lord thy God giveth thee'. In practical terms that meant that children were to 'obey their parents in the Lord' in expectation of a time when they too could exercise such authority. Since girls were more likely than boys to remain under the family roof until marriage or the removal of that

---

[2] There was available at this time a wide variety of published sermons and religious books and articles, some particularly aimed at the adolescent girl, others such standards as Thomas à Kempis, *The Imitation of Christ*, given to large numbers of girls on their Confirmation in the Anglican Church.

roof, the need for filial obedience in small everyday matters as well as large ones was likely to be more dominant in the ordering of their lives. Religion also emphasized the particular duty of women. With the family as the material secular foundation in which the female stereotype was traditionally fixed, Christianity was presented to children as providing the long-standing spiritual authority for the family unit and the domestic feminine role therein.

It was always admitted, though, that not all parents were good or wise, or even capable of acting in the best interests of their children. This in itself was not seen as a reasonable excuse for disobedience for either sex, so long as parental commands did not conflict with other elements of the commandments. Again, though, the dependent element of a girl's life meant that this was most likely to bear more hardly upon her than her male counterparts. Didactic authors do give many examples of the problems of male conformity, such as in choice of career, partly to show that it was not just one-sided and partly to encourage girls to urge brothers or friends to a due submission. Sisters like Griselda in Emma Marshall's *Laurel Crowns* point out first that parents as experienced adults are better able to judge potential and openings. In addition, they show that obeying the parental will until independence was achieved was only just, and that after that, a young man would probably be justified in altering his career in line with personal inclination if he could do so without damaging his family.[3]

More time, however, was spent on recounting the plight of girls facing such a crisis. A well-trained girl could rely on her conscience and the wide availability of written matter, including didactic fiction, which could inform her on points where it was permissible to stand firm. It was, for instance, no duty of a good girl to marry simply to oblige her family. As L.E. Guernsey's Lady Thornyhaugh reassures her niece:

> no parent has the right to make his child perjure herself by promising to love and honour a man whom she hates and despises, or to promise to love one man while her heart is another's ... if a father bids his child to bow down before an idol, she is not bound to obey.

[3] Mrs Emma Marshall, *Laurel Crowns, or, Griselda's Aim: A Story for Brothers and Sisters* (Nisbet, Welwyn, 1889), pp. 345–7.

Equally, it was not her duty to marry to *dis*oblige that family. In the case of Viola de Grey in *The Sunny Side of the Street*, she has 'fallen in love in a quarter entirely disapproved by my parents' and refuses to give up her undesirable lover. Her defiance of parental command is plainly shown as a 'selfishness' likely to be disastrous to both her family and herself if she persists (which after getting to know Reginald better she does not).[4] In all other respects of life, including the question of leaving home it was generally considered that religion settled the question satisfactorily and effectively on the side of girlish submission.

This leaves open, however, the question of why religion was considered to be such a particularly powerful tool of social control in the case of women, even when it came to wider issues than those centring on the domestic hearth. One reason is that it was already axiomatic in Christian ideology that good girls of any social class had a strong streak of piety as well as virtue, unselfishness and family loyalty in their nature. It was part of a genuinely old tradition in both English life and literature: with saintly girls like Lady Jane Grey and a range of well-known and loved heroines including Chaucer's Patient Griselda, Shakespeare's Cordelia, Richardson's Pamela and Scott's Jeannie Deans standing as landmarks along the way. Equally, modern maidens of fiction, like Ellen Montgomery or Lily Mohun, were recognizable as such partly because of their recourse to prayer and praise at moments of crisis or triumph. Good girls always had their Bible and prayer book close to hand. When Ellen Montgomery's mother was helping Ellen to choose her Bible, Mrs Montgomery insisted that the Bible be of a size and weight to be comfortably carried, and with a print size that would let it be easily read, because the book was intended to be Ellen's companion and mentor in life.[5]

However, there was rather more to religion when viewed as a tool of gender-based social control. Women were firmly established in the minds of society as being ruled more by emotion than reason; while with some exceptions the opposite was the

---

[4] Lucy Ellen Guernsey, *The Foster Sisters: A Story of the Days of Wesley and Whitfield* (Shaw, London, 1882), pp. 401–2; Evelyn Everett Green, *The Sunny Side of the Street* (RTS, London, 1895), pp. 22–5.
[5] Elizabeth Wetherell, *The Wide, Wide World* (Bliss, Sands & Co., London, 1896), 1st edn (1852), pp. 17–18; pp. 26–7.

case with men. It was for this reason that the intellectual discipline of theology was allotted to the male preserve, with the emotional reaction of simple piety being considered more typically feminine amongst those social orders with a developed capacity for both thought and feeling.[6] For women, therefore, religion was viewed as fundamentally an emotional experience, and consequently, was a useful channel through which to guide them.

Concentration by the individual of either sex on self was seen as being a danger to the welfare of society as a whole, and Christianity was useful in combatting selfish tendencies with its message of self-abnegation as the way to happiness on earth and afterwards. Men, however, were better off than women because the use of reason to motivate their actions and the demands made on them by their participation in the public sphere meant that they were less at the mercy of their emotions and so less likely to fall into the trap of emotionally fuelled selfishness. Both the more limited feminine capacity for logic and the more restricted sphere available to them meant that women were particularly susceptible to this unless their emotions were properly disciplined from the start. Moreover, scientific theories, especially after Darwin, put forward the widely-accepted hypothesis that single women were especially, though not uniquely, prone to emotional outbursts because of physical frustration. To avoid this, it was necessary to train all women while still young to discipline their emotions and channel any surplus energy away from self-centred projects and ideas. This was where self-sacrifice came in.[7]

It was easy to interpret Christianity for women in emotional terms, and to suggest that religion demanded of them sacrifices of self in patient imitation of the Christ. The result of whole-

[6] This is still a period when members of the lower classes of society were widely presumed to have less intellectual and emotional capacity than those in the middle and upper classes. Hence it is common in fictional terms to see men as well as women from a working-class background, urban as well as rural, living their lives by rules of a simple, emotionally founded piety. Hymns aimed at this rank of society also tended to evoke this sort of idea.

[7] Herbert Spencer, *The Principles of Ethics*, 2 vols (Williams & Norgate, London, 1892); Henry Maudsley, *The Physiology of the Mind* (Macmillan, London 1879), 3rd edn, p. 164; Martha Vicinus (ed.), *Suffer and Be Still: Women in the Victorian Age* (Methuen, London, 1977).

hearted self-immolation of personal ambition was presumed to result in conversion of feelings of frustration into more constructive emotions from the viewpoint of the community as a whole. Experience and tradition both taught that self-sacrifice was sweet in its results, and thus likely to prove a major aid in overcoming personal discontent. Such an exercise was also of real benefit to women in confirming their moral superiority. It was the sustained practice of such daily abnegation that was commonly presumed to set them apart from, and in this respect, above men. At any period during the nineteenth century, sight of the good woman marked by the halo of self-sacrifice axiomatically called forth feelings of male adoration. Olive Roscoe in Evelyn Everett Green's novel of the same name appeared before a suitor who viewed her with 'something very like adoration, in the thought of her self-sacrificing womanhood'.[8]

However, it was also important that women did not become too fervent in this direction. Even self-denial had to be kept within reasonable bounds if women were still going to be able to operate successfully within the domestic sphere. Sackcloth and ashes were not likely to add to fireside comfort. Equally, the motivation had to be genuinely felt if the immolation was to be sustained for a life-time. Women had thus to be prepared to regard self-sacrifice in a balanced, or professional way, avoiding extremes of either kind in the interests of their allotted role in life. Mothers 'over-anxious to instruct', for instance, had the opposite of a good effect on their children, who could even be 'driven far on the way to scepticism' by too much well-meaning 'energy and fervour'.[9]

It was important to take a proper attitude towards the life God laid out for you. The professionalization of the masculine sphere during the nineteenth century, affecting particularly the middle-class male, has been much discussed by historians. Fiction of all kinds, including that for the adolescent girl, picks up on this theme. Carelessness and idleness, for instance, were

[8] Evelyn Everett Green, *Olive Roscoe, or The New Sister* (Nelson, Walton-on-Thames, 1896), p. 267.

[9] Evelyn Everett Green, *The Heiress of Wylmington* (Nelson, Walton-on-Thames, 1886), p. 150.

portrayed as being the antithesis of professionalism in men.[10] Being a woman was seen as a career in itself and therefore responsive to professionalization, especially when the opportunities of domestic usefulness presented themselves. Thus judgements of behaviour as set against ideal standards in the male sphere were increasingly matched by similar grounds for judgement of feminine demeanour, especially among the middle classes. In origin it was largely a natural spread of attitude from the masculine sphere. As a professional attitude developed towards the performance of the increasing variety of male occupations, from clergymen to politician, men involved in this process began to expect the same attitude towards the running of their domestic backgrounds from their wives. Once accepted by adult society it was inevitable that professionalism should form part of the training of young girls – indeed it could be argued that the use of literature to inculcate various ideas was part of an attempt to indoctrinate the next generation in a professional manner.

The increasing emphasis on this aspect was one of the factors that lay behind the proliferation, throughout the last sixty years of the nineteenth century, of books dealing with subjects such as household management, training of children, and attitudes towards husbands. The majority of these manuals were primarily intended for the adult woman already established in a position of domestic responsibility and increasingly required to tackle her duties in a properly professional manner. This professionalization of the domestic role was also one of the core themes of stories written for girls of this class, backed up by exhortations in manuals, books of essays and articles in periodicals showing not only how but also in religious terms why girls as apprentice *Household Fairies* or *Home Goddesses* could learn their multifarious duties.[11]

[10] W.J. Reader, *Professional Men: The Rise of the Professional Classes in Nineteenth-Century England* (Weidenfeld & Nicolson, London, 1966); Carol Christ, 'Victorian Masculinity and the Angel in the House', in Martha Vicinus (ed.), *A Widening Sphere: Changing Roles of Victorian Women* (Methuen, London, 1980).

[11] See, for example, Sarah Stickney Ellis, *The Daughters of England* (Fisher, Son and Co., London, 1845); *Girls and Their Ways by One Who Knows Them: A book for and about Girls* (John Hogg, London, 1881).

These duties went beyond the obvious practical elements of professional housekeeping. As advancing adolescence brought with it the necessity for girls to develop a sense of refinement and modest restraint didactic fiction made it clear that these elements made their presence felt in a combination of spiritual and in physical ways. For one thing, religion provided the finishing touches to a pleasing appearance for such damsels. A saintly expression could provide a ladylike gloss that would cover the defects of irregularly formed features or impoverished, if neat, dress.

True refinement and restraint rested on possession of the genuine Christian feeling that overcame any thought of self. Miss Yonge's Ethel May, for instance, reveals her selfishness and thus, her imperfect Christianity, by her lack of physical control over her movements. Her skirts get dirty on a country walk, thereby embarrassing her brother and father (one feels that on this showing Miss Yonge can have had little faith in the Christian principles of Jane Austen's Elizabeth Bennett, with her dirty petticoat after her walk to visit her sick sister). As Lilias Mohun in *Scenes and Characters* found, only a firm Christian faith could provide the foundation on which the essential feminine qualities of duty and self-sacrifice could be built. Even the more independent stereotype of a good girl was shown as needing to be guided by a nice sense of religiously inspired restraint in manner and duty in action in all aspects of her life. A corollary to L.T. Meade's Bel-Marjory becoming a better Christian was her development of a sense of good taste in dress and decorum in bearing – a fact that brings her under the approving notice of Philip Edgar.[12]

Stories for adolescent girls aimed also to remind them of their social responsibilities. Men required more from their womenfolk than fireside comfort. They relied upon their womenfolk to maintain the social network that was seen as an essential part of their work and the foundation for their social status. Women's talents, or lack of them, reflected upon their

[12] Charlotte M. Yonge, *The Daisy Chain* (Macmillan, London, 1856), p. 52; Jane Austen, *Pride and Prejudice*, Penguin English Library (Penguin, Harmondsworth, 1967); Charlotte M. Yonge, *Scenes and Characters, or Eighteen Months at Beechcroft* (Macmillan, London, 1886), p. 315; L.T. Meade, *Bel-Marjory: A Story of Conquest* (Shaw, London, 1878), p. 191.

family as a whole quite as much as those of men. In many ways, the Victorian equivalent of the business lunch was the family dinner at home. In such a setting, the efficient and smooth running of a well-equipped household could be displayed as an additional statement to professional efficiency in the public sphere. As Mr Carew in Emma Marshall's *Constantia Carew* implies when giving instructions to 'be sure to be well prepared, and put out the silver on the sideboard', a wife who was also a good hostess added immeasurably to a man's respectability in the eyes of those around him.[13]

It was necessary for the woman, be she wife, daughter or sister, to maximize the resources available to her and entertain guests in the way most suited to the family social station and surroundings. In addition, they had to be prepared to make a good impression at short notice. Mrs Vale Deveron in *For Honour's Sake* is a well-educated and clever young woman, but she fails to see why she should apply that education to the making of a blancmange for dinner 'in case' her husband should bring home a guest whom he wants to admire his menage. The resulting meal was so bad that the guest 'nearly killed himself with laughing' and the humiliated husband scolds his wife so much for her lack of domestic tastes that she faints. It is plainly shown that if she was not prepared to sacrifice her personal interests for her husband's credit, she should not have married.[14]

In addition to evening entertaining, the good middle-class woman and her apprentices in all but the poorest of such households were required to develop and maintain a network of suitable social contacts. This entailed participation in an elaborate ritual of regular receiving of callers and visiting amongst people in the neighbourhood who could in some way support or add to the credit of the family unit. While men were also involved in the process to some extent, it was women who bore the brunt of the exercise, particularly in the last years of the century in urban or suburban areas which usually found themselves denuded of middle-class males during the week-

[13] Mrs Emma Marshall, *Constantia Carew: An Autobiography* (Seeley, London, 1883), p. 16.
[14] Jennie Chappell, *For Honour's Sake* (Partridge, London, 1890), pp. 120–5; pp. 144–5.

days. Calling was the mechanism of social contact in a neighbourhood. Any family not involved in it was debarred from participation in the social activities of the area, and from meeting a suitable range of people, including eligible young men and women. Girls striking up a friendship on chance meeting, as happened with Mrs George de Horne Vaizey's Betty Trevor and Cynthia Alliot cannot continue that relationship until sanctioned by the formal calling of their respective mothers on each other, leading to the consequent assessment that the families, as well as the individuals, are well-suited to further acquaintance. A district, whether rural or urban, would contain a number of social sets comprised of family or household units which would entertain amongst each other, and the limits of those sets were defined almost entirely through the efforts of the womenfolk. Unfortunate indeed was the *pater familias* without the feminine resources to oversee this element of his life.[15]

Thus for reasons of professionalism, social prestige and self-interest, it was important to indoctrinate girls in the correct procedures involved once they were emancipated from the schoolroom. As Madge Roscoe in *Olive Roscoe* finds, lengthening skirts was a signal to good mothers or their substitutes that these maidens on the brink of adult status should begin to accompany them on their social rounds and bear their part in entertaining visitors in the drawing room.[16] Calling was a ritual which took both time and trouble, often with little apparent reward for the woman, especially if young. In less wealthy households where wives and daughters took more than a supervisory role in the running of domestic affairs, the time that had to be set aside for this process ate into periods available to maintain the professional standards demanded by the male members. Also, the necessity for setting aside certain afternoons for being 'At Home' to callers entailed providing suitable refreshments for them. In some households this could entail a considerable strain on the household budget, and in all it required a nice demonstration of housekeeping ability to provide a sufficiency without being ostentatiously lavish for an

[15] Mrs George de Horne Vaizey, *Betty Trevor* (RTS, London, 1907), 1st edn (1905), p. 115; p. 133.
[16] Evelyn Everett Green, *Olive Roscoe*, p. 290.

unknown quantity of guests. The new young bride, Mrs Gervase Vanbrugh in *Betty Trevor* finds herself left with a small army of refreshments from cakes to blancmanges when expected numbers do not turn up and walks in the humiliation of it before her husband for days.[17]

The majority of afternoons would be set aside for the returning of calls for various reasons or the instituting of new ones. For all this it was necessary to dress carefully, in a due indication of one's age, station and resources in life. Lady Blunt in *Laurel Crowns* insists to her stepdaughter that before going out to call she 'change [her] hat, and put on suede gloves, and bring your parasol, the one with lace', because it was essential to be 'presentable' at all costs.[18] Moreover, the social niceties meant that it was important to be on formal polite terms with all the women who comprised a particular social set in a neighbourhood, regardless of personal likes and dislikes and time spent in more enjoyable, informal visits. Books like Agnes Giberne's *Miss Con* abound in episodes of the horrors of trying to entertain unpopular women who could not, however, be ignored because of their social status. It was also demonstrated as being a question of judgement whether strangers should be called on by the matrons of a particular social set in a district. A mistake either way was a serious matter. In the case of Annie E. Armstrong's Mrs Lawrence, the foolish woman holds aloof from some newcomers, only to find herself at odds with the rest of the circle and open to severe rebuke for her failure from her husband.[19]

Here again, if unobtrusively and even indirectly, religion had a role to play as religion was, in so many ways, the oil in the wheels of society. For one thing, the parson's wife, sister or daughter, with a dispensation to visit freely amongst all ranks of society, was frequently shown to be the arbiter of where

[17] Mrs George de Horne Vaizey, *Betty Trevor*, pp. 131–2. See also Carol Dyhouse, 'Middle Class Mothers and Daughters' in Jane Lewis (ed.), *Labour and Love: Women's Experience of Home and Family, 1850–1940* (Basil Blackwell, Oxford, 1986) for further discussion of this social ritual.

[18] Mrs Emma Marshall, *Laurel Crowns*, p. 342.

[19] Agnes Giberne, *Miss Con, or All Those Girls* (Nisbet, Welwyn, 1887), pp. 283–5. Annie E. Armstrong, *Violet Vereker's Vanity* (Blackie, Glasgow, 1897), pp. 150–2.

newcomers fitted into a particular social circle, particularly if little or nothing was known of the strangers' social antecedents.[20] The wife of the Reverend Paul in May Baldwin's *A Plucky Girl* found herself required, despite comparative youth, to take a lead and then advise other matrons whether or not a family was likely to fit into their particular calling circle. For another, girls frequently found the detailed rituals of visiting, including the formal dressing, tedious and pointless. This element became increasingly strong from the 1880s on, as girls questioned the limited nature of their domestic sphere and philanthropic exercise in the community led them to question also the righteousness of socializing in the consciousness of poverty and distress around them. Religion could be called on to explain why girls should acquiesce in the continuation of these social obligations, as in the case of Gwendolyn Maltby in *The Heiress of Wylmington*. The clergyman, Mr Carlingford, tells his refractory subject that conformity in this respect was part of the duty and gratitude owed to God for placing her in a social position where social obligations were part of her life. After all,

> who dare say that it is wrong to take a lively interest in 'worldly matters', when we know who has made the world, and who has never said that such interests are wrong, unless they grow so strong as to exclude all else. The more I see of the world . . . the more do I see . . . the deep need for earnest, conscientious Christians to take up their place in social circles, in the gay round of what always must and will prove the duties entailed by wealth and position, and to show whilst so doing that . . . '*whatsoever* they do they do it unto the Lord'. That . . . would do more . . . than many a crusade against the evils of the day.[21]

Such speculations led on to questions of class. In Mrs Alexander's well-known words:

[20] The nature of middle-class society meant that most people moving into a neighbourhood would be able, through friends or relations, to send advance warning of their family status etc.

[21] May Baldwin, *A Plucky Girl, or The Adventures of 'Miss Nell'* (Chambers, Edinburgh, 1902), p. 102; Evelyn Everett Green, *Heiress of Wylmington*, pp. 361–2.

The rich man in his castle
The poor man at his gate,
God made them high or lowly
He ordered their estate.[22]

It was not for mortals to question the dispensations of Almighty Providence, but merely to accept and be grateful for whatever they were doled out in the divine lottery. The higher the class, the greater the social responsibilities placed on the shoulders of the members thereof.

In questions of class, professionalism and religion acted very much in concert. Because it was both irreligious and unprofessional to question or rebel against the station which God had ordained, it was necessary also to be fully aware of both personal social station and the relative position of those encountered, to maintain stability and avoid mistakes which might embarrass a family. It was imperative that girls realize that it was not 'right to lower oneself by associating with people who are beneath us in station', but that presupposed an ability to recognize social merit in this respect.[23] Throughout this period, the question of class was a potential minefield for the middle classes, becoming increasingly complex as the twentieth century approached. The feminine responsibility for the smooth running of social affairs entailed a great reliance on the presumed female 'instinct' for assessing rank as well as character.

Obviously, though, to work effectively this instinct had to be cultivated and trained, and authors of didactic fiction aimed to help good girls develop their faculties in this respect. The broad question of belonging to the middle orders was settled on the basis of qualifying as a 'lady' or a 'gentleman' – terms which were in themselves open to much interpretation. Authors generally settled their definitions on the basis of possession of 'refinement'. The more genuine refinement one possessed, the more assured one was of being termed socially acceptable. In Agnes Giberne's *Kathleen*, the second Mrs Joliffe was 'not quite a lady by birth or early training' but her 'fine natural character' and later training had raised her perceptions and enabled her

[22] Mrs Alexander, 'All Things Bright and Beautiful', verse 2. See *Hymns Ancient and Modern* (W. Clowes and Son, London, 1875).
[23] Annie E. Armstrong, *Violet Vereker's Vanity*, p. 74.

to claim status, as the aristocratic Lady Catherine Ritchie approvingly noted.[24]

It tended to be agreed that birth and breeding carried with them a greater capacity (not always fulfilled) for developing that certain 'high-bred tone and finish' which was the usual mark of a refined nature in either sex. No matter how good and worthy, an individual of humble origin was less likely to be able to acquire the finer aspects of mental and spiritual distinction, which so often made themselves felt in appearance and deportment. Evelyn Everett Green's Olive Roscoe (who took after her aristocratic mother and was brought up by a maternal aunt) discerned the one man 'of birth and inherited breeding' she met amongst her father's circle of males 'of the money-getting and trading class'. While she had no 'supercilious feelings' towards the latter, she recognized the superiority of the well-named Everard Dacre.[25]

Certainly it was agreed that it was important to emphasize on girlish minds that material possessions, no matter how vast, did not entitle the owner to social status unless linked with the mental and spiritual capacity that should ideally accompany them. As in *Violet Vereker's Vanity*, it was a case of 'Money don't make the gentleman, Miss Voilet'. In fictional terms, the usual mark of successful social mobility was the marriage of a scion of a family of humble background and relatively newly-acquired wealth to a good girl, or good man depending on sex, of established and impeccable breeding, with or without money. In *Violet Vereker's Vanity*, the soap-manufacturing Sugdens acquire the accolade of a 'charming family' after the marriage of the head of the family to 'a lady of rank – the Honourable Constance Dalrymple' who is also acknowledged to be a truly good and refined lady.[26] Yet at the same time, as Mr Carew reminds his children in *Constantia Carew*, 'The day is gone by for anyone to despise trade'. Foolish girls like Violet Vereker, tempted to try to despise 'common tradespeople', need to learn that 'Good honest trade is thought nearly as much of as anything else in these days'. God was responsible for rewarding

[24] Agnes Giberne, *Kathleen: The Story of a Home* (Nisbet, Welwyn, 1883), p. 184.

[25] Ibid., p. 184: Evelyn Everett Green, *Olive Roscoe*, p. 129.

[26] Annie E. Armstrong, *Violet Vereker's Vanity*, p. 2; pp. 19–20.

honest industry and recent peers stood 'side by side with our nobility, and in most cases they are worthy of that high privilege, for they are honourable, upright men, and some of them have done inestimable good with their wealth'. After all, 'if the good Queen thinks these men worthy of the honour' she showed them in various ways, it was not for her subjects to demur, but rather to follow her lead.[27]

The developing 'woman' question added a new dimension to the need for professionalism amongst women as early as the end of the 1860s. This dimension then became increasingly important as time went on. Women clamouring for more fulfilling and more responsible work than was traditionally assigned to them were initially reminded that they already had a career of considerable responsibility. They had a clear duty to remain in a sphere where only they could perform properly the essential tasks. To neglect this prime responsibility would be both unChristian and unprofessional, and selfishly to demand a right to do so showed how unfit such women were to move into the public sphere. As the century advanced and it became necessary for increasing numbers of women and girls to earn their own living outside the domestic circle, this stance was modified, though never abandoned. It became instead a question of whether or not any particular woman or young girl was needed to keep her own domestic circle going. If without any domestic duties, because homeless or if her wages were needed to keep a home going, then it became a duty to seek work outside the home. Otherwise, it remained a prime duty to remain as a self-sacrificing angel in the house rather than indulging personal desires, as will be discussed in greater detail in chapter 6.

For the English middle class during the nineteenth century, religion had implications beyond all this. The vast majority of this class was Protestant, both Anglican and Nonconformist, and the tenets of Protestant religion were considered to be essential in the maintenance of the values and traditions of that class, particularly the domestic ones. Recent studies have shown the emphasis placed by middle-class Protestants of all denominations on the role of family religion as well as public

[27] Mrs Emma Marshall, *Constantia Carew*, p. 141; Annie E. Armstrong, *Violet Vereker's Vanity*, p. 18.

worship.[28] It was generally held that the Protestant religions raised the social status and moral nature of women, by providing them with a natural sphere of action suited to their capabilities, *viz.*, within the home.[29]

It was a fundamental statement in this fiction that the historical development of the home in the English sense was of enormous importance to civilized society as a whole. Men had a 'God-given instinct' to acquire a home of their own. After all, domestic bliss was, as Cowper put it, the 'only bliss/ Of Paradise that has survived the Fall'. That bliss, however, was only attainable through the work of a good woman who was herself possessed of the qualities and support that would enable her to create such an earthly reflection of joys to come.[30] Consequently it was shown as an unquestioned tradition that fictional heroines would automatically turn first to their Bibles for solace and inspiration in times of domestic difficulty. The reliance of the heiress of Wylmington, Gwendolyn Maltby, on her Bible, the last gift of her father before an untimely death, is demonstrated as occurring naturally in the course of daily life. At hand when she woke or slept, or went to her room to order her dress; it was 'a true and unchanging friend and companion, whose teaching grew dearer to her day by day'. She would glance at it in order to find support for her daily actions. In sadness or in happiness its teachings were described as 'words which seemed to her (as when do Bible promises not?) as the echo of her own heart'.[31]

Such a recourse was the foundation on which women were to

[28] See Leonore Davidoff and Catherine Hall, *Family Fortunes: Men and Women of the English Middle Class, 1780–1850* (Hutchinson, London, 1987), Part I, pp. 73–192; A.D. Gilbert, *Religion and Society in Industrial England: Church, Chapel and Social Change, 1740–1914* (Longman, London, 1976).

[29] The author is not aware, despite an extensive survey, of any popular author in this genre writing from a Roman Catholic viewpoint, and can give few examples where the Roman Catholic religion is given much respect. By contrast there are many books in which Catholicism is presented as a threat to established society and its values. See Laura Barter Snow, *Honour's Quest, or How they came home* (RTS, London, 1903).

[30] Cowper, 'Retirement', *The Complete Poetical Works* (Henry G. Bohn, London, 1849); Ellen Louisa Davis, *Asceline's Ladder* (RTS, London, 1892), p. 69; p. 97.

[31] Evelyn Everett Green, *The Heiress of Wylmington*, p. 474.

regulate the informal place of religion within a household. The
fiction of this genre makes plain the emphasis that was placed
by middle-class society regardless of denomination on the need
to found prayer on close knowledge of the Bible. Only petitions
made on that basis could teach people to pray properly and
effectively. Gwendoline Maltby, for example, believes in God,
but her prayers are initially ineffective because they are not
properly based. Seeking help on this point she is told to go and
study the Bible as she would:

> an ordinary history . . . to bring home to yourself that you are
> reading a real history of a real Man. Some people are afraid of
> taking Bible narratives in too practical and matter-of-fact a way.
> This is a great mistake. The Bible is the most practical Book in
> the world, and the gospel narratives cannot be too literally
> accepted. They were written by plain men for plain people, and
> are simple unvarnished facts, which the fact of their inspiration
> does not in any way lessen.

It was, however, also desirable in women to seek certain aids to
Bible interpretation, which effectively meant a male view.
Theology, as an abstract intellectual discipline, was considered
to be outside the scope of the feminine mind, as the next
chapter will discuss.[32]

It was expected that both men and women would pray
regularly, but it is made plain that such regular habits of prayer
were particularly important for women because of their responsibility for the domestic atmosphere. It was crucial for
women to ensure 'the coming of religion into the common little
things of everyday life' in the domestic sphere; for 'If our
religion doesn't do that, it is not worth much'.[33] This was, in
real life, the place and purpose of prayer. In the fictional
echoes of ordinary life, heroines found help, consolation and

[32] Ibid., p. 159; p. 169.
[33] Formal religion within the household, as out of it, was largely a
male-directed and supervised activity. Family prayers, for example, were the
responsibility of the male head of the household, and only if that figure were
absent, or it was an all-female menage, would formal religion pass, by default,
under female direction. But it was the responsibility of women to ensure that
their menfolk maintained regular habits of *private* prayer. Agnes Giberne,
Miss Con, p. 56.

PLATE 3   'ABSENTLY SHE TURNED THE LEAVES.'

The path to becoming a good girl – Bible reading. From *The Heiress of Wylmington* by Evelyn Everett Green (1886)

inspiration in personal prayer, and it was plainly expected by
the authors that this would strike a chord in their readers. In
unhappy surroundings, inspired by the text 'ye have not,
because ye ask not', L.T. Meade's Bel-Marjory prayed that she
would grow up 'refined and gentle and good', and her prayer
was answered. As a result, 'The love, gratitude, faith, awakened
by that first consciously-answered prayer, never died out of the
heart of Marjory Fraser'.[34]

The results of this style of personal faith so carefully fostered
in women and girls of the middle classes had to be spread to a
wider circle within the home. Mothers and elder sisters were
expected to pass the benefits of their Christian experience on to
all members of their household, regardless of sex or rank.
There was, it was widely agreed, nothing like the influence of a
good woman (or several good women) in the home. Alice
Corkran, for instance, wrote a book entitled *The Romance of
Women's Influence* on the 'theme of the helpfulness of women to
men as mothers, wives, sisters and friends'; which dealt with
women who were 'inspirers of some of the greatest work done
[by men] for the [human] race, referred to by a male reviewer
as 'A healthy, helpful volume for any thoughtful girl'.[35]

The reasons for the perceived necessity for linking secular
domestic duty with religious motivation were compelling. Failure to perform the former could be construed as a failure in
Christianity: hence the paramount importance in stories for
adolescent girls of soundly based early religious training for
children of both sexes from the age of first lisping speech. The
conviction was that proper early indoctrination in Christianity
and its precepts as interpreted by middle-class English society
would make religion an effective behavioural constraint on
adult behaviour, and evidence exists which must have encouraged proselytizers to applaud the efficacy of their approach.[36]

Once again, girls' stories focus on the central significance of
the maternal role in middle-class society. With few exceptions,
middle-class children throughout the period taught in Sunday

[34] L.T. Meade, *Bel-Marjory*, p. 133; p. 136.
[35] Alice Corkran, *The Romance of Women's Influence* (Blackie, Glasgow, 1906).
[36] See, for instance, evidence given in Carol Dyhouse, *Girls Growing Up in
Late Victorian and Edwardian England* (Routledge & Kegan Paul, London,
1981), pp. 29–30.

Schools, they did not themselves learn their religion in them. The onus lay on the home primarily, and failing that a daily educational establishment for inculcating religious principles. No hard and fast fictional rules were laid down, but it is axiomatic that the daily occurrence in the domestic timetable of some form of religious instruction to her household was the goal that the good woman should strive for. If domestic or social duties gave the mother little time, then under her supervision a deputy such as an elder daughter or other female relative should substitute for her. Only dangerous illness could excuse failure on the part of a mother to fulfill these almost paramount duties. Certainly physical weakness was no excuse, as instruction could be given from an invalid couch. In *The Daisy Chain*, Mrs May's first sign of a return to her normal duties after recovering from her confinement was a resumption of her religious teaching and 'It was pleasant to see that large family in the hush and reverence of such teaching, the mother's gentle power preventing the outbreaks of recklessness to which even at such times the wild young spirits were liable'.[37]

Even youthful participation in public acts of worship such as Sunday services needed to be founded in maternal teaching, because such lessons were better learned and understood if enforced by the explanations of motherhood, as Mrs Pennington in *Winning the Victory* knew. She gathered her children around her while they 'read the chapter amongst them, verse by verse, according as they sat, and the mother explained all that was hard to understand, and answered all the questions put to her by one another'.[38] It was assumed that biblical references, particularly those in sermons or collects, could be made more contemporary and relevant to individual children and their daily life through carefully directed conversations with strong didactic overtones:

> '"Little children, keep yourselves from idols. Amen." Mamma, what does that mean? ... Was it written only for people long ago? or has it anything to do with us? People never worship idols

[37] Charlotte M. Yonge, *The Daisy Chain*, p. 5.
[38] Evelyn Everett Green, *Winning the Victory, or Di Pennington's Reward* (Nelson, Walton-on-Thames, 1886), p. 33.

now, do they?' Mrs. Pennington looked at her daughter with a smile. 'What do you think about it, all of you? Are there any idols left in the world still?'

'I suppose there are, in some countries . . . but there aren't any in England, I'm sure . . . I didn't know anybody but heathens worshipped idols.'

'But St John says a little more than that . . . What I think St John meant to teach us all is, to take great care that God shall always come first . . . if . . . something else is occupying and absorbing most of our time and thought and affection, then it is time we paused to think what we are doing, for then we are in great danger of making an "idol" of that same thing.'

In such ways, Mamma could make it 'all clear', and warn her children away from sins of idleness and self-indulgence etc.[39]

Society viewed the responsibility of women and adolescent girls for children of both sexes as a divinely appointed mystery; it was to be cherished by women for that reason. Women like Charlotte Yonge's Rachel Curtis find motherhood an experience that resembles religious conversion. When the spinster Miss Abbot tries to bring up a child in *Margery Merton's Girlhood*, the reason behind her failure to make Margery a good, obedient child is that Miss Abbott is not a mother: 'It is because you are not a mother than you cannot manage your little Margery . . . Ah! with the anguish of maternity comes the divine gift of understanding children'.[40] It was considered rare for a maiden lady who had not undergone the heaven-sent sufferings of birth to receive so blessed a reward. But it was neither a light nor a short-term burden, for all the rewards it might bring.

It was necessary to bring Christian judgement to the affair in order to avoid ruin. The vast range of examples of the often disastrous results of lack of early training or of unduly fond and overindulgent maternal love, particularly for boys, in these books indicates both popular concern with the theme, and the fact that it was a very distinct contemporary problem. Mrs Emma Marshall, herself a mother of a large family, wrote in *Violet Douglas*:

[39] Ibid., pp. 33–5; p. 40.
[40] Alice Corkran, *Margery Merton's Girlhood* (Blackie, Glasgow, 1888), p. 35.

> We must needs take our maternal lot to the Great Refiner; we
> must needs cry to Him for wisdom and for help, not only when
> our babies lie upon our knees . . . happy is the son who has a wise
> mother – wise in the wisdom which commeth from above, strong
> in the strength which God alone can give.

Violet's weak, but not intrinsically bad, brother, Willie, is shown
to have brought shame on his family and misery on himself and
his mother because of faults stemming from early training.
Equally, L.T. Meade's apparently unloving and unsympathetic,
if understandably harried, mother in *Miss Nonentity* is shown as
being to blame for her daughter's scandalous conduct. Clarissa
Rodney abstracts a sovereign from the missionary box and sells
a ring which she has been given, all without her parents'
knowledge, to get medical help for her father. She does 'wrong
that good might come', but the fault is more that of the mother
than the child that Clarissa feels when in difficulty she cannot
trust or confide in that repository of right-thinking.[41]

Yet the maternal role was not perceived as an entirely
one-sided process. The presence of a good child, with the
childish innocent capacity for blind faith was often presumed to
act as a reminder, or even a rebuke to the doubting and
questioning adult woman who might, due to the burdens of her
household or sorrow, forget the simple truths in which she was
reared. Amy Le Feuvre was something of a specialist in this
line. In *Odd*, for example, the supposedly unselfconsciously
pious little Betty talks to the grief-stricken mother, Mrs Fairfax,
of her wish that God will send her 'tribulation' so that she can
overcome it faithfully and make Him love her better. As a
result, 'for the first time for many a long month, the sorrowful
woman knelt in prayer. 'God help me!' she cried; 'I have been
an unfaithful servant, and have refused to turn to Thee for
comfort.' Thus duly 'led by a little child' to an emotional high
she returns to the paths of righteousness and is, naturally, a
much happier woman.[42]

Despite the wide acceptance by society of the existence of a
natural childish faith in God, at least amongst good children,

[41] Mrs Emma Marshall, *Violet Douglas, or the Problems of Life* (Seeley,
London, 1868), pp. 51–2.
[42] Amy Le Feuvre, *Odd* (RTS, London, 1910), 1st edn (1894), pp. 103–4.

didactic fiction needed to accept the existence of personal religious doubt as a factor that many good girls had to overcome, sooner or later, in the course of life, particularly once they had left a protected childhood behind. It was a factor that was present throughout the period. Many authors for an adult audience, from Mrs Gaskell to Mrs Humphrey Ward, tackled the problem; but it is an indication of how widespread it was and how seriously middle-class adult society took the question that it should form such a regular feature in the fiction of this genre. In earlier works like those of Charlotte Yonge it tended to be a matter for pity, and certainly heroines like Lily Mohun who never went through such a crisis were spiritually more perfect and better able to display the workings of religion in their everyday life. However, girls such as her Rachael Curtis who did have problems in making their faith a living, breathing reality receive sympathy, not condemnation, so long as they make earnest efforts to overcome the problem.[43]

Later works, such as those of Mrs Meade, can even display a certain approval of a girl passing through a phase of religious doubt. This approval would seem to indicate that by the 1880s there was an acceptance by society that the increasingly independent womanly stereotype would no longer maintain the purely child-like and largely unquestioning acceptance of orthodox Christian doctrine. Her attempts to explore the boundaries of her sphere was almost certain to involve questioning of faith in the process of, hopefully, coming to terms with her sphere in life. As Evelyn Everett Green indicated, this process could actually be used as a means to strengthen rather than weaken faith, as well as to confirm existing social divisions. The clergyman, Mr Carlingford, exclaims of Gwendoline Maltby:

> Thank God for honest doubt and humble determination to struggle after the truth. If those two unhappy girls, her cousins, would honestly admit their doubts and fears, and give one the

[43] Charlotte M. Yonge, *The Clever Woman of the Family* (Virago Press, London, 1983), 1st edn (1865), p. 275. Elizabeth M. Sewell herself went through such a crisis of faith in her youth. Elizabeth Sewell, *The Experience of Life* (Blackie, Glasgow, 1854). Eleanor L. Sewell (ed.), *The Autobiography of Elizabeth M. Sewell* (Longman, London, 1907). See also, A.D. Gilbert, *Religion and Society in Industrial England*.

chance to lay them to rest, they might be happy and useful women.[44]

The conviction seems to have been that so long as doubt was openly acknowledged, interested members of established society, usually priests but occasionally older women, could provide satisfactory answers to the doubters' problems, and thus enable them to become, like Gwendoline, full and useful members of that society.

Religion was also a constant factor in reconciling both men and women to death or serious illness leading to permanent incapacity, with women being particularly vulnerable to the latter. To an active girl it must have been an uninviting prospect. Yet the invalid female lying on her couch, or possibly moving from it with difficulty in later versions, but still taking part in, or even controlling, the life of her household was a stock character in fiction because of the reality that lay behind it and the need to point readers to the positive aspects. In Mrs Marshall's *Grace Buxton* Mrs Buxton was:

> a prisoner to her sofa, day after day, year after year, and yet superintending everything, watching all her children, and exerting untold influence over them . . . It was always customary to put the adjective 'poor' before Mrs. Buxton's name. But few people were less to be pitied . . . Mrs. Buxton was . . . happy in that only true sense – happy because she held the treasure within of which no earthly hand could deprive her.

While later authors preferred less passive resignation, there was essential agreement about the idea of the female invalid acting as the heart of the home. These books also reveal the extent to which girls or women facing an invalid future were offered the consolations of religion to give them strength and purpose and give the sweetness to self-sacrifice that the blind Grace Buxton discovers. Nor was it just resignation to divine will – it was religion that inspired later fictional invalids like Mrs Pennington in *Winning the Victory* to improve as far as possible.[45]

[44] Evelyn Everett Green, *The Heiress of Wylmington*, p. 165.
[45] Mrs Emma Marshall, *Grace Buxton, or The Light of Home* (Nisbet, Welwyn, 1869), pp. 15–16; p. 198.

In practical terms, death was ever-present, particularly in the domestic circle. From the earliest age of comprehension children had to be trained to meet and accept death as a regular part of their life, and again, women inevitably bore the brunt of this. Not only did they have to face the possibility of death for members of their family circle or for potential lovers and husbands, but also, they had to come to terms for themselves and their babies with a high mortality rate during childbirth. It was an important exercise in common sense, therefore, to view death as a transition to a higher and more desirable state, and to encourage grief to be expressed through prayer and religious resignation to the will of God; lightened and comforted by the Christian security of a meeting again in heaven – if you were 'good'. In this respect, the frequent depiction of death beds or narrow escapes therefrom in the fiction of this genre takes on a deeper meaning, particularly when written with a certain skill and restraint as well as genuineness of feeling.

Charlotte Yonge was famous for her depictions of death or serious illness fitly borne by both victim and witnesses. Margaret May spent seven years of *The Daisy Chain* dying slowly and beautifully. She expired with a vision of her mother and her dead lover, 'a consoling smile, on her father' with the words 'Over now!':

> all was over; nothing left, save what they had rendered the undying spirit, and the impress her example had left on those around her. The long continuance of the last suffering had softened the actual parting; and it was with thankfulness for the cessation of her pain that they turned away, and bade each other good night. Ethel would not have believed that her first wakening to the knowledge that Margaret was gone, could have been more fraught with relief than with misery.[46]

Such a description was obviously intended to give readers a guide to comporting themselves under such circumstances, when grief needed to be tempered with relief for the sufferer as well as to evoke feelings of sympathetic sorrow. A later author in *Ruth's Path to Victory*, carefully described a rather sadder, though hardly less common scene, that of a little sister's

[46] Charlotte M. Yonge, *The Daisy Chain*, pp. 575–6.

death from scarlet fever. Again, the scene is clearly intended to evoke emotion, but to evoke it in a positive sense:

> our darling lay dying. Yes, dying! Children though we were, we understood that. She was half upright in bed, supported by mother's arms, and nurse stood weeping beside her ... Her breath came in short gasps, and she now and then turned her blue eyes pitifully from one to another, as if begging for help, but she could not speak. .... Thank God it did not last long! In a few minutes the gasps ceased, and she lay back exhausted, but with such a smile. .... When we saw our little loved one for the last time ... it seemed to us then that we could never, never be happy any more. But God knew better. He gave us comfort first, enabling us to comfort our father and mother, who stood in sorer need of it than we, and by and by we were all happy once more.

Yet they were never so 'unthinkingly gay' as before.[47] The morbidly over-sentimental death scene with exhortations to salvation accompanied by floods of tears that is thought of as typical of this genre was, in fact, far more a feature of the fiction designed for the more emotional working-class evangelical market. Throughout the period, the scenes for imitation by middle-class girls preferred a modicum of restraint in expression as well as a reliance on the meeting in the hereafter as being more in keeping with the orthodox values required by established society.

Generally, this fiction serves to emphasize the central place that religion occupied in middle-class ideology; a factor sometimes overlooked in social history studies of the nineteenth century. Christianity worked as a broad cultural foundation for this society in the nineteenth century. As this genre plainly shows, even those members of orthodox middle-class society who were not convinced Christians found it useful to present a Christian face to the world to conform to social useage; it was part of the subscription to society. Books depicted a world with significant numbers who merely paid lip-service to Christianity in order to conform outwardly. Fictionally, the more significant of these characters either reformed after contact with a 'good' character, often the heroine, or were left discontented with life

---

[47] Evelyn L. Thomas, *Ruth's Path to Victory* (RTS, London, 1898), pp. 124–5.

and facing the prospect of eventual death with fear and trembling. A typical example of the former is provided by the worldly and rather cynical Lady Kingsley in *Joint Guardians*, who is jolted out of her complacence by a brush with death. She becomes aware of the hollowness of her life, that she has been 'a scheming, ambitious woman all my life, for myself and for my children, thinking of nothing but their worldly advancement and mine'. Conscience-stricken she agrees to an unworldly but Godly love match for her daughter and asks her pious stepson how to find her 'better self'. He helps to set her on the right path in time to face the fatal consequences of a carriage accident in a suitable way.[48]

Constrained by the need for reality, the writers of these books also openly acknowledged in their stories the existence of many members of society who paid only lip-service to the tenets of religion and never became true Christians. The fictional characters of this persuasion were generally depicted as objects of pity who concentrated on purely material things and were without a real capacity for enjoyment of the finer pleasures in life. However, their presence also reveals a conception of such people as a social problem, particularly in the case of women. Lovely Constance Douglas's greatest sorrow was the tearing of a new dress, while she could take no joy in the possession of her fine little son, only in her personal appearance. By their poor example, such women could undermine the fitness of the nation as a whole as well as that of their own family unless they were exposed for what they were.[49]

In the main, authors writing for such a market were able to incorporate religious messages that can currently seem over-done or irrelevant into their fictional situations; but that then actually enhanced rather than destroyed the reality of that situation in the eyes of their audience. It should not be forgotten that authors working within this genre generally displayed a keen appreciation of the nature of life and its preoccupations as lived and understood by the class from which, for the large part, they themselves sprang. They tended to keep the examples of high-flown piety in novels like *On*

[48] Evelyn Everett Green, *Joint Guardians* (RTS, London, 1887), pp. 254–6; pp. 303–4.
[49] Mrs Emma Marshall, *Violet Douglas*, p. 99.

Angels' Wings for the supposedly naturally less discerning lower classes.[50]

The way in which religion was expressed in the text of such popular tales did vary with time and fashion, as well as denominational stance. The religious message was much more explicitly expressed by earlier authors. Charlotte Yonge and Elizabeth Sewell both enjoyed a considerable command of suitable biblical mottoes which they used to embellish their stories. But even writers responsible for the creation of the more independent female tradition, like L.T. Meade, used texts that were well known to their readers from other educational sources to reinforce their moral messages in some of their books, particularly the earlier ones.[51]

This general approval of Christian inspiration in the didactic fiction written for girls does not obscure the additional fact that these books fairly faithfully mirror the major Protestant theological divisions of the day, from Unitarian to Anglo-Catholic. By the 1840s, evangelical ideas had had an impact on most areas of Christianity in England, though not necessarily the same kind of impact. The Church of England, for instance, developed a strong band of clergymen fired by an Anglican evangelical fervour; but others within that Church were disturbed by some of the attitudes and beliefs of such men. The Oxford Movement of the 1840s and 1850s was the most notable example of men within the Church seeking an enthusiastic Christianity within the traditions of the old order, rather than looking to the rather emotional enthusiasm of the evangelical clergy, an enthusiasm which linked them with the various dissenting sects. Within the dissenting tradition, the Unitarian Movement equally distrusted the zeal of the evangelical movements, believing they led to a narrow intolerance rather than a broad Christian conviction based on logic and philosophy.

Novels aimed at the growing girl throughout the last half of the nineteenth century picked up on this conflict to a significant

[50] Hon. Mrs E. Greene, *On Angels' Wings* (Nelson, Walton-on-Thames, 1885), p. 280. It must be admitted, though, that even normally competent writers like L.T. Meade were capable of producing books which rather went 'over the top' as regards the religious message, as in *The Beresford Prize* (Blackie, Glasgow, 1890). Often such books were 'pot-boilers', however.

[51] Evelyn Everett Green, *Winning the Victory*. This was built around 1 John v. 21. See title-page and p. 33.

extent. Authors like Evelyn Everett Green and Charlotte Yonge blamed the prevalence of religious doubt on the 'paradoxical position', doctrinally speaking of Unitarians, for instance.[52] Some authors, particularly those publishing mainly with Nisbet & Co. like Agnes Giberne, were firmly in the low Church evangelical tradition. Her tales share the common evangelical preoccupation with conversion leading to salvation that marked this religious preoccupation. Miss Giberne made, for instance, frequent reference to the need for her characters (and by implication, her readers) to be 'washed in the blood of the Lamb' in order to achieve a state of grace with great emphasis being laid on the need to incorporate Christianity into every facet of daily life, and to trust one's fate entirely to God without question. Stranded with a broken ankle by a rising stream, Constance Conway is self-consciously assured of heaven and content to leave the question of rescue to divine will.[53]

By contrast, Charlotte Yonge and Evelyn Everett Green equally deliberately acted as representatives of a continuing Anglican tradition that was more influenced by the Oxford Movement than anything else. A regular reliance by a household on the formal and public rituals of religion were seen as an essential aid in the maintenance of the happy home. Charlotte Yonge saw herself primarily as a tool of Church policy in her fiction, hence her heavy emphasis on the central role of baptism, for instance. The great tragedy in *Scenes and Characters* is that Lily Mohun's selfish actions result in the needless death of a small child. For Evelyn Everett Green, regular celebration of the approved sacraments in the approved ritual always forms an important part of Christian support as well as the social picture she presented for emulation by her readers.[54]

In addition, and more significantly in respect of the gap between these two stances, writers in the moderate Anglican tradition distrusted outbursts of evangelical religious fervour, especially if Nonconformist — reflecting a feeling shared by

---

[52] Evelyn Everett Green, *The Heiress of Wylmington*, p. 163; Charlotte M. Yonge, *The Daisy Chain*, pp. 459–61.

[53] Agnes Giberne, *Miss Con*, pp. 230–7.

[54] Georgina Battiscombe, *Charlotte Mary Yonge: The Story of an Uneventful Life* (Constable, London, 1943), p. 43; Charlotte M. Yonge, *Scenes and Characters*, p. 49 and pp. 203–7. Evelyn Everett Green, *In Pursuit of a Phantom* (RTS, London, 1906), 1st edn (1905), p. 135.

many members of the middle classes. Members of even the moderate Anglican tradition feared that the evangelical movement ran the danger of trivializing Christianity. The latter's reliance on an unrestrained emotional faith was felt to be detrimental to professionalism and clear judgement. It was agreed that it was important to make religion a part of daily life; but many moderate Anglicans feared that the over-emotional fervour of evangelical Christians led them into the danger of debasing certain elements of the sacred in this respect.

Such Anglicans preferred a faith founded on a practical appreciation of the Gospel narratives and a judicious application of certain elements such as regular prayer and Bible reading – but at suitable times and in suitable places. Evangelical fervour, though a stereotypical lower-class habit and admirable in some ways, was, as many Anglican writers made plain, inappropriate to the normal exigencies of middle-class life and pandering wrongly to the whims of the lower classes. It was also not always conducive to respect for social mores amongst working-class Christians.[55] It is a reflection of the factor that families often found it expedient to discard Nonconformist allegiances as they rose up the social scale that the majority of the fiction written for the middle classes, especially the wealthier and more socially prominent portion after the 1870s, was Anglican in tone. There are few fictional examples of Nonconformist families with gentry aspirations! People like the manufacturing Sugdens in *Violet Vereker's Vanity* with the opportunity to be presented at Court, leave Dissent behind.[56]

Despite these differences picked up in fiction of the era, there were fundamental areas on which all parts of the English Protestant middle-class religious community marched hand in hand, throughout the period. The Nonconformists might be more outwardly fervent in their pious support, reinforcing their ideas by singing more hymns both in public and private and eschewing strong drink to a greater degree, but ultimately all the English Protestant denominations were able to find certain important areas of common ground. For all, religion

[55] Evelyn Everett Green, *Temple's Trial, or For Life or Death* (Nelson, Walton-on-Thames, 1887), p. 111.
[56] Annie E. Armstrong, *Violet Vereker's Vanity*, p. 50.

reinforced the family within by preaching damnation to those who tried to undermine the domestic sphere. Salvation and bliss, heavenly if not earthly, were the portion of those who enhanced the Family, particularly women.

However, the necessity for authors of popular fiction to cope with an ever-widening set of social issues meant that from the 1880s on, realism was increasingly preserved by lessening the emphasis on details of religious form, and even on particular texts which might be considered apt illustrations that reinforced a fictional situation. Generally it became more useful to apply religion as a standard against which the merits of certain aspects of life might be measured.

The presentation of orthodox religion had always, in the nineteenth-century fiction of this genre, reflected a social attitude that saw it as the only valid medium through which women might interpret a world outside the immediate household circle. From the 1880s, this attitude became increasingly dominant. This does indicate, in part, simply a device for social control – a necessarily hopeful means of controlling and guiding the energies and ambitions of a new generation into acceptable channels using the teachings of Protestant Christianity to give extra validity and authority to the secular messages of didactic fiction. From this point of view again, the divisions between the sects were less significant.

Anglicans and Nonconformists agreed on the fundamentally distinct and separate roles of men and women in society. Didactic fiction for girls both emphasized the religious sanction for this separate development, and indicated the correct feminine attitude towards members of the male sex, as well as a male estimate of their own role. The starting point was the conviction shared by a majority of the members of the middle classes, that God had made the world for man and, as Charlotte Yonge put it bluntly in a magazine article, subsequently 'woman was created as a helpmeet to man'. Thus women like her Rachel Curtis who attempted to rebel against this and develop a role based on equality of the sexes violated divine law. As Mrs Craik commented, 'Man and woman were made for, and not like one another'.[57] In practical terms, the male role was the superior

[57] Charlotte M. Yonge, 'Womankind', *Monthly Packet*, vol. 17, p. 24; Mrs Dinah Mulock Craik, *A Woman's Thoughts About Women* (Nisbet, Welwyn, 1898) 1st edn (1856), p. 6.

role, in that men had a more active part to play in life – but that did not mean that the place of women was to be seen as inferior in any demeaning sense. The feminine sphere was a complementary, though not necessarily a passive one, particularly after the 1870s. However, though the division of society into two distinct spheres remained constant throughout the period, many significant elements, particularly with regard to the feminine, were questioned and modified as time went on; a process illuminated by the evolution of the feminine stereotype in girl's fiction.

Ruskin provided a popular early reference point for writers such as Charlotte Yonge when it came to delineating the womanly role in its rightful context. In *Sesame and Lilies*, a favourite book of reference for the period, Ruskin commented that the 'true constant duty' of women was not profitlessly to waste their powers on the active roles of invention and creation, but instead to use their uniquely feminine talents for 'sweet ordering, arrangement, and decision'. Ideally, women were 'protected from all danger and temptation', and in return for this, women had to be 'enduringly, incorruptibly good; instinctively, infallibly wise'. A woman 'in any rank of life, ought to know whatever her husband is likely to know, but to know it in a different way' – basically, a more limited, applied one! Women should 'know the same language, or science, only so far as may enable her to sympathise in her husband's pleasures, and in those of his best friends'. Equally, piety, not the knotty points of theology was to be her brief.[58]

By the 1880s, the force of religio-philosophical arguments for the separation of the spheres was reinforced by the appearance of an additional, quasi-scientific school of thought, largely based on Darwin's theories of evolution. The implications of Darwin's ideas as used by the majority of commentators were that women were biologically on a lower evolutionary level than men; and thus were inferior in both physical and mental capacity. The last 30 years of the nineteenth century saw an increase in the status and authority of sciences such as biology, geology and anthropology. As one commentator wrote, these sciences, especially biology, 'threatens to invade and annex

[58] John Ruskin, *Sesame and Lilies* (Smith, Elder & Co., London, 1865), p. 73; p. 87; p. 89; pp. 95–6.

every province of thought'. It is not surprising that established society, for all its doubts about Darwin, used the pronouncements of these respected disciplines on women and their capacities to bolster the conventional position.[59]

Writers working in these fields, almost invariably male, took as an unassailable fact that women were naturally inferior versions of humanity. Commentators pointed to small brain sizes etc. in women and argued that they therefore needed to operate in a different and subordinate social sphere. Books were written specifically on the scientific authority for such judgements, including *The Evolution of Sex*, published in 1889. Coming at a time when there were increasing protests by women against the limited spheres assigned to them, such writings were a great boon to an establishment seeking to preserve a status quo. Science added new weight to a useful tradition that had already called on the powers of religion to enhance it. Moreover, most of the influential writers of scientific treatises were Christian in outlook. Thus men like Herbert Spencer, one of the foremost intellectual authorities of the late nineteenth century on the differences between the sexes, quite unashamedly associated their scientific message in their writings with established theological ones; reinforcing and giving an apparently unarguable new authority and logic to the traditional Christian arguments for separate male and female spheres in life.[60] (It is worth noting, as a counterpoint, that John Stuart Mills' refutations of such theories were, in the eyes of conventional society, devalued and discredited by his religious position.)

An interesting development reflected in fiction that seems to have resulted from this was a considerable increase in the moral status accorded to doctors. Stories written for the adolescent girl after the mid 1870s frequently used medical men in ways more reminiscent of parts previously played by clergymen.

[59] Robert MacIntosh, *From Comte to Benjamin Kidd: The Appeal to Biology or Evolution for Human Guidance* (Macmillan, London, 1899), p. 2.

[60] Patrick Geddes and J. Arthur Thompson, *The Evolution of Sex*, Contemporary Science Series (Walter Scott, London, 1889); Havelock Ellis *Man and Woman: A Study of Human Secondary Sexual Characters*, Contemporary Science Series (Walter Scott, London, 1894); Herbert Spencer, *The Principles of Ethics*, 2 vols (Williams and Norgate, London, 1892); Brian Eastlea, *Science and Sexual Oppression* (Weidenfeld & Nicolson, London, 1981).

Charlotte Yonge's Dr May, for instance, though a good and devout man never reached the heights of saintly nobility and selfless dedication reached by practitioners in the fiction of L.T. Meade or Evelyn Everett Green. Dr Philip Edgar in *Bel-Marjory* is fuelled by a sense of divine mission, and his medicine is as much spiritual as paregoric. One particularly important aspect of this development was the way in which doctors were seen in stories as alternating with clergymen in acting as guardians of the feminine sphere.[61] Doctors were increasingly responsible for warning women, on danger of complete physical and mental collapse, of the perils of going beyond their powers in attempting work and activities suited only to the male frame and brain. Yet such doctors rarely restrain women from working themselves into a state near exhaustion in respect of their accepted feminine duties! In many ways doctors thus became additional bastions of the values of established society.

It has been suggested by Jane Lewis that the shock given to conventional religion by the theory of evolution, made it even more important to a male-dominated middle-class society that women should place the domestic hearth and the moral values centred thereon before attempts to fulfill themselves in a wider sphere, as men were more upset by the detailed implications of the theory than were women.[62] The fiction designed for adolescent girls seems to bear this out, revealing a swift feminine acceptance of the stance that evolutionary theories could be portrayed as being compatible with orthodox Anglican Christianity and then employed to give intellectual authority to existing ideas about women and their social context. Writers like Evelyn Everett Green took it as scientific fact, revealing a sense of divine order, that the brains of women were operated by patterns of emotion and instinct rather than reason. Since morality of the type tradition assigned to good women was an emotional, instinctive reaction to the divine, the moral ordering of daily life was obviously marked out for women. Men were more prone to use logic in their thinking, with their piety being based on a system of carefully con-

[61] Charlotte M. Yonge, *The Daisy Chain*; L.T. Meade, *Bel-Marjory*, pp. 118–21.
[62] Jane Lewis, *Women in England 1870–1950: Sexual Divisions and Social Change* (Wheatsheaf Books, Brighton, 1986), pp. 81–2.

structed theology – which was why men were more susceptible to having their faith shaken by new scientific ideas![63]

However, the demands of fictional 'realism' linked with the progression of the 'woman question' by the end of the 1870s required a shift in the attitudes of authors, reflecting that of established society as a whole. The numbers of women taking a prominent public role of some kind was still comparatively small, but it was growing. Moreover, these women were proving that they could be successful in their undertakings, and the publicity surrounding them meant that this could not be suppressed. Instead, it had to be interpreted as far as possible to fit in with existing stereotypes of femininity. It is noticeable that there was a growth industry from the late 1860s in books for girls containing collections of brief biographies. Such collections, frequently written by popular authors of girls' fiction, found it necessary to discuss the contributions of outstanding contemporary independent women; but surrounded them with accounts drawn from history and modern life of outstanding female contributions to the community through their traditional role. Florence Nightingale, for instance, was surrounded by mothers, sisters and wives of great men – like St Monica, Caroline Herschel, or Mrs Gladstone.[64]

There was also a reworking by women writers of didactic fiction of parameters and emphasis in the relationship between the sexes, as part of a perceived need to impress on girls the importance and influence of continuing within the traditional feminine sphere in response to the growing female pressure for wider and more obviously exciting roles in the community at large. Feminine rebellion might be curbed if not destroyed by scientific advance which came forward so convincingly to reiterate old truths. It resulted, in the later novels, in a discernible increase in the responsibility vested in the feminine

---

[63] Evelyn Everett Green, *The Percivals, or A Houseful of Girls* (RTS, London, 1903), 1st edn (1890), p. 44. Ellen Louisa Davis provides a rare example of an author in this genre writing, in books like *Asceline's Ladder* (RTS, London, 1892), in opposition to Darwin.

[64] For Example, Charlotte M. Yonge, *A Book of Golden Deeds* (Macmillan, London, 1888). Caroline Herschel was a sister of William Herschel the astronomer, and St Monica the mother of St Augustine, and it is worth noting that biographies of St Monica make little mention of her intemperance, though she is the patron saint of alcoholics.

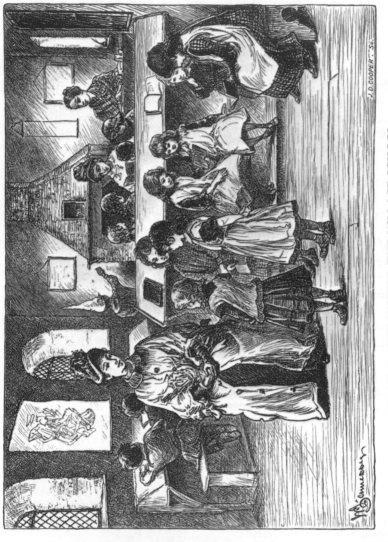

PLATE 4   SHE VISITED THE VILLAGE SCHOOL

An exercise in philanthropy: visiting the lower orders. From Scenes and Characters, or Eighteen Months at Beechcroft by C.M. Yonge (1886)

sex in social terms. First, the modest disinterest that good girls of the earlier era had been ideally required to display in reaction to the male sex until avowals of devotion had been made and accepted was largely dispensed with. Instead, girls were reminded that it was natural that they should be interested in the affairs of the opposite sex, as attraction between the sexes was divinely approved: 'God designed it as one of the great forces in His universe, and an almost omnipotent power it is, either for good or evil.' However, it was up to women more than men to regulate the nature of such intercourse, to ensure that the interest stayed innocent and did not get out of hand.

> Do the girls who frivol and jest with the young men with whom they are brought into contact, realise their responsibility in all they say and do? Do they ever reflect that the beauty and charm which they possess are weapons with which God has endowed them – weapons which may have more power in the battle of life than a two-edged sword? Remember . . . to preserve your dignity as women, knowing that by so doing you will not lose, but trebly strengthen your hold on any man worthy of the name. Say to yourself, dear girls – 'With God's help I will be a good angel to this man, who has to meet trials and temptations from which I am exempt. So far as in me lies I will make him respect all women and help, not hinder him in his work.'[65]

Faced with such unequivocal statements of the harm that women could do by rejecting their traditional role, as well as the good they could do by making the best of it, the more 'advanced' fictional stereotype typical of later authors acquiesced in her separate development; if not always cheerfully at least in a spirit of conviction about the scientific inevitability of her fate leading to acceptance of the moral burden laid on her. It was hoped that by exposing in fiction the dilemmas facing many dissatisfied girls longing for a more exciting life and rebelling against the constrictions of the traditional feminine sphere, and then showing the reasons why such dissatisfied heroines finally compromised their ambitions by settling for a version of the traditional role, readers would be encouraged to empathize with and ultimately emulate such fictional models.

[65] Mrs George de Horne Vaizey, *Betty Trevor*, pp. 166–7.

As before, the role of sister, increasingly extended to include the category of sister-friend, was seen as an important training for adult relations with the opposite sex.[66] For instance, Cynthia Alliot, the sister-friend in *Betty Trevor* grumbles mournfully about the limited opportunities for adventure presented to girls as opposed to men. Miles Trevor, about to head out for adventure in the mines of South America, disposes of her complaints in a fashion characteristic of such clear-sighted fictional men:

> 'And who makes the men?' he asked simply and Cynthia peered at him in startled eager fashion and cried –
> 'You mean – *we* do? Women, mothers and sisters and wives? is *that* what you mean? Oh I *do* think you say nice things. . . . I shall remember that, next time I see a plucky boy pass by rattling the railings, and looking as if the world belonged to him.'[67]

Miles goes out to work for the sake of his mother and Cynthia, and they wait for his return in the knowledge that 'They also serve who only stand and wait'.

As part of this thread in the novel, Betty Trevor is enabled to act as a 'good angel' to a chance-met, fog-bound gentleman who nobly undertakes to escort her home before fulfilling his intention of hiding his shame at a misspent past in the river. He no longer believes in God, but Betty modestly comes to him like a voice from heaven and persuades him, in sisterly tones, to give up his suicidal notions and go abroad to make a fresh start and suitable reparation. When, six years later, he returns out of the blue, with a new name and as the chum and partner of her brother in a successful gold-mining venture in Mexico, he tells Betty that it has been her words and her solicitude that has inspired and carried him on. Once he has revealed his real identity, Betty can do no other than continue the role of

[65] Ibid., pp. 166–7.

[66] Ibid., The term 'sister-friend, is used to describe a girl within the canonical tables of marriage whose adolescent relationship with a boy is considered by authors to be devoid of 'romantic nonsense'. It may, as with Cynthia Alliot, develop into a romance. It may remain an essentially sisterly relationship into maturity.

[67] Ibid., pp. 63–4.

self-appointed guardian angel, but in the persona of wife rather than sister.[68]

On the whole, the view of men presented for the understanding of girlish readers towards the end of the century differed little in essentials from that presented in an earlier period. Men were still presumed to be best fitted for the active, logical world of politics, business and industry, and the army or navy. They were, in stereotype, still courteous and reverential towards women and protective of them against potentially contaminating contact with the public sphere. It was often noted in this later fiction that headstrong girls would try to redefine the parameters of their gender role by rejecting such protection, but almost invariably needed to avail themselves of it in times of crisis.

Overall, it was hoped that the majority of girls would continue to imitate fictional models by continuing to react to men very much as established tradition suggested, despite the growing independence of the womanly stereotype. On this basis, men were still to be respected and deferred to by women in terms of their strength and capacities in the wider community, while still in need of encouragement, comfort and support from women in the morally ordered domestic circle. In turn, men continued to respect and be influenced by good women, whose essential strength lay in the emotional and not the physical realm. In Evelyn Everett Green's *Sister*, Lady Joan Royal runs her estate successfully. Her managerial capabilities are acknowledged to be large – her nephew and heir accepts he can learn much from her in many ways. However, it is also emphasized that she is not 'in the least masculine', in either appearance or ways, and that is the basis of her success. By being a good woman and exercising the influence of a good woman, she is able to persuade her male workers into carrying out her wishes, rather than setting their backs up by ordering where she cannot rightfully enforce.[69]

This all sounds as if writers, and established society, viewed the relationship between the sexes as a particularly gloomy one. What is interesting is the emphasis laid by virtually all authors

[68] Ibid., p. 310.
[69] Evelyn Everett Green, *Sister: A Chronicle of Fair Haven* (Nelson, Walton-on-Thames, 1898), p. 137.

writing in this genre from start to finish on the fun side of it. From Charlotte Yonge to L.T. Meade they showed brothers and sisters, young men and young women, playing games together and having jokes. They did their best to show the characters in their books as enjoying life. Indeed it was quite categorically stated that there was a religious duty for women and girls in particular to cultivate their happier emotions under normal circumstances. As Mrs de Horne Vaizey wrote, 'Laugh and be merry – enjoy the sunshine of your youth; it is a sin to see a young thing sad'. There was a considerable awareness of the danger that a well-brought up girl might turn into a prig, and of the corresponding fact that men were not likely to return to a fireside that was sunk in moralistic gloom. Consequently Mrs de Horne Vaizey went on to warn readers that in order to fulfill the divinely appointed feminine role as regards men professionally:

> It isn't necessary to be prim and proper – don't think that! The Misses Prunes and Prisms, who are always preaching, weary rather than help, but when the bright, sweet-natured girl, who loves a joke, and can be the whole-hearted companion of a summer day, speaks a word of reproof, or draws back from a proposed enterprise, her action carries with it a treble weight of influence.[70]

It is a factor often overlooked in assessments of the Victorian age that for a large number of people, especially those categorized as middle class, life in general contained a considerable degree of wholesome merriment. The frequent occurrences of family jokes, practical jokes, and the laughter that surrounded physical games or activities of various sorts in fiction mirrored a real-life enjoyment amongst most readers. Life might be 'real' and 'earnest', to paraphrase the popular Victorian hymn, but it did not mean you could neglect your duty to enjoy what God had provided for you! And if you were of a merry disposition anyway you had the comfort of being able to indulge in cheerful behaviour in the assurance of pleasing God as well as people around you.

In the face of the growing need to accept the expansion of

[70] Mrs George de Horne Vaizey, *Betty Trevor*, pp. 166–7.

women's roles into a wider sphere, religion acted from early on in the period to provide a 'suitable' channel for women's participation in activities outside the immediate household. Women traditionally acted behind the scenes to sustain the role played by church and chapel in the life of the community. Initially, their role was seen as little more than an extension of the part of their household duties that involved religious instruction of children and servants. It was a short step from this to teaching at the local Sunday School, an activity much indulged in by middle-class good girls, and proposed in fictional terms as a duty where possible.[71] It was seen as an exercise in the personal emotional influence so intrinsically part of the feminine sphere and an acceptance of the responsibilities of their social station. In addition, it was a major contribution to the good of the community. Charlotte Yonge claimed that 'A century of Sunday Schools has saved the populace from heathenism'. Moreover, it was a contribution that was firmly under the supervision and direction of members of the male sphere. Clergymen could be relied on to keep enthusiastic teachers within bounds by due reference to theology.[72]

But the opportunities offered by Sunday School teaching were limited unless women took up the opportunity to follow up their scholars in their home settings. From this it was a small step to full-scale philanthropy. In general terms philanthropy was viewed as part of the social and religious responsibility of the middle classes, and it was apparent that certain aspects of philanthropy were particularly suited to women with their talent for domestic detail, so long as their efforts were supervised by men. They could assess the home situation of any candidates and judge their real needs in a way that a man could not, at the same time as reminding them of the lessons of orthodox Christianity. Didactic fiction without exception showed immense disapproval of girls who, without any religious conviction, still tried to improve the lot of the lower orders. Cicely Allardice in *The Heiress of Wylmington* visits the poor conscientiously both in London and on the Allardice

[71] Evelyn L. Thomspon, *Ruth's Path to Victory*, p. 86.
[72] Charlotte M. Yonge, *Practical Work in Sunday Schools by Charlotte M. Yonge, A Teacher of Many Years' Standing*, Religious Knowledge Manuals (National Society's Depository, London, 1881).

estate. A man dying of consumption craves spiritual comfort as well as the food and firing she brings, but Cicely holds back from giving it. Asked why she did not 'give him comfort?' because 'religion is just as much for the poor as for the rich' she admits to having no real personal belief. Cicely is businesslike in her comprehension of their material wants, but totally fails to give them the real help they seek.[73]

It was a fairly natural progression from assessment of need and the handing out of material things designed to help the needy poor to taking steps to help them in the way that they used this dole and in general, made the best of their lot in life. Authors catalogued the fecklessness and lack of thrift of so many of the working classes, especially those in industrial areas. Fiction indicated the good effect a well-meaning and well-prepared middle-class girl could have on the lives of those lower down the social scale. Lamenting the irreligious ways and unsatisfactory private lives of the mining community, Evelyn Everett Green's Basil Roscoe concludes that 'to train the women kind seems the best chance for a better regimen in the future ... they ... will be the wives and mothers of the rising generations'. So, sanctioned by male authority, Olive Roscoe sets to work to teach them 'object lessons' in domestic economy and subtly thereby, religion.[74] Acting in this way, a woman could develop a very active role in life in a way suited to her talents and her sphere, and, in addition, have a considerable influence for good on her menfolk in greater philanthropic activities. In *Temple's Trial*, also by Evelyn Everett Green, the good results of the efforts of Molly Melville to improve the lives of the wild, ignorant and giddy mill girls leads to a radical change in the attitude of the mill owner and his son:

> My old idea was, that to give a man his wage was all that a master need think of – that his duty ended there. It seems to me now that he can't well stop short with a clear conscience until he has taught him how to spend it.[75]

Fiction shows that by the 1870s it was commonplace for girls

[73] Evelyn Everett Green, *The Heiress of Wylmington*, pp. 112–16.
[74] Evelyn Everett Green, *Olive Roscoe*, pp. 149–51.
[75] Evelyn Everett Green, *Temple's Trial*, pp. 308–9.

to be involved in such philanthropic schemes. It was a mark of
growing maturity when they were permitted to join mothers or
other older women in this work. However, a professional
approach was essential, and in effect this meant acting under
male direction. Being emotional, women were all too likely to
let their emotions distort their judgement, with a consequent
bad effect on those they wanted to help. Ideally, thus, girls and
women would be assigned their spheres of work by men such as
clergymen or doctors; men in a position to have the most
intimate acquaintance with a community as well as the ability to
put it in a proper context. The Beresford sisters in *The Percivals*
want to utilize part of their patrimony (as directed by religion)
to buy some slum cottages and put up model houses for model
tenants. Being sensible girls they immediately admit that 'of
course' they must first bring in male advice to approve and
oversee the scheme. Mr St Aiden agreed it was a good idea
though 'womanlike, you have done so upon impulse', but
insisted that the girls charge proper rents for as they would
find:

> by practical experience, it never answers to do such things for
> nothing. It teaches people to be importunate and discontented.
> Let them feel that they are paying for their privileges ... and
> they will value them accordingly, and preserve their independ-
> ence at the same time.

The troubled reaction of the girls was met by his statement that
it was 'a clear-commonsense rule'. It was essential to be 'business-like even in your charities, or you will soon find yourself in
a mess', and if there were difficulties in paying rent it was better
to put work in the way of able-bodied members of the family
rather than giving morale-sapping alms. In philanthropy as in
all else 'Nothing can really prosper that does not stand on a
sound economic basis': profits could be reinvested in further
and greater philanthropic schemes.[76]
     One of the other important reasons why it was necessary to
keep a close watch on the philanthropic activities of women was
that inevitably such activity would bring women into contact

[76] Evelyn Everett Green, *The Percivals*, p. 117; pp. 128–30.

with undesirable ideas in an age which many feared was becoming increasingly secular. Women maintained the moral purity of society, yet outside their natural sphere women were vulnerable, and would all too readily fall victim to mistaken ideas about society. They might even feel less assured about the role of religion in social problems unless carefully directed. It was part of a major, and an increasing, problem after the 1870s. Since it would be impossible and wrong to stop women taking an interest in philanthropy, it could thus be advantageous to use fiction to forewarn and forearm the youngest, and most impressionable members of the sex. Here again, regardless of period, the fiction of all denominations and all shades of class acted in concert. The 'truth' about socialism, about trade unions and their aims, for instance – two issues which were particularly dominant by the 1890s – had to be demonstrated to combat the insidious appeal that such issues might have for the inexperienced, well-meaning middle-class girl uneasy with her comfortable life in the face of incredible poverty.

In the opinion of didactic authors concerned with industrial problems in particular, such as L.T. Meade and Evelyn Everett Green, 'socialism and atheism always walk hand in hand'. From there it was an easy step to 'prove' to readers that socialism was only very superficially in the interests of the working classes. Fiction was used to show that it trained them in habits of idleness and carelessness, and reduced the capacity to take a moral responsibility for individual actions – all of which was anathema to the good Christian. Also, socialism had a 'levelling' tendency which was in both religious and social terms anathema. In Evelyn Everett Green's *Temple's Trial*, the state of affairs amongst the mill hands was shocking. Fully 80 per cent of them were described as atheists and they not only 'scoffed openly at all forms of religion' but also regarded the State as 'a great engine designed to crush and grind them down to the lowest state of subjugation'. Yet the fault was shown to lie also with the employers who would not take their workers into their confidence and would not encourage religion amongst their labour force. It required slow and patient missionary work to combat the problems of 'red-hot socialism' and return the lower classes to the paths of righteousness and content with their place in the social order, and was, indeed, such a difficult task that years would be required to achieve the goal.[77]

Equally, trade unions were an exuse to fool the poor, foolish, working man into seeking the redress of what were admitted to be often very genuine grievances from the wrong sources. Ignorant of the real economics of business (like all too many of the readers of this fictional genre, it was implied), the existence of times of slump as well as boom, such men were misled into turning away from their employers, and seeing trade unions as the only way to improve wages and conditions. While fiction agreed that employers could be greedy and harsh, the majority were driven by imperatives beyond the vision of their workers. Girls were shown how the best results for those workers were achieved by good management techniques. Trade unions grew up because of bad masters like Edward Lawson in Florence Witts' *In the Days of His Power*, who underpaid and overworked his workers sinfully. It was up to women like his daughter, Freda, to influence their menfolk so that they became good masters. Her influence, and that of her religion, overcome her greedy parent's heart in a far more lasting fashion than any forced settlement of the strike could have done. The reformed man institutes as his motto 'A fair wage for a fair days' work', and his workers become 'the envied ... members of the Templeton population'.[78]

The role of middle-class women was also important, because of the presumption that working-class women were, like their social superiors, more open to religious influences. Good women of all classes were supposed to have an instinctive distrust of both socialism and trade unions, and properly encouraged and guided, could all act together to convince the poor misled men. In addition, any foolish girl whose soft heart led her astray could be convinced by shrewder and older members of her sex. As one woman points out to the anguished young philanthropist in *Olive Roscoe*, strikes were merely a recipe for family misery in view of the 'bit of a wage' allowed by the unions which was 'not enough to keep body and soul together'. But, the wife comments bitterly,

you might as well talk to a doited pig as to a union man when

[77] Evelyn Everett Green, *Temple's Trial*, p. 111; pp. 118–19.
[78] Florence Witts, *In the Day of His Power: A Story of Christian Endeavour* (Sunday School Union, London, 1902), p. 80; pp. 85–6; p. 142.

he's got the union maggot in his brain. He can't see no further
than the end of his own nose ... At such times I do think the
Lord Almighty has given all the strength to the men and all the
sense to the women.[79]

As Olive Roscoe finds on investigation, it would be no kindness
to give in to 'the tyranny of these monstrous organisations'.
Miners are 'a well-paid race on the whole', deservedly so in view
of the nature of their work, but 'to force the price up [of coal]
... would be to cause suffering and depression and misery all
over the country'. It was presented to readers as 'a very
complicated and difficult matter to strike the balance of perfect
justice in such matters', but good men did their best to achieve
it, and were only hindered in their attempts by the interference
of unions. At best, trade unionism was a short-term remedy,
and at worst, a channel for atheism and the decay of civilization
via the promotion of class hatred and the collapse of the social
hierarchy.[80]

This emphasis on the pivotal social role of women of all ages,
and the need for them to be professional in all aspects of their
daily lives provided a major concern for established opinion. In
this respect, Christianity was presumed to be the best safeguard
against any catastrophic erosion of moral standards, by controlling and guiding those members of society most susceptible
to moral damage. It was a time of concern about the poverty
and squalor associated with industrialization and the apparent
decline of religion amongst the working classes, as well as
assaults on English civilization from movements such as socialism. It was also a time when women were making increasing
forays into a wider world and meeting such dangers through
the exercise of, for instance, their philanthropic instincts. In
order to ensure the continuance of secular and spiritual civilization in England, women had to continue to play a central role as
well as being properly trained to undertake their vast, and
increasing, responsibilities. Only by thorough education would
girls appreciate how significant a quiet and self-sacrificing
feminine role was, influencing them, it was hoped, to consent to
take a long-term view. It is thus not surprising that education
thus formed a major preoccupation in didactic fiction.

[79] Evelyn Everett Green, *Olive Roscoe*, pp. 300–1.
[80] Ibid., pp. 301–2.

3
Education for Model Maidens

Be good, sweet maid, and let who will be clever,
Do noble things, not dream them all day long[1]

Of course, the truly noble things for a 'sweet maid' were not the same as those for a man. Kingsley (a great admirer of Charlotte Yonge, who even admitted to being moved to tears by one of her works)[2] did not see English maidens performing the essentially masculine deeds of high chivalric action. The view of the bastions of established society throughout the period was that women had an essential and fundamental contribution to make to the maintenance of society, by the efficient perform-ance of noble deeds within their own domestic sphere. This for the vast majority of sweet maids referred to the duties that pertained to a devout good girl who was an *Angel in the House* and, within limits, in the community. But to function properly in this respect, sweet maids had first to be educated; informed as to what their duties and responsibilities were and how they were to be fittingly performed. In other words, girls could only be transformed into professional *Household Fairies* or *Home Goddesses* via a rigorous training that by no means concentrated on formal academic lessons.

---

[1] Charles Kingsley, 'Farewell', *The Poems of Charles Kingsley* (Dent, London, 1927).

[2] Georgina Battiscombe, *Charlotte Mary Yonge: The Story of an Uneventful Life* (Constable, London, 1943), p. 87. Kingsley was apparently moved to tears by Charlotte M. Yonge, *Heartsease, or The Brother's Wife* (Macmillan, London, 1865).

Recent studies on the schooling of girls of all classes during the nineteenth century have emphasized the extent to which established opinion regarded education as a broad concept, including personal qualities as well as grammar and mathematics in its scope. A well-educated girl in this period was one who had been successfully instructed in the performance of her social and domestic responsibilities as well as in lessons in academic subjects. Scholars such as Carol Dyhouse and Felicity Hunt have pointed to the major role played by gender expectations in the selection and presentation of appropriate lessons for girls and boys.[3] As the century progressed it became increasingly acceptable for girls to study the same subjects as their male counterparts, so long as teaching was coloured by a feminine approach. Ruskin argued that 'a girl's education should be nearly, in its course and material of study, the same as a boy's; but quite differently directed'.[4] The changes in the field of girls' education advocated by thinkers like Ruskin and so energetically worked for by educational pioneers such as Maria Grey, Sara Burstall and Mary Beale are fundamentally linked to the modifications occurring in conventional attitudes towards the role of women in the community; in the things that a good woman could do and the talents she could exercise without upsetting the basic concept of the relationships between the two sexes. Without such advances, the cause of improved female education would have met with much stiffer resistance. Generally, therefore, any scholarly survey of the nature of education in this period must lead to the conclusion that the end purpose of education was assessed on the basis of gender-based expectations of roles in adult society.

That, however, does not mean that education was totally gender-based or biased. A second major plank in nineteenth-century education was character training, many aspects of

---

[3] See Carol Dyhouse, *Girls Growing Up in Late Victorian and Edwardian England* (Routledge and Kegan Paul, London, 1981); Felicity Hunt (ed.), *Lessons for Life: The Schooling of Girls and Women 1850–1950* (Basil Blackwell, Oxford, 1987); Josephine Kamm, *Hope Deferred: Girls' Education in English History* (Methuen, London, 1965); Joan N. Burstyn, *Victorian Education and the Ideal of Womanhood* (Croom Helm, London, 1980).

[4] John Ruskin, *Sesame and Lilies* (Smith, Elder & Co., London, 1865), p. 95.

which were essentially genderless.[5] The place of 'character' in understanding middle-class social values in nineteenth-century Britain has been sadly, if understandably, obscured by the emphasis on gender in recent discussions. It is necessary to have a consciousness of the role played by gender in social development in this period. It is also necessary, if the picture is not to be distorted, to retain a sense of the role of character in education. In many ways Kingsley took the femininity of his maids for granted in his quoted poem; he addressed himself primarily to their character, exhorting them to be before anything else, 'good', achieving that by 'noble' behaviour. Gender constraints meant that in practical terms nobility of character would manifest itself in different ways in men and women. Thus gender and character considerations were both elements in the successful training of children: complementary elements, but requiring specific educational approaches to cultivate them suitably.

Character concerned itself with temperament rather than sexual nature; it was 'character' that marked people out as good, bad or indifferent. It encompassed the attributes that helped people either maintain their original station in life or where fitting, rise to a higher one. Equally it was the factor that explained the downfall of people who were, in a superficial way, blessed by possession of natural talent. Character provided the element that could alone reinforce and underpin inborn temperament and talent. Both of these implied potential, but character summed up the merit, or lack of it, that accompanied them and ultimately, made them socially useful and worthwhile: one reason why middle-class society in this period accepted merit as an arbiter of fortune in life, and something that could overcome established class barriers.

In didactic fiction, for instance, those of humbler background who achieve social heights are shown to deserve their worldly rise in rank because of their fine characters. The hero

[5] Imprecise nineteenth-century usage of the term has tended to confuse the issue for modern scholars. Certain attributes usually classed under the heading of character were undoubtedly traditionally gender-orientated: aggression being perceived as a male trait, and maternalism as a feminine one. Yet most of the most significant attributes of humanity placed by contemporaries under the heading of character applied to both sexes.

of Mrs Craik's much-loved popular novel, John Halifax, rose from a humble tanner's apprentice to a wealthy mill-owner and adorned his new social status with his imposing figure and dignified bearing, but the clear-sighted observer realized that John Halifax's 'true dignity' lay 'in himself and his own personal character' which had been responsible for all his success.[6] His character had been rightly moulded when young, and in maturity it stood him in good stead. He possessed the desirable elements of goodness, strength and selflessness, which overcame any other educational deficiencies and established his credentials as a gentleman.

To achieve the best and most permanent results, character, like a sense of religion, had to be fostered and trained from early childhood. Careful, cogent early nurture was vital. Indifferent education in these respects in the formative years could prevent the development of a strong character, while a sound one could impart lasting strength and resilience of character to a weak nature, masculine or feminine. Even more significant, a bad childhood education could produce from a temperament lacking in a strong natural moral sense a character that was strong but evil, something very difficult to overcome in later years. Therefore, education was important initially as a device which could develop the character traits that were positive and 'good', while eradicating those traits which would generally be described as 'defects' or weaknesses.

Character building had to be the primary goal of education, because without that as a foundation, any other training would be fruitless. the Principal of L.T. Meade's St Benet's College tells her promising student that:

> character ranks higher than intellect . . . You may never get this great earthly distinction [success in the tripos], and yet you may be crowned with honour – the honour which comes of uprightedness, of independence, of integrity.

This applied regardless of gender: Sarah Tytler summed up majority opinion with her comment that the basic character principles such as virtue and honesty 'are as incomparably

---

[6] Mrs Dinah Mulock Craik, *John Halifax, Gentleman* (Nisbet, Welwyn, 1898), 1st edn (1856), p. 173.

superior to any mere mental organism in a woman as they are in a man'.[7] Viewed in this light, the emphasis on character training in girls' didactic fiction becomes more socially significant than a mere patriarchally inspired plot to restrict women to a limited sphere. Estimation of character for both sexes is established as one of the fundamental elements of the spirit of the age.

Religion formed a fundamental element in that spirit, and for conventional opinion was inextricably linked with character. Fiction echoes the agreement that from the time that a child could lisp his or her first collect, he or she was the major custodian of his or her salvation. It was necessary to be good in a Christian sense before aspiring to secular nobility. Being good was a personal responsibility that took no real account of practical circumstance or even age. Adversity was presumed, in object lessons and in stories, to increase moral rectitude, or the longing for it, rather than the reverse. Suffering had a refining effect on a good person of any age, purging the character of less worthy elements. It was agreed that it was often better to suffer from a misfortune of circumstance than to have a happy easy life. Good girls whose lines had fallen in pleasant places, like Molly Melville in *Temple's Trial*, believed that undeserved suffering was a mark of divine grace and favour rather than anything else.[8] The defrauded heiress in *Madeleine* had to take a place as a nursery governess but her friends took comfort in the idea that behind it all was 'some mysterious, though doubtless a wise and good reason', suggesting that 'Perhaps in poverty may be developed noble traits in the dear child's character which, as a petted heiress, might never have come to light. God thinks more of the wealth of the soul than of the pocket'.[9] It was not safe or prudent to rely on the chance of divinely inspired misfortune as a teacher, however. It might never come: so more earthly methods needed to be employed as well.

[7] L.T. Meade, *A Sweet Girl Graduate* (Cassell, London, 1891), p. 251; Sarah Tytler, *Papers for Thoughtful Girls: With Sketches of some Girls' Lives* (Daldy, Isbister & Co., Edinburgh, 1862), p. 27.

[8] Evelyn Everett Green, *Temple's Trial, or For Life or Death* (Nelson, Walton-on-Thames, 1887), pp. 220–1.

[9] Jennie Chappell, *Madeleine, or The Tale of a Haunted House* (Partridge, London, 1894), p. 307.

The usual approach to character education involved a more or less sophisticated use of the carrot and rod theory, using those most basic human emotions, love and fear. Love was considered to be the most effective sanction in the long term, particularly for children; the wisdom of ages supported the case that judiciously wielded there were few more powerful methods of control and few rewards more prized. Love was seen as the cohesive power that had throughout history bound individuals together, as well as communities and the secular and divine spheres. Montagu Tempest in *Joint Guardians* commented: 'it is love that is the greatest power in the world. We can bear anything if only we are loved'. In agreement his bride commented that 'that is why God is love'.[10] In practical terms, the religious implications of love could be used to give a deeper authority to pronouncements made in its name, especially to the young: the parent stood as God's deputy to the child. It was firmly stressed that genuine love was, like God, never blind. True affection was selfless and there was no kindness in overlooking faults, especially those of character.

This belief in love as an effective didactic tool meant that women had to take a prominent role in education. As mothers, or their substitutes, they were the first objects of a child's love and they had a duty, religious and social, to use that power wisely and with an eye to long-term effect rather than short-term personal gratification; one reason why it was so necessary to approach the emotions of motherhood in a responsible manner. It was desirable, if not essential, to set before children an early example of self-denial in order to make it an ingrained principle in adult life, and who better to perform this task than women, the professionals at domestic self-sacrifice. It might not always be easy, but failure was still harder. Evelyn Everett Green's Eugenie Durley 'so craved' her son's love that she tried to mould his character by 'tenderness and gentle forbearance' alone. She learned with tears that such a self-indulgent attitude damaged both her son's character and her power over him. Lady Durley was a wise teacher: her love for her grandson made her stern and so 'he became shame-faced and conscience stricken before his grandmother, and was eagerly anxious to propiate her'. Eugenie realized that:

[10] Evelyn Everett Green, *Joint Guardians* (RTS, London, 1887), p. 262.

Love was not synonymous with weak indulgence. The best mothers were those who had conquered themselves and their natural reluctance, and had brought up their sons with loving yet resolute firmness . . .

Daughters, of course, benefited equally from a similar course of action.[11]

It was, however, admitted that love did not always succeed in achieving the desired end of a well-educated character. In such cases it was necessary, with the sanction of religion as authority and usually in the name of love, to call upon the power of fear to help instil the necessary lessons. Death was a regular feature of daily life for many, so fear of not being 'good' enough to go to heaven was presumed by adults to be an effective sanction over childish naughtiness. Tina Fellowes in *Little Mother Bunch*, with an unconfessed sin hanging over her, found the night full of terror. Listening to the night noises she is convinced that 'ghosts always come to naughty people' and awakes adult authority to make due confession in case death overtakes her unawares. Fear of forfeiting parental or other adult love was also seen as a regular sanction. L.T. Meade's schoolmistresses successfully brought recalcitrant pupils to heel with the threat of withdrawing their regard. As Mrs March said of one such sinner 'I do not propose to punish Alison in any way but by the loss of my favour' because this would be 'the hardest punishment of all'. So deprived, Alison naturally drooped and pined.[12]

The central role of character training in the genre of the nineteenth-century didactic fiction is emphasized by an examination of the output of major authors writing for girls. Most, like Mrs Molesworth, Charlotte Yonge and Emma Marshall, felt a need to write for the juvenile as well as the adolescent market, in order to maximize the impact of their adolescent message.[13] They employed much the same approach in their character lessons for both markets. After all,

[11] Evelyn Everett Green, *Her Husband's Home, or The Durleys of Linley Castle* (Shaw, London, 1887), pp. 335–6.

[12] L.T. Meade, *The Beresford Prize* (Longman, London, 1890), pp. 302–4.

[13] It is difficult to find an author for the middle-class adolescent market without an output designed for the juvenile market as well.

good women were considered to remain essentially child-like, viewing life through the heart rather than the brain and thus responding better to education accomplished through an appeal to the emotions instead of cold logic. Stories for older girls made a more sophisticated appeal to those emotions, while the fiction written for the juvenile market encapsulated less complex lessons, using traditionally popular formats like fairy stories and allegories to aid easy childish digestion of the message. One of the most popular and widely read Victorian tales for the younger child, *Down the Snow Stairs*, provides a useful insight into the nature of the pre-puberty indoctrination presented to girls throughout the period, with a clear relevance to the message for adolescents.

Alice Corkran's little tale reveals not only the stress laid on early character training, but also the fear that was used as a sanction therein and the message of the all-conquering, self-sacrificing power of love. On Christmas Eve, eight-year-old Kitty is in considerable distress. Her crippled little brother, Johnny is dying because she disobeyed her mother and took Johnny out into the garden to see her snowman. Forbidden to visit him she again selfishly disobeys, whereupon Johnny gets worse. In Kitty's despair her mother comes to 'comfort' her by telling her:

> 'You were naughty. I should not love you if I did not say you were naughty', the sweet voice continued, talking in Kitty's ear. She sometimes lost what it said, but she heard the sound like a lullaby. 'Punishment always follows naughtiness. . . . It may not be in pain to your body that it will come. It may come in grief for seeing another suffer for your fault; but punishment must follow wrongdoing.'[14]

It is to modern eyes not surprising that the result of such comfort is an allegorical nightmare where Kitty goes 'Down the Snow Stairs to Punishment Land'. There she sees the fate of children with character faults they wilfully refuse to mend: children who are untruthful and dishonourable, greedy, idle, vain or worst, unloving towards their families. The 'appropri-

[14] Alice Corkran, *Down the Snow Stairs, or Between Good Night and Good Morning* (Blackie, Glasgow, 1887), pp. 32–4.

ate' punishments for all these are graphically described, with a touch that a current writer of horror fantasy might envy, all intended to send a shiver of horror down the spine of a less than perfect child.[15] Along with these youthful transgressors, Kitty is then given the chance to earn a Christmas Blessing – in her case, Johnny's life – if she returns home without succumbing to the pleasant temptations she may meet on her way. Necessarily for the moral of the story, she fails in her task of self-denial because she has not developed the character to overcome temptation – 'No Christmas! No blessing! No Johnny!' cry the successful voices of temptation. Love personified bars the way home. Face down in the snow, terrified and humiliated, Kitty breaks down before this lovely figure with a last-minute full comprehension of her selfishness, and because her humiliation is so complete, Love relents. Though Johnny is saved, this new self-awareness is her true Christmas blessing as morning dawns. Kitty has overcome her temperament, and learned the central lesson that true affection has not only to be 'severe' to be kind, but also that its essence is self-sacrifice.[16]

Kitty may have won her battle young, but authors of adolescent girls' fiction were at pains to point out that this was not always the case, and that unless it was won true success and happiness would elude the unhappy struggler. There were always going to be children who had failed, for whatever reason, to take in the essential messages before puberty and whose battle would continue, perhaps into adult life. Annie Forrest in L.T. Meade's *A World of Girls* and its sequel, *Red Rose and Tiger Lily*, was a delightful girl in many ways, 'love and kindness had developed all the best side of her character'. However, she did not possess 'steady principles'. Despite all her efforts to overcome her natural temperament, lacking those she 'would always be influenced, whether for good or evil, by her companions' and not her own judgement.[17] There was much foreboding in fiction for the future of the Annies of the world and those who came in contact with them, for sorrow was bound to result from their lack of resolution and religion in

---

[15] For instance, children who have failed to show proper affection to their parents are shown as having their legs frozen. Ibid., pp. 123–52.

[16] Ibid., p. 240; pp. 247–54.

[17] L.T. Meade, *Red Rose and Tiger Lily* (Cassell, London, 1894), pp. 16–17.

the rosy lips, the tiny ears, hands, and feet. The child did not stir; it remained quiet in its gray, filmy prison. But there were other children in the fog, some entangled in webs almost as large and strong, while others had but a silver thread or two

gleaming about their necks and brows. These played merrily about, not seeing the black wary spider watching above their head, and every now and then shooting out, spinning and knotting a thread about them.

"What is that dreadful cobweb?" asked Kitty in a whisper, drawing nearer to Love.

PLATE 5

Never too young to learn: in Punishment land — the Fate of those who tell Falsehoods. From *Down the Snow Stairs, or Between Good Night and Good Morning* (1887)

crises and full happiness would elude them in the end.

It was far more serious for men and women when self-discipline had not been learned in any real degree before maturity, particularly as it was so often associated with either a lack of religion or a very confused sense thereof. At that stage, the lessons were far less easily learned, and the impact of the undisciplined character on those around them often far greater. For them, a life of joyful content with the confident prospect of a deserved heavenly reward was a virtual impossibility. Remorse was always likely to peer over their shoulders at inconvenient moments. The weak Willie Douglas created by Emma Marshall finally repented of his ill-doing on his death-bed, but his mother was also prey to that uncomfortable emotion, remorse, because she knew she had failed in her duty to teach him properly in this respect. It was necessary to point this out to adolescents, partly as a warning to acquire the necessary qualities before it was too late and partly to ensure that these attributes would be passed on by the impressed reader wishful of avoiding the reproach of future generations.[18]

Charlotte Yonge's Rachel Curtis is a classic example of an undisciplined character, who inevitably follows a course of action which leads to misery for herself and those around her. Of a naturally robust temperament, Rachel becomes overbearing and self-sufficient despite her desire to be good, because she is lacking in self-discipline and the elements of self-sacrifice; to such an extent that one observer considers her to be totally unwomanly. Rachel's admission of her faults is made in bodily weakness and spiritual humiliation, but she is redeemed to some extent because she has fallen in love and that belatedly teaches her self-denial and restores her Christian faith. However, despite her attempts to reform, her happiness is never as complete as it might be. Such fundamental faults can only be partly remedied in adult life and Rachel is only prevented from further outbursts, and that with difficulty, by her religious faith, memories of the past and her genuine love for her husband.[19]

[18] Mrs Emma Marshall, *Violet Douglas, or The problems of Life* (Seeley, London, 1868).
[19] Charlotte M. Yonge, *The Clever Woman of the Family* (Virago Press, London, 1983), 1st edn (1865).

Girls' novels operated on the supposition that women were in particular need of strength of character and selflessness in order to cope with the increasing demands made on them by their gender expectations. One significant difference between the juvenile and adolescent markets is the lack of gender emphasis in the former. Little attention seems to have been felt necessary in delineating different standards of the ideal for the childhood, largely pre-12 market. This is not to say that authors did not clearly perceive a difference between girls and boys. Many fictional little girls were feminine to the core, with a taste for feminine pastimes like dolls and sewing and the requisite dainty fastidiousness about their appearance, while little boys were rough, tough and disposed to torn clothes, dirt and insects. But much less emphasis was laid on the importance of gender typical behaviour, as is borne out by the indulgence shown to tomboys in this age-group even by early writers such as Charlotte Yonge.

Puberty brought with it the necessity for developing the attributes of femininity, as boyish behaviour became unbecoming in the face of the physical changes that took place in girls' appearance. Charlotte Yonge's Ethel May was rebuked for maintaining her tomboy behaviour into her teens, not for behaving in such a manner in her childhood. Esther Egerton, in her childhood 'a bit of a tom-boy herself' explained to her 13-year-old niece Trixie in *Greyfriars* that it was 'a pity to be too much the tom-boy at your age' because such behaviour was both 'unladylike' and 'disgusting' and upset the feelings of people around her, a thing no good girl wished to do.[20] Understanding of this helps to explain the puzzle of seeming contradictions in behavioural ideas for females to be found in stories written for different age groups.

Some stories written for girls just achieving adolescence indicate the transitional stage, such as L.T. Meade's epic *Four on an Island*, where two related sets of brother and sister find themselves cast away and forced to rely on their own resources to survive. Unlike the Swiss Family Robinson they did not find everything necessary conveniently to hand and had to over-

[20] Charlotte M. Yonge, *The Daisy Chain*; Evelyn Everett Green, *Greyfriars: A Story for Girls* (Leisure Hour Monthly Library, London, 1905), 1st edn (1890), p. 199.

come considerable difficulties. The elder girl, Isobel, who had been something of a tomboy but is becoming increasingly conscious of her femininity, proves herself of sterling worth. Her religious faith and resolution of character help her to take the lead in many ways. She finds that 'being thrown on her own resources led her to make all kinds of discoveries', about herself. She develops ways to make them all comfortable, cheering the others in times of danger and depression, and without falling into the trap of self-sufficiency and conceit. Ultimately, the experience is character-forming for all the castaways, including the older, temperamentally less equable boy who develops both his masculinity and his character on the island. Yet the apparent departure in gender expectations due to the prominent role taken by Bell diminishes neither her femininity nor her brother's masculinity.[21]

While temperament could be modified, gender was an unalterable aspect of nature that no education could alter or overcome. The feminine or masculine nature was inborn and inescapable, and from adolescence it was seen as asserting its influence to an ever-increasing extent. The limitations this awakening of the gender nature brought with it to women, especially those who had had a taste for boisterousness in childhood, were agreed to be hard to accept. Education thus had a major role in persuading young women of the necessity to conform to conventional standards of femininity in their ambitions and actions, and so the education of the adolescent girl involved a complex mixture of continuing character training and the teaching of gender expectations. Religion played a prominent role here, particularly with those whose as yet incompletely trained temperaments rebelled against the constraints of the traditional role open to them. As the century progressed, the authority of divine ordination of this view was increasingly called into play against girls with desires awakened by education to walk new paths. They were to be consoled for their self-denial by the promise of a reward in Heaven such as Ethel May looked forward to.[22]

[21] L.T. Meade, *Four on an Island: A Story of Adventure* (Chambers, Edinburgh, 1892), p. 241.
[22] Charlotte M. Yonge, *The Daisy Chain* (Macmillan, London, 1856), pp. 593–4.

Yet they were additionally supposed in fictional theory, and life-supported fiction, to get earthly pleasure from sacrificing themselves and subordinating their talents for the love of others, be they parents, siblings or sweethearts.[23] This promise of happiness was of considerable importance for the maintenance of the existing, female-bolstered society. Few girls would in practice be quite so masochistic as to deny themselves any chance for contentment in their daily round in order to sustain the great abstract goal of continuing social harmony. Backed up with the undeniable presence of real-life models, fiction could act as both a warning of the problems they would have to overcome, and a sympathetic guide on ways to tackle them. It could also be a reminder of the pleasurable rewards to be gained in life – such as the complacent glow that came from problems overcome and ambitions slain on the altar of affection.

Tales for the adolescent market therefore abound in plots dealing with the most common and likely scenarios that were likely to strew obstacles in the path of the well-intentioned but ambitious maiden. These certainly increased in complexity, as well as variety and scope as the century and education for women advanced. Heroine of *The Daisy Chain*, Ethel May in the 1850s only desired to have time to acquire more knowledge at home: and her path to victory over her personal ambitions was relatively straightforward as compared with the trials facing her intellectual counterparts later in the century. Aveline Armitage in *Too Dearly Bought* had to come to terms with a resignation of the wider possibilities to which her intellectual talents seemed to entitle her, to fulfil the duty that lay before her of caring for the deaf child of her unattainable hero.[24] The happy endings of these novels hinted that the only method by which their problems could be resolved remained self-denial brought into being and fuelled by Love, divine and secular.

[23] Women like Mrs Gladstone, Caroline Herschel and even a number of the authors of this genre of fiction like Elizabeth Sewell or Emma Marshall lived lifestyles that provided testimony to the extent to which women were capable of living lives dedicated to the comfort and ambitions of others around them, and yet appearing to enjoy their lives quite as much as less self-sacrificing sisters!

[24] Jennie Chappell, *Too Dearly Bought* (Partridge, London, 1901).

This, raised to ever higher stages of perfection, was capable of overcoming all obstacles. Fiction aimed sympathetically to show that readers were not alone in their hopes and their trials. Other people had had similar ones and triumphed through the power of love. Fiction also aimed to assure readers that, like Aveline, in overcoming, it was possible to achieve security and degrees of happiness that had eluded them in more selfish times.

It was advances in female education, particularly in its scope, that undoubtedly fuelled the ambitions of growing numbers of girls to perform tasks traditionally considered outside their sphere and even competence during this period. Ironically, these advances were advocated in essence by the increasing demands made by conventional society on the domestic capacity of the *Household Fairy* as she modified into the *Home Goddess*. The growing emphasis on professionalization within all elements of society entailed a consciousness that the disciplined habits of thought instilled by a careful education of the intellect could be immensely valuable to aid efficiency in the domestic, feminine as well as the public, masculine sphere.

Sarah Tytler exhorted her thoughtful girls to remember that, all other things being equal, 'a clever good woman is a finer, abler being than a stupid good woman'. The opinion of Mr Carleton, the English hero in Elizabeth Wetherell's *Queechy* in this respect amplified this. The view was put to him that 'a woman's true sphere is in her family – in her home duties, which furnish the best and most appropriate training for her faculties – pointed out by nature herself'. Mr Carleton responded that as women's duties were 'some of the very highest and noblest that are entrusted to human agency, the fine machinery that is to perform them should be wrought to its last point of perfectness'. He added that:

The wealth of a woman's mind, instead of lying in the rough, should be richly brought out and fashioned for its various ends, while yet those ends are in the future, or it will never meet that demand. And for her own happiness, all the more because her sphere is at home, her home stores should be exhaustless – the stores she cannot go abroad to seek. I would add to strength beauty, and to beauty grace, in the intellectual proportions, so far as possible. It were ungenerous in man to condemn the *best* half of human intellect to insignificance merely because it is not his own.[25]

It was in male interests to ensure that women had the opportunities to be as well-educated as their minds and bodies would allow.

However, there was no intention of using education to promote a revolution in women's role in the community. The majority of educational reformers, male or female, and certainly the most influential of them, looked on girls' education as a way to get the best out of the existing situation. Even those amongst this majority that advocated a single curriculum for both sexes saw that curriculum achieving different ends according to sex.[26] As Carol Dyhouse has pointed out, no attempt was made by these reformers to reform the concept of different spheres of occupation for men and women. The domestic circle remained woman's highest, holiest goal and a good liberal education fitted her to maximize the opportunities offered her within its legitimate bounds. Yet this should not be held to minimize the reforming zeal of women interested in female education or the firm conviction that women like L.T. Meade possessed, that it was in the best long-term interests of the female sex to maintain the *status quo* in this respect. Stories like *A Sweet Girl Graduate* or Mrs George de Horne Vaizey's *Sisters Three* insisted that women were neither mentally nor physically capable of operating in the same world and on the same terms as men, but equally, the consolation was that no man could substitute for a woman in her own sphere.[27]

A key assumption by most writers presenting their thoughts to adolescent girls was that there was a difference in tone between the male and the female mind. The male mind was creative, with an ability to produce original thought and artefacts of great artistic mastery that in a chosen few

[25] Sarah Tytler, *Thoughtful Girls*, p. 27; Elizabeth Wetherell, *Queechy* (Warne, London, 1877), p. 279.

[26] Mrs Maria Grey and Sara Burstall, for instance, saw the married state as the ideal for women, and education as fitting women primarily for that, and only secondarily for undertaking suitably 'womanly' employment. See Maria Grey, *Old Maids. A Lecture* (William Ridgeway, London, 1875), for instance.

[27] Carol Dyhouse, *Girls Growing Up*, pp. 139–50; L.T. Meade, *A Sweet Girl Graduate*; Mrs George de Horne Vaizey, *Sisters Three* (Cassell, London, 1900).

amounted to genius. The female mind was essentially imitative, and at its best incapable of the heights to which men could aspire. Thomasina Bolderstone in Mrs George de Horne Vaizey's *Tom and Some Other Girls* poured scorn on the 'ordinary blunt, straightforward questions manufactured by the masculine mind'; girls were tested better by questions that required them to use their wits and feminine insight.[28] Consequently it was permissible for clever men to cultivate their intellectual abilities to the highest level they could attain for the love of it, because of the possibility that their efforts might produce some outpouring of genius that would improve society's quality of life. It was very different for women. Girls should certainly 'honour and cherish their intellects', but they had to avoid 'cultivating intellect for intellect's sake' as there was 'No more barren toil; no more bootless harvest'. There simply was no possibility that anything comparable to the peak of male genius could result from a woman's brain. More, self-indulgence by women in this respect would sap their qualities of self-sacrifice and that was tantamount to being wilfully unwomanly. For them the intellect was 'a gracious faculty, but no more to engross them than beauty'.[29] It was thus necessary to find alternative reasons for educating the feminine mind and for selecting the subjects that would form part of the curriculum.

The traditional role marked out for women provided many answers to this problem. Girls could find 'some definite object' in their studies by relating them to the needs of the other members of their domestic circle. In *The Daisy Chain*, Ethel May would have done better to concentrate on learning Latin and Greek to help her brother in his studies than to seek to learn to indulge her own desires. Her selfishness blinded her for a while to the needs of her siblings. In a house where papa was a business man with a continental connection, modern languages might do much to aid his success. Miss Bickersteth's Frances Leslie reminded her sister that 'papa sometimes brings French people home with him, and if we hadn't learnt French, we couldn't even ask them what they would like at table, or understand the stories they tell'. A facility in some branch of

[28] Mrs George de Horne Vaizey, *Tom and Some Other Girls: A Public School Story* (Cassell, London, 1901), pp. 112–20.
[29] Sarah Tytler, *Thoughtful Girls*, pp. 27–9.

music, or the art of reading aloud, would help to make an evening pass pleasantly for papa or brothers, preventing any temptation on the part of the menfolk to wander outside the security of home in search of more dangerous pastimes.[30]

It was also necessary to realize that lessons could help in the efficient performance of household duties at all levels of middle-class society: 'sums are very useful ... else one could never keep the accounts'.[31] Some scientific knowledge would aid a woman in keeping a hygienic house, in keeping a watchful eye on her own bodily health and that of those around her, and even, depending on her status, in cookery or the supervision of it. Beyond that, the discipline involved in education was a lasting help to a good woman in all areas of her life because the nineteenth-century approach to learning required both orderly habits and feats of memory for success. When young Ina complained to Aunt Jeannie in *Frances Leslie*, 'I can't see the good of lessons', it was explained to her that 'it is not nearly so much the *things* which you have learned ... as the effect which your schoolroom hours have had on your character, which will really prepare you for life's grown up duties'. While Aunt Jeannie doubted she could conjugate a French verb the time she spent learning them in her youth was not wasted as:

> I gained thereby a power of fixing my mind on a thing which was not at all interesting in itself, simply because I ought to do so. This power is invaluable in housekeeping ... and nearly every good useful work that you can mention, and I believe it is only acquired by long training such as is secured in the school-room.

The message for the female mind is clear. Girls were not to think of lessons as 'a mere stowing away of certain dry bits of knowledge'. Education was 'the polishing, and sharpening, and perfecting of the ... living, loving heart and soul'.[32]

In a class-conscious age which looked to merit as well as breeding in order to determine social station, an academically

[30] Charlotte M. Yonge, *The Daisy Chain*, pp. 155–7; pp. 181–3; Miss E. Bickersteth, *Frances Leslie, or The Prayer Divinely Taught* (RTS, London, 1867), p. 89.

[31] Miss E. Bickersteth, *Frances Leslie*, p. 89.

[32] Ibid., pp. 95–6.

orientated education could operate as a means either of maintaining rank or of fuelling a drive for upward social mobility. This was particularly the case where Greek and Latin were concerned, because of the prominent role that these subjects took in the select public schools combined with the invaluable mental discipline involved in their learning. The initial impact on middle-class educational ideas of this philosophy was on boys' education, linked with the emphasis on the role of the public school ethos in ideals of Victorian masculinity.[33] However, the mental discipline of learning Classics was seen as being useful to the feminine character as well, when time could be spared from other more traditional female occupations and duties to permit such studies. Charlotte Yonge's Ethel May, it should be remembered, found her increasing household duties entailed a yielding up of her classical studies.[34] Yet the necessary investment of spare time supposedly required for girls to achieve high standards in the Classics, coupled with the presumption that the necessary mental equipment was most usually to be associated with fine breeding, soon marked it out as desirable for families with talented daughters and the money to support a concentration on more esoteric study. Greek and Latin did not, in this period, become universals of female education. Where parental prejudice supported the idea, the Classics thus increasingly operated in female education as a mark of superior family social status as well as individual academic ability.

It is interesting to note that the women authors of didactic fiction clearly accept by the 1870s that the intellects of individual members of their own sex could well be superior to those of the menfolk immediately around them. A girl could be better at mathematics or Greek, and even more adept at science than her brothers. It is an indication of the self-imposed limitations of many educational pioneers, whether their ideas appeared in stories or official reports and pamphlets, that such women generally do not try to bring their assessment of female intellectual power to its logical conclusion. They do not seem to consider that there might be no gender-based difference

[33] See W.J. Reader, *Professional Men: The Rise of the Professional Classes in Nineteenth-Century England* (Weidenfeld & Nicolson, London, 1966).
[34] Charlotte M. Yonge, *The Daisy Chain*, p. 163.

between the potential capacity of male and female brains, merely a limit to potential imposed by differing expectation.

Such authors fell back instead on the scientifically backed supposition that a great man would always outstrip a great woman in mental capacity – if only because the female frame was less robust and more complex than that of the male and would collapse under the strain of too much brain work. The intellectually brilliant Maggie in L.T. Meade's *A Sweet Girl Graduate* admits that the male students in the University have superior minds – and proves it by marrying the Senior Wrangler, 'one of the cleverest men at St Hilda's'. Equally, working too hard at an academic discipline frequently brought a fictional girl to the brink of either brain fever or a physical breakdown. Rhoda Chester in Mrs George de Horne Vaizey's *Tom and Some Other Girls* has justifiably high hopes of a splendid showing in the University of Cambridge local examinations, but ends up failing miserably because she has studied too hard. Only liberal applications of sal volatile kept her from physical collapse during the examination. It is, moreover, agreed that it would be dangerous to let her take any more exams, effectively barring her from further study.[35]

For all the opening up to women of the realms of higher education and competitively assessed tests of knowledge, the debate over the nature of the curriculum that should be available to girls was still not settled at the end of the century (if it is now, in some quarters). Certain subjects were unquestionably considered to be within the female educational compass, with clear applications to the domestic sphere, including English, both grammar and literature, arithmetic, general information via the medium of history and geography, and modern languages. Music and drawing were considered accomplishments rather than academic subjects, at least for the vast majority of girls. It became increasingly acceptable to teach girls Latin and Greek, and success in those subjects even at higher levels was not seen as inherently damaging to the female psyche. There was less complacency over other academic disciplines. Miss Beale nearly faced a parental mutiny in the interests of their daughters' femininity when she started to

---

[35] L.T. Meade, *A Sweet Girl Graduate*, p. 253; Mrs George de Horne Vaizey, *Tom and Some Other Girls* p. 175; p. 181.

teach the higher branches of mathematics to pupils at Cheltenham Ladies College.[36] Mathematics led to logic, after all,
and logic represented the antithesis of the emotional feminine
nature.

Certain branches of science were, at least at elementary level,
perfectly acceptable: geology was considered unlikely to arouse
speculations which might be damaging to feminine modesty,
while making and classifying collections of specimens could
usefully encourage orderly mental habits. Many heroines of
fiction such as Mrs George de Horne Vaizey's Peggy Saville
made assiduous and carefully collated collections of rocks and
pebbles. Botany and certain branches of zoology fell into this
category also. Girls were also likely to be useful to boys here,
developing their skills with the opposite sex, helping brothers
or friends in forming interesting collections of plants and
insects and looking after them while a brother was at school, as
Marjory did for her adopted brother, Jack in Mrs Ewing's *Six to
Sixteen*.[37] There were even things to be said for teaching a girl
elements of basic anatomy. Properly directed it need not
encourage unwomanly thoughts but could be used at a higher
level to reinforce theological and Darwinian ideas about female
inferiority to men, to say nothing of the opportunity, as taken
by Rob Darcy in *About Peggy Saville*, to show her how fragile her
bodily system really was.[38]

However, many conventional thinkers remained rather un-
convinced about the usefulness of mathematics and science at
any advanced level, and very alive to the possibilities that
speculation in these topics might damage feminine acquiescence in their divinely appointed role in society. The argument
was that women generally lacked the power of reaching conclusions step by logical step, arriving at their goals by instinct not
reason, and were thus notoriously vulnerable to faulty logic. In
addition, those rare women who possessed the mental capacity
to cope with such subjects were made narrow-minded and
unfeminine by their attempts to make their minds work on

[36] Josephine Kamm, *How Different from Us: A Biography of Miss Buss and Miss
Beale* (Bodley Head, London, 1958), p. 30.
[37] Mrs George de Horne Vaizey, *About Peggy Saville* (RTS, London, 1900),
p. 15; Mrs Juliana H. Ewing, *Six to Sixteen: A Story for Girls*, Queens Treasures
Series (Bell, London, 1908), 1st edn (1876), p. 113.
[38] Mrs George de Horne Vaizey, *About Peggy Saville*.

such unnatural lines.[39] Clearly, however, the underlying fear
was that mathematics and science encouraged women in intellectual realms that bordered dangerously on the realms of
theological speculation.

There was even less enthusiasm for ladies with a desire to
enquire into theology itself as an academic discipline instead of
accepting the established interpretations. The role played by
religion in authorizing established social mores and 'traditional'
gender divisions in the community meant that it was presented
to women in the light of a divinely sanctified and scientifically
endorsed tradition that they were dependant being. Reinforcing that, male-interpreted religion was presented to the vast
majority of them as the lens through which they should
interpret most of the reality that surrounded them and the
duties and opportunities open to them. Feminine inquiry into
the intricacies of theology at a time when women were making
some headway in modifying the boundaries of their legitimate
sphere must run the risk of endangering social stability by
encouraging a dangerous level of self-sufficiency amongst the
'fair' sex. Ruskin had inveighed against permitting women to
study theology on these grounds:

> Strange, and miserably strange, that while they are modest
> enough to doubt their powers, and pause at the threshold of
> sciences, . . . they will plunge headlong and without one thought
> of incompetency, into that science in which the greatest men
> have trembled and the wisest erred.

The women who did so formed 'habits of mind which have
become in them the unmixed elements of home discomfort' as
they elevated vice and folly and stupidity into religion, alienating men and destroying the moral fabric of society with which
they were so specially entrusted.[40]

It was accepted, as was pointed out in the previous chapter,
that women could be subject to religious doubt, but fiction was
used to demonstrate to readers, as in the case of Rachel Curtis
in *The Clever Woman of the Family*, that they were not able,
without serious damage to their minds and souls, to seek the

[39] See, for instance, 'Thoughts on the Higher Education of Women', by A
Man, *Girls' Own Annual*, XII, Oct. 1890–Sept. 1891, p. 714.
[40] J. Ruskin, *Sesame and Lilies*, pp. 94–5.

answers for themselves by indulging in religious philosophy. Rachel's 'cleverness' led her to question the traditional womanly duties to such an extent that she tells her lover, piteously, that the result of her inquiries was that her 'faith – it is all confusion. I do believe . . . but my grasp seems gone. I cannot rest or trust for thinking of the questions that have been raised.' Her womanliness and peace of mind only reasserted themselves once she had abandoned her self-sufficiency and returned both to a trusting acquiescence in a male-interpreted theology and suitably 'womanly' occupations. A danger to later heroines such as Ellen Louisa Davis's Asceline Barclay was 'theosopy', the quasi-scientific philosophical treatment of the divine, which in male eyes, seemed intended to lead the less critical feminine mind astray.[41] Areas such as these, after all, were ones where even great men had floundered in their thinking, in the eyes of conventional society. The potential danger of letting the guardians of moral purity go astray was too terrible for most to contemplate.

Physical education was another area of debate for those concerned to protect established gender standards. Ruskin had early advocated the building up of feminine bodily stamina as a pre-requisite to mental training – but he made no real suggestions as to the methods by which this should be done. A central consideration in regulating the limits of female physical exertion was the necessity, in the eyes of conventional opinion, of co-ordinating useful exercise with a womanly decorum appropriate to the stereotypical pattern of English womanhood. As this pattern modified with time, so too, to some extent, did ideas of decorous behaviour. It was agreed that it was a good thing that 'the prim walks . . . constituting their [girls'] only exercise . . . are over'. But the majority assumption remained that women and men retained different standards of physical as well as mental deportment. The essential 'rules of morality and decency' could not be infringed, and that meant that any activity which tended to an uninhibited excess of energy, and required movements or the wearing of clothing which displayed too clearly the outline of the post-adolescent female body to the 'personal and familiar' gaze of men was unacceptable. It was also unattractive and undesirable to

[41] Charlotte M. Yonge, *The Clever Woman of the Family*, p. 275; p. 316. Ellen Louisa Davies, *Asceline's Ladder*, p. 139.

indulge in exercise which altered the 'womanly' outlines of the body by hardening the muscles into a more masculine appearance. The message was to use 'moderation' and 'remember the obligations of your sex and of your self-respect'.[42]

One problem in selecting appropriate pastimes was the continuing conflict over the amount of physical exertion that, from adolescence on, the well-bred female frame could endure. Even science could not agree here, as doctors resorted to 'scientific fact' to bolster personal bias in this respect. The school which believed in great innate feminine physical fragility, originating in the 'mysterious' feminine capacities for menstruation and motherhood, tended to dominate in the early period. Elizabeth Wetherell's heroines, such as Ellen Montgomery and Fleda Ringgan were in adolescence notoriously given to physical collapse after only moderate exertion. However, by the 1880s, this had changed. For one thing, the stereotype of the model maiden was by this time rather more vigorous in appearance and resource; heroines were permitted to indulge in a greater variety of modes of physical exertion in reflection of the greater opportunities open to most readers. The good girls in novels by Evelyn Everett Green or Mrs George de Horne Vaizey were invigorated rather than exhausted by reasonable exercise. The Floy Rivers and Peggy Savilles of later fiction retained a healthy glow and cheerful spirits as a result of suitable activity, and few things told on them more than being confined to a sofa for any reason. Yet activity which involved really violent exertion or immodesty was still considered damaging.[43]

Certain types of activity were indulged in throughout this period. For instance, healthy English heroines were almost always good walkers, capable of covering several miles at a stretch when the nature of the landscape or the opportunity allowed. Most girls from Anglican backgrounds, and even some from less strict Nonconformist ones, with any access to society

---

[42] S.A. Caulfeild, 'Some Types of Girlhood, or Our Juvenile Spinsters', *Girls' Own Annual*, XII, Oct. 1890–Sept. 1891, pp. 4–5.

[43] Elizabeth Wetherell, *The Wide, Wide World* (Bliss Sands & Co., London, 1896), 1st edn (1852), p. 256; *Queechy* (Warne, London, 1877), pp. 347–8; Evelyn Everett Green, *The Jilting of Bruce Heriot* (RTS, London, 1904), pp. 237–40; Mrs George de Horne Vaizey, *More About Peggy*, p. 254.

could expect to learn how to dance from childhood. It was both an accomplishment and exercise. Properly performed, dance was seen as peculiarly suited to display feminine grace and there was no longer any majority fear that the waltz was a moral danger.

The better-off country dweller had also the resource of riding. It should be noted, though, that there was by no means universal agreement, even at the end of the period, over the desirability of hunting as a feminine pastime for those girls with the financial and social resources to indulge in it. Many considered that 'the hunting field' was no place 'for ladies'. There was the association with violence and hard energetic riding, for one thing. For another, choice of the members of the hunt was left up to men, who were notoriously frequently unable, or unwilling, to exercise the same degree of 'nice discrimination' about people that women did. Many fictional men of refinement were permitted to say that they preferred women not to hunt. Those girls in stories who do hunt are always fine horsewomen, and if good girls, invariably escorted by male members of their family who will protect them from annoyance or physical danger. Otherwise, their determination to hunt, as in Evelyn Everett Green's *A Difficult Daughter*, was the mark of the unwomanly hoyden.[44]

Callisthenics and other forms of gymnasium-style exercise designed to develop feminine stamina aiding deportment and grace, without overdeveloping feminine muscle, became popular. Even swimming, if learnt in childhood and properly supervised from adolescence was not considered to be incompatible with notions of femininity. There was a growing idea that, if not indulged in to excess and properly played, organized games such as lawn tennis or croquet were pastimes which could develop useful character attributes like self-control, obedience to rules and a cheerful demeanour under disappointment.

It is worth comparing the growth of higher education for women with the growth of a perceived need for vigorous physical exercise for girls in the shape of organized team games

[44] Evelyn Everett Green, *The Head of the House: The Story of A Victory over Passion and Pride* (RTS, London, 1886), p. 11; Evelyn Everett Green, *A Difficult Daughter* (Sunday School Union, London, 1895), pp. 158–62.

like hockey, lacrosse and even cricket to build up as far as possible the necessary stamina and spirit for school life in general, and competitive examinations in particular. 'Pluck' and commitment were demanded of the individual girl if she was to play well, and the team nature of the game required unselfishness and even generosity of spirit from individuals to draw out the best from all the players. It was pointed out that 'The result of unselfish play' is often that the 'weaker team wins simply because they play well into one another's hands': and 'these qualities help towards a healthy mind, even as the vigorous exercise helps towards a healthy body'.[45]

In both fiction and life, it was the same large schools which promoted academic learning, the possibility of higher education on university lines and the use of the same competitive examinations for both sexes, that also took the lead in promoting the development of organized team sports. At Hurst Manor, Mrs George de Horne Vaizey's fictional counterpart of Wykeham Abbey, games were compulsory every afternoon except in cases of illness. It was seen by the authorities as the only way to keep the female body healthy enough to cope with the academic demands of the system. But Mrs George de Horne Vaizey made sure that her readers were aware of the drawbacks to overindulgence in organized sport, such as the temptation to be too masculine. Rhoda's brother tells her to 'Be ... as hardy as you like – that is all to the good – but, for pity's sake be pretty too, and dainty, and feminine! We don't want to have all our womenkind swallowed up in athletes'. She was not to forget that a woman's highest role in life was at the centre of a home.[46]

For this reason, a girl's education had to cover many lessons that could be best learned outside the schoolroom. A good girl was, first and foremost an apprentice in the art of being a *Household Fairy* or *Home Goddess*, and she needed to be trained in the numerous arts involved in running a household that would, if life was kind, comprise her major duties in adult life. Many good girls were not academically clever, but if they were competent at their domestic duties, they were no less valued. Indeed it is often overlooked in modern studies of nineteenth-

[45] 'Girls at Hockey', *Girls' Own Annual*, XII, Oct.–Sept. 1890–1, p. 186.
[46] Mrs George de Horne Vaizey, *Tom and Some Other Girls*, p. 71; p. 130.

century education for girls that not every girl was interested in academic learning, or saw the burgeoning opportunities in this field as a good thing for them. There were girls who were happy with their traditional lot and even resented the increasing pressure to acquire more scholastic knowledge, and didactic fiction needed to sustain them also. Miss Bickersteth's Ina Leslie was one of many fictional heroines who found her schoolroom lessons both difficult and uninteresting, while "The things that I shall do when I am a woman *are* interesting to me now; I love learning them'. For Ina, the 'horrid drudgery' was not in domesticity but in French and arithmetic. The idea of learning Latin would have horrified her. She was reconciled to her lessons by the knowledge that it would please those she loved, and that it was 'right' and would please God – exactly the reasons which was supposed to hold girls in love with academe to more mundane household tasks.[47]

From Charlotte Yonge to Mrs George de Horne Vaizey, the didactic genre of fiction emphasized the importance of learning how to perform the domestic tasks appropriate to one's social station. These women saw no disgrace in the performance of humble practical tasks whatever the level of education. The better the education, the more orderly habits instilled. A major responsibility was the supervision and training of servants, for the vast majority of middle-class households could expect to have at least one servant to do the roughest work, even if not living in.

In order to ensure that work was properly done, it was important that every mistress of a household should know precisely how to do properly every task that ensured its smooth running, so she could teach her servants how to do it. The *Girl's Own Paper*, for instance, produced a series on the theme of professional performance of household duties, with the message that there was 'a right way and a wrong way of doing everything in the house'. All sorts of things from dusting to scrubbing were covered, with helpful and scientifically labour-saving hints for the model maiden.[48] The mother in Mrs George de Vaizey's *Houseful of Girls* had 'strong ideas on the

[47] Miss E. Bickersteth, *Frances Leslie*, pp. 95–7.
[48] Dora de Blaquiere, 'How to Help in the House', *Girls' Own Paper*, XIII, Oct. 1891–Sept. 1892, p. 84.

subject of domestic education'. It was a mark of her successful training of her active, intelligent girls that she entrusted them, once old enough, with the task of spring-cleaning the house from top to bottom. Moreover, the girls rejoiced at the trust and the opportunity to lighten their mother's tasks: 'I love rushing about in an apron, using my muscles instead of my brain'. Of course 'the servants scrubbed and scoured' while the girls 'performed the lighter duties, washing the ornaments, polishing pictures, turning faded draperies, sewing on new lengths of fringe'. It was, however, up to the daughters of the house to ensure things were properly done. They, for example, had to take over the re-laying of the drawing-room carpet because the maids had failed.[49]

A thorough acquaintance with stitchery of all kinds was desirable, if not always attainable by heroines. If a girl was wealthy enough to make it unlikely she would need to make her own clothes she should know how to make garments for those unfortunates who were poor enough to need such frequently indifferent needlework as girls like Charlotte Yonge's Ethel May or Lilias Mohun produced in pursuit of their philanthropic duties. Some paragons, like Elizabeth Wetherell's Ellen Montgomery enjoyed all types of needlework, but most fictional characters were human enough to enjoy the prettier forms of embroidery which could be used to decorate their persons or their homes. Equally cookery could be useful not only for those girls who would have to share in the production of meals but also for those who might wish to teach the lower classes how to cook, as did Olive Roscoe who took a class in 'artisan cookery' being horrified at the wasteful habits of the poor.[50]

Of course, it was not expected that girls should neglect any part of their academic lessons in order to practice their more domestic skills unless there was no alternative. Ethel May was scolded for failing to spend time on producing an orderly copy of her French exercise in order to fulfil her philanthropic urges. The time for such practices would come when the

[49] Mrs George de Horne Vaizey, *A Houseful of Girls* (RTS, London, 1902), pp. 38–9; pp. 44–6.

[50] Charlotte M. Yonge, *The Daisy Chain*, p. 18; Charlotte M. Yonge, *Scenes and Characters, or Eighteen Months at Beechcroft* (Macmillan, London, 1886), p. 192; Elizabeth Wetherell, *The Wide, Wide World*, p. 343; Evelyn Everett Green, *Olive Roscoe, or The New Sister* (Nelson, Walton-on-Thames, 1896), p. 350.

schoolroom was left behind. Emancipation from the school-room was not at any time in this period presumed to herald the end of a good girls' education. Education was, after all, seen as a process of self-improvement, and constant practice and continued application was necessary not only to keep up standards in subjects already acquired but also to keep up standards of discipline. It was all too likely that if the hours of scholastic discipline were not replaced by hours of rigid self-discipline, the kind of unproductive apathy such as that which overtook Emily Mohun in *Scenes and Characters* would overtake weaker natures.[51]

It was, however, not only for reasons of continued self-improvement that a continuation of the learning process was desirable. Life was not given to 'amuse ourselves – just to let things drift on . . . without caring for or thinking of the deeper meanings and larger duties'. The girl on the brink of woman-hood was expected to take her place in the community, whether as ornament or worker, and it was essential that she was able to make a material contribution thereto if she was to fulfil properly her divinely instituted womanly role. What else was she given her talents for? In *Vera's Trust* Vera Carmichael warned her sister that she was disappointing her family and God by her trivial attitude: 'You must not stop learning just because you have left the school-room, but you may choose for yourself what subjects you would best like to take up'. For instance, the discipline involved in learning new languages was considered useful, while practice at accomplishments like music and art were essential if a girl in society was to be able to use these suitably to enhance family status. Evelyn Everett Green's Esther Egerton had trained her drawing-room talents 'by years of patient labour' and, for instance, performed on the piano 'with the ease and accuracy that only comes as the result of earnest effort'. Her playing thus 'deeply mortified' the titled Overton family because it contrasted with their daughter's unpracticed and stumbling attempts.[52]

It is worth noting that it was not even enough to be a drawing-room ornament: a modicum of general information

[51] Charlotte M. Yonge, *The Daisy Chain*, pp. 160–1; *Scenes and Characters*, p. 315.

[52] Evelyn Everett Green, *Vera's Trust* (Nelson, Walton-on-Thames, 1889), pp. 125–7; *Greyfriars*, p. 120.

was also necessary in order to converse with men and not bore them. Vera Carmichael was ashamed to take her sister out with her as it was plain 'how little you can find to say on any but the most trivial topics'. It was necessary for a good girl or woman to have 'an intelligent comprehension of the leading questions of the day, to show a little interest in your country, in the great movements of these stirring times'.[53] For one thing, the expansion of the feminine sphere as a result of the growing involvement of women in public life via philanthropy and the support for any male interest in politics demanded an informed mind. For another, lack of comprehension constituted a reproach to the education and training given by her family, and there could be few worse sins for a girl whose main responsibility still lay with the home.

It was equally bad for a girl to shame her upbringing by trying to urge too much information on her audience, and trying, like Charlotte Yonge's Rachel Curtis, to impose her point of view instead of deferring to those older, wiser and masculine. That could only make her and to some extent her family foolish. The end aim of continuing education was as gender orientated as earlier lessons. There was even a backlash at the end of the century against too academic an education for girls because it was felt by some conventional observers that experience now showed that such an education unfitted girls for their adult duties.[54]

This backlash tended to blame the venue in which education was conducted as much, if not more, than the content of the curriculum. It is a movement which forcibly demonstrates the worry felt by the sizeable section of middle-class opinion that the boundaries between the feminine and masculine spheres were being dangerously eroded, with the consequent threat to social stability, and that changes in the style of female education were much to blame. For instance, Mr Cardew in L.T. Meade's *The School Queens* feared that school life unfitted girls for home duties and responsibilities, and was convinced that a home education was best.[55]

[53] Evelyn Everett Green, *Vera's Trust*, pp. 125–6.
[54] See Deborah Gorham, 'The Ideology of Femininity and Reading for Girls, 1850–1914', in Felicity Hunt (ed.), *Lessons for Life*, pp. 39–59.
[55] L.T. Meade, *The School Queens* (Chambers, Edinburgh, 1903), p. 58.

The traditional, gender-based middle-class expectations of the role women needed to perform in society seemed to establish that the mother was unquestionably the best person to teach a girl the lessons required to fit her for adult life. As Oscar Wilde noted, it was (and still is) a truism that girls turn out like their mothers. In a hero-conscious age, the best and the most accessible heroine and role model for a girl was the good woman as *mater familias* and accomplished head of her household. It was felt that girls were more likely to learn of a loving but demanding mother the necessary, if at times uninviting, feminine lessons. An additional factor was the general agreement that the emotional nature of girls made them peculiarly vulnerable to baleful influence. Only in the home could girls be fully protected from outside influences that might damage the innocent bloom of their moral health and the strains that might damage the frailer female physique.

By contrast, didactic fiction for girls emphasized that from adolescence, boys flourished best away from an overwhelming feminine presence. They needed men to act as role models, to help them develop their nascent masculinity. Physical stamina played a great part in this, via reaction to the greater stresses involved in participating in the rough and tumble of school life. Examinations, for instance, sharpened a natural masculine competitiveness while testing in logical fashion their acquisition of necessary knowledge. Becoming a schoolboy thus stereotypically marked a rite of passage when gender took over and inevitably sent boys and girls down different paths. Evelyn Everett Green's Dorrie wept as she realized that school had given her beloved brother a taste for bloodsports, while she remained emotionally attached to animal life.[56]

Such expectations of the role that schools should perform for boys seemed to make it impossible to reconcile use of such institutions for female education. At best, such an institution, even if run on small and intimate lines, could only imitate a home setting with all its benefits and at worst, damage the careful groundwork of early years. The school atmosphere could harden girlish natures and stultify their essential emotions by encouraging masculine qualities – if the girls did not

[56] Evelyn Everett Green, *Dickie and Dorrie: A Tale of Hallowdene Hall* (Wells, Gardner & Co., London, 1906).

first break down under the sheer physical strain of the regime. After all, a good girl eschewed a self-sufficient assurance in her own powers, and the competitive spirit associated with male public school education seemed to encourage personal display. Few things were considered more odious than a girl complacent in her own powers in this respect. Certainly it must be remembered that a home education did not necessarily debar a girl from taking up academic subjects like Greek, Latin or mathematics and pursuing them to a high standard. Priscilla Peel in *A Sweet Girl Graduate* went to St Benet's College on the strength of sound teaching at home and not at school.[57]

The fiction written in the period up to the 1870s by authors like Charlotte Yonge and Elizabeth Sewell indicates that it was initially rare for middle-class girls to receive their education away from the domestic circle. Elizabeth Sewell, who herself received most of her education at school, both as a boarder and a day pupil, and even ran a successful small school herself, emphasized the advantages and merits of home education for girls in her works.[58] The minimal role played by schools in fiction of the earlier period would seem to indicate a feeling on the part of authors that a school setting was generally less realistic and contained less relevant lessons for their readership than the depiction of education in the domestic setting, particularly when the book was aimed at a rural readership since boarding schools were still relatively few in number and even day schools suitable for middle-class girls were not plentiful.[59]

Yet girls' schools did exist and were not ignored in didactic fiction, even in the early period. The reasons for this were often more pragmatic than principled. The most common of these, in and out of fiction, was the lack of a suitable home background and the need to find a substitute. This remained an imperative into the twentieth century. In some cases a girl like L.T. Meade's Betty Falkoner needed to go to school due to the death or total incapacity of a mother and the lack of any available female relative to substitute.[60] For many schoolgirls,

[57] L.T. Meade, *A Sweet Girl Graduate*, p. 51.
[58] Eleanor Sewell (ed.), *Autobiography of Elizabeth Sewell* (Longman, London, 1907), pp. 33–41.
[59] Carol Dyhouse, *Girls Growing Up*, pp. 40–4.
[60] L.T. Meade, *Betty: A School Girl* (Chambers, Edinburgh, 1895), p. 60.

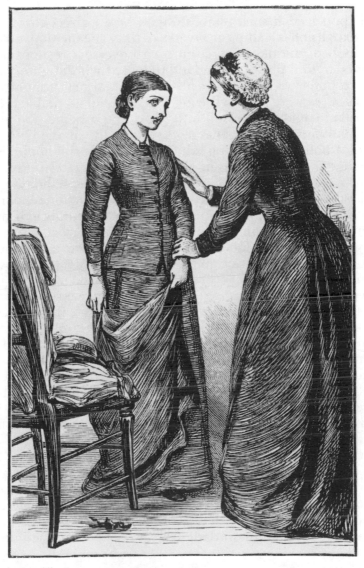

PLATE 6 "'YOU WILL NOT FORGET MY WORDS, WILL YOU, CORA?'"

Lessons for life: the Headmistress's last admonition. From *Cora, or Three Years of a Girl's Life* by M.M. Pollard (1882)

their presence at such establishments was a direct corollary of the expansion of empire. Overseas duty meant that growing numbers of middle-class parents with overseas responsibilities needed to find places in England to leave their daughters, even before puberty. Imperial orphans like Marjory Vandaleur in *Six to Sixteen* were also on the increase. Even if a suitable relative or friend could be pressed into providing a home, the age or commitments of that personage frequently entailed the children of both sexes seeking education outside the home. Some attended a day school, as in Mrs Molesworth's *Robin Redbreast*. Many more went to boarding schools, spending holidays with a variety of relatives or friends. It is rare for a fictional boarding school after 1870 not to contain a significant number of pupils with Indian or other colonial backgrounds requiring their presence at such establishments, and in quite a number of school stories the plot originated in parental death or absence abroad.[61]

A proportional shortage of suitable home-care in middle-class families cannot, however, be held realistically to account for the accelerating growth of schools throughout the last half of the century. A number of other factors made significant contributions. Even where a comfortable home was available, education within its environs undoubtedly became more difficult as the century progressed. Highly qualified governesses were becoming more expensive and difficult to find as numbers of this elite found it preferable to seek employment in schools rather than take an equivocal status in private homes. The plight of Evelyn Everett Green's Roscoe family who found their treasured governess leaving as a result of 'an offer of a very good second mistress-ship in some excellent school' became a fictional commonplace.[62] In particular those families with moderate incomes and immoderate offspring increasingly found it necessary to send their daughters to school instead of em-

[61] Mrs Juliana Ewing, *Six to Sixteen*. Marjory's parents both died of cholera. Mrs Mary Molesworth, *Robin Redbreast: A Story for Girls* (Chambers, Edinburgh, 1892).

[62] Evelyn Everett Green, *Olive Roscoe*, pp. 403–4. See M. Jeanne Peterson, 'The Victorian Governess: Status Incongruence in Family and Society', in Martha Vicinus (ed.), *Suffer and Be Still: Women in the Victorian Age* (Methuen, London, 1977), pp. 3–19 for the invidious position of governesses throughout this period.

ploying a governess for at least part of their education if reasonable academic standards were to be reached.

A problem for the parents of talented girls living in the provinces regardless of income was the availability of qualified masters (and masters they almost always were in fiction) to polish the standard of feminine accomplishments such as music, art or languages. Told by his wife that their daughters were 'not getting the advantages their rank in life and their talent demand', even the wealthy landowner Mr Cardew in L.T. Meade's *The School Queens* could not overcome this problem without sending his girls to school in London. It was impossible outside London or other large centres like Manchester 'to command the services of the best masters'.[63] The continuing importance of accomplishments in the womanly stereotype, plus the increasing stress that was laid on professional performances, encouraged growing numbers of parents with active social lives to despatch their girls to school for a year or two to round off their education.

This gives a key to another factor that was of considerable importance to parents. The majority of girls' schools designed for the middle-class market took their pupils on a class basis rather than an intellectual one if the headmistress was wise. Wealth was definitely of less importance than family status. Daughters of tradesmen could not expect to mix indiscriminately with daughters of professional or service families, for instance, but poor pupils were perfectly acceptable in such a background if they brought with them the less tangible wealth of good connections. L.T. Meade's headmistresses specialized in taking girls of impeccable but impoverished backgrounds, to give them the training appropriate to their breeding, as in the case of Alison Hilyard in *The Beresford Prize*.[64]

Boys' public schools had shown the enduring nature and the power of friendships formed in such surroundings, as well as the opportunities to practice role playing in preparation for the adult world. A good school could, it was hoped, perform much the same service for girls. Hester Thornton in *A World of Girls*, one of the most popular of the early school stories, was told that school life 'has its trials', but that she would 'find a miniature

[63] L.T. Meade, *The School Queens*, pp. 36–7; pp. 65–6.
[64] L.T. Meade, *The Beresford Prize* (Longman, London, 1890).

world around you' and how she reacted to it would be a measure of how she reacted to later life. At Lavender House she would be 'surrounded by temptations; and you will have rare chances of proving whether your character can be strong and great and true'. It was also a time of discipline: 'We are earnest in our work, we are earnest in our play. A half-hearted girl has no chance at Lavender House', just as she would fail in the wider world.[65]

As Mrs Dering in another of L.T. Meade's tales told her daughter, 'life is only being placed in a higher school ... take the good that the little school gives in order to be strong enough for the greater'. School provided girls with a unique opportunity to 'find their own level' before the pitfalls of adult life. For this reason, there was a growing acceptance by the end of the century, reflected in fiction, that even competition could be a positive force for girls, and this was where a school could score over an education totally conducted in home surroundings. Rightly regulated, competition could provide a 'healthy' stimulus to sustained effort. It was simply necessary to ensure that it did not get out of hand.[66]

It was, as has already been said, an age of hero-worship: biographies of the good and the great men and women appeared in enormous numbers during this period. The problem was that few families or neighbourhoods provided much in the way of available objects for adoration or emulation in this respect. A good school, however, could provide such role models for girls in much the same way it could for boys. This factor acquired increasing force as the womanly stereotype modified, and it was seen as necessary to show girls that it was possible to take an active role in the community while still being the acme of femininity. As more girls were either forced to think of paid employment or did so from choice, headmistresses and teachers provided examples of women with an acceptable remunerative feminine role or vocation in life who remained perfectly womanly in the performance of their tasks. Schoolgirl adoration of their mistresses was thus seen as a

[65] L.T. Meade, *A World of Girls: The Story of a School* (Cassell, London, 1886), p. 32.
[66] L.T. Meade, *A Madcap: A Story for Girls* (Cassell, London, 1904), p. 157.

positive and healthy force. The vast majority of fictional headmistresses were noble figures, occasionally bending down from a figurative height to embrace or laugh with their charges. All the good girls at either L.T. Meade's or Mrs George de Horne Vaizey's schools professedly adored their headmistresses, and were acutely influenced by them. The girls at Lavender House, for instance, thought Mrs Willis the most wonderful woman in the world. It did not prevent them getting up to mischief, but it did ensure their penitence and a genuine desire on the part of her pupils to please her. Miss Phipps in Mrs George de Horne Vaizey's *Pixie O'Shaughnessy* won Pixie's whole-hearted love and admiration and converted her into a reasonably decorous young woman as a result.[67]

The reputed influence of headmistresses over their pupils even provided a further reason why occasionally a girl was sent to school. If she was a rebellious character who had failed to respond to home teaching, she might well respond better to a powerful character with wide experience in training recalcitrant specimens. Thus school could figure as the ultimate threat for a rebellious girl. Evelyn Everett Green's Gypsy (or Gertrude) Challoner was warned that if she could not behave as a lady she would have to 'go to school to be taught those manners that you have deliberately elected to disregard' and to learn 'to appreciate the advantages of your home'.[68]

Models for emulation could also be provided, though often less convincingly, from amongst the pupils. Within the microcosm of fictional school society, certain girls were more perfect pattern damsels than others in terms of character and sometimes attainments as well, and were given a pre-eminent position by staff and their schoolmates because of it. Alison Hilyard in L.T. Meade's *The Beresford Prize* is a somewhat extreme example. At the end of her school career, she wins her prize for 'exceptionally noble conduct' and is presented with a locket inscribed:

In honour and maiden purity, and in deep thankfulness of heart for a special and great deliverance, I, Alison Hilyard, have won

[67] L.T. Meade, *A World of Girls*; Mrs George de Horne Vaizey, *Pixie O'Shaughnessy* (RTS, London, 1903).
[68] Evelyn Everett Green, *Head of the House*, pp. 265–6.

the Beresford Prize. I dedicate myself to the service of honour
and truth, and pray to God to help me to walk worthily to my
life's end.

Her influence will supposedly stay with her schoolmates for the
rest of her life. As they applaud her a 'ringing cheer rang up to
the old rafters!' but it 'died away into a minor note' as Alison
'kneeling there, so pale, so sweet, so saint-like, was going
away'.[69]

However, the majority of L.T. Meade's good girls were not
quite so unrealistically removed from ordinary humanity and
enjoyment of life as that. While Hester Thornton of *A World of
Girls* surmounts many difficulties to become a good girl whose
presence is greatly missed, and whose memory stays with her
schoolmates, she also displays a considerable capacity to enjoy
picnics and jokes with her fellows. The heroine of *A Sweet Girl
Graduate* gives up her chance for high academic honours for
the sake of family duty, but she still takes part in amateur
theatricals. Overall it is agreed that 'no girl did more honour to
Heath Hall than she'. Priscilla Peel is plain and shabby, and she
spreads an 'influence on the side of all that was good and
noble', through 'Extreme earnestness, the sincerity of a noble
person, the truthfulness of a nature which could not stoop to
deceit', but she can also enjoy honest fun. Women like her 'live
at the heart of the true life of a worthy nation'.[70]

Equally, Mrs George de Horne Vaizey's record wall at Hurst
Manor, containing tablets put up by the students honoured
previous pupils like Eleanor Newman – 'Beloved by her fellow-
students as the kindest and most loyal of friends, the most
unselfish of competitors. Held in grateful remembrance for the
power of her influence and example'. Eleanor was 'quite stupid
. . . yet everyone loved her'. She 'wasn't a bit goody, but she
always seemed waiting to do kind things', and in the years after
she left her fellows 'immortalised her name in words of grateful
loyalty'.[71] This element of work associated with enjoyment
becomes increasingly the dominant keynote of school fiction in

[69] L.T. Meade, *The Beresford Prize*, pp. 355–6.
[70] L.T. Meade, *A World of Girls*; L.T. Meade, *Red Rose and Tiger Lily*, p. 16; *A Sweet Girl Graduate*, pp. 287–8.
[71] Mrs George de Horne Vaizey, *Tom and Some Other Girls*, pp. 76–8.

the post-1905 period, witness the tales of Angela Brazil.[72]

Yet while at least a year or two at school became increasingly seen as a desirable addition to a girl's education, there was still a feeling that home was the core of female education. As one headmistress put it 'The first years of a young girl's life should always, in my opinion, be spent in a happy home' if she was to grow up to be a happy, useful and modest woman. The gender element in educational assessment assured that most girls' schools remained conscious of a need to avoid the threat of comparison in their impact on their pupils with boys' schools. Enormous efforts were thus constantly made by the former to demonstrate the lengths to which they went to reproduce a private, suitably harmonious, well-protected, essentially domestic atmosphere. Day schools benefited particularly from the continuation of this theme; being able to provide a venue where girls could receive the bulk of their formal teaching outside the domestic circle while ensuring the constant advantage of home life outside school hours. Good quality day schools, however, were more likely to be found in sizeable urban centres and girls from a rural background often needed to find a different solution to their educational needs in the shape of boarding schools.[73]

Most boarding establishments also did their best to create a quasi-domestic, sheltered atmosphere. As numbers in such institutions rose a number of strategies could be employed to this end: division into 'houses' supervised by women who would act as 'big sisters' or mother-substitutes according to age and temperament, for instance. Where there were dormitories instead of individual or two-bed rooms, the dormitories were still usually cosy small affairs, dividable up into private cubicles with chintz curtains and dimity-draped beds in the interests of preserving that precious feminine modesty. At L.T. Meade's Briar Hall, pupils were given their own room unless sisters, all simply but daintily furnished in maidenly white, 'White enamel, white paper, white beds', with a crimson carpet which gave 'a sense of warmth'. Pixie O'Shaughnessy arrives at Mrs George de Horne Vaizey's Holly House School to find she is in a small

[72] Mary Cadogan and Patricia Craig, *You're a Brick, Angela! The Girls' Story 1839–1985* (Victor Gollancz, London, 1986).
[73] Carol Dyhouse, *Girls Growing Up*, pp. 40–4.

dormitory where 'an arrangement of curtains hung on rods made each little cubicle private from the rest'.[74]

However, during the last decade of the century fiction began to reflect the growing acceptance of girls' schools that deliberately aimed to move away from this cosy educational system and to parallel more closely in organization and administration the long-established and successful boys' institutions. It is probable that in this respect didactic fiction was reflecting a trend that was more acceptable to the pupils than to many conventional middle-class parents. The private, small to medium school was seen by many model maidens in the stronger mould as old-fashioned and worse, limiting to their ambitions: a factor which had been meritorious in the eyes of parents. Faced with the prospect of school, Mrs George de Horne Vaizey's Rhoda Chester repudiated her mother's desire to send her to a school taking only 10 girls which was 'just like a home'. She announced that if she went she would 'do the thing properly and go to a real school, and not a hot-house'. What she desired was to 'go to a nice, big, sporty school, where they treat you like boys, and not young ladies, and put you on your honour'.[75] Angela Brazil and her ilk seem just over the horizon from this statement, but the ambience of Hurst Abbey is still remarkably feminine in all traditional respects, and no self-respecting Eton or Rugby boy would have owned it.

However, it should not be assumed either that character training was any less important in these new regimes, or that the former type of establishment vanished. There was no fundamental change in majority attitudes towards the essentials of feminine education, and schools needed to take this into account to retain parental goodwill. Many parents still preferred to send their cherished daughters to the small private schools with a proven pedigree of producing good girls. In addition, the large establishments, with all the modern advantages, were more expensive and without some form of aid, numerous parents simply could not afford to send their daughters to these 'go-ahead' places even if they did so desire. Consequently publishers still found it worthwhile to produce

[74] L.T. Meade, *A Madcap* (Cassell, London, 1904), p. 172; Mrs George de Horne Vaizey, *Pixie O'Shaughnessy*, p. 34.
[75] Mrs George de Horne Vaizey, *Tom and Some Other Girls*, p. 14.

fiction by authors like L.T. Meade that portrayed the more old-fashioned types of school.[76]

Moreover, the major educational thrust, even at schools with a high academic record, continued to be towards character moulding. Equally, the teaching methods continued to rely primarily on affection, prayer and personal influence to inculcate the necessary lessons. Rhoda Chester finds her headmistress relies as much on love and personal influence to enforce discipline among her girls as any L.T. Meade headmistress. True she also uses the type of boys'-school inspired prefect not found in the Lavender House style of school. But such prefects are actually ideally loveable, if stern, big sister types, again relying on personal influence rather than the letter of the law. One prefect, Thomasina Bolderston, is remembered by her fellows for 'the kindly justice of her rule, and the unfailing cheerfulness which was a stimulus to them in work and play'. Religion is also still omnipresent, if less overt. Rhoda's moment of self-revelation about the self-indulgence behind her failure to make a mark at school comes through the impact of listening to an apposite morning hymn.[77]

The fictional counterparts of Girton, Newnham et al needed to be quite as circumspect as girls' schools in their context and emphasis on femininity. L.T. Meade's *A Sweet Girl Graduate* and Alice Stronach's *A Newnham Friendship* are clearly intended to demonstrate to parents and girls that colleges for the higher education of women continued the fostering of their femininity and the training of their characters as much if not more than their intellects. In the latter work, emphasis is laid on the pretty and dainty rooms and attire of the best students like Betty Leslie and Carol Martin. The Vice-Principal of Heath Hall in the former tome is another, if younger, Mrs Willis. She is 'all that is good', and she works to influence her students into the paths of righteousness by love rather than reason. Moreover she will not divert a student from the paths of dutiful self-sacrifice in order to assure the attainment of first-class honours. In comparison with the noble coronet of self-denying human

---

[76] But L.T. Meade herself approved of schools like Cheltenham. See, 'Girls' Schools of Today', *Strand Magazine* X, pp. 283–8; pp. 457–63.

[77] Mrs George de Horne Vaizey, *Tom and Some Other Girls*, p. 213; pp. 250–2.

love, the intellectual 'crown of bay looks quite tawdry' as a prospect.[78]

Education remained for the majority of girls simply the road to character improvement. It was, in the eyes of established opinion, most ideally a demanding apprenticeship for the role of *Household Fairy*. Development of the female intellect or talents for their own sake was a form of unrealistic self-indulgence, what Alice Stronach termed 'a dream-world', which struck at the core of presumptions about the nature of a woman's role, and was therefore to be avoided at all costs. Throughout the period, girls who took to that form of selfishness came to grief, and often enough, involved others who were innocent in their misery. From Charlotte Yonge's Ethel May to Evelyn Everett Green's Ursula Tempest, girls were shown that happiness could never be achieved through learning alone.[79] As Miss Arundel told her pupil in Lily Watson's *A Fortunate Exile*, education was a preparation for life, and both were 'made up of duty, not of pleasure only'. While education for girls remained a vast and complex subject, in terms of venue and curriculum the overall aim remained to produce at the end a 'good girl'. Education modified in detail, such as the role of physical education, to take account of the minor changes in the stereotype of a good girl, but its major thrust did not alter. Indeed the emphasis on being 'good' meant that for most girls education continued outside the classroom, into recreational hours, and even after formal schooling had ended. In this respect, history provided a useful medium of continuing education.

[78] L.T. Meade, *A Sweet Girl Graduate*, pp. 249–51; Alice Stronach, *A Newnham Friendship* (Blackie, Glasgow, 1901), pp. 199–200.

[79] Charlotte Yonge, *The Daisy Chain*; Evelyn Everett Green, *Joint Guardians* (RTS, London, 1887), pp. 140–2.

[80] Lily Watson, *A Fortunate Exile: A Story of Swiss School Life* (RTS, London, 1896), p. 62.

4
History with a Purpose

All our past proclaims our future: Shakespeare's voice and
Nelson's hand,
Milton's faith and Wordsworth's trust in this our chosen
and chainless land,[1]

History with a purpose was a favoured device of nineteenth-
century middle-class society: providing through scholarship
and literature an apparently ideal vehicle for passing on
cherished ideas and values to a rising generation. By this time,
history was firmly established as a respected scholarly pursuit.
It was also presumed to have an important part to play in
promoting an understanding of the current age. Not surprisingly, therefore, the study of history was seen also as an
important educational discipline for young children. Its importance is testified to by the considerable numbers of history
textbooks that were produced for this market. Mrs Markham's
History of England, originally written for her own children and
embellished with aids to sound historical interpretation in the
shape of 'Conversations' at the end of each chapter, was an
early nineteenth-century standard, as was *Little Arthur's History*

[1] A. Swinburne, 'England: An Ode', *Collected Poetical Works*, 2 vols (Heinemann, London, 1924). The Victorians also looked to Cicero: *'Historia vero testis
temporum, lux veritatis'* (History indeed is the witness of the times, the light of
truth), *De Oratore*, Book 2, 9.36; or 'Nescire autem quid antea quam natus sis
acciderit, id est semper esse puerum. Quid enim est aetas hominis, nisi
memoria rerum veterum cum superiorum aetate contexitur?' (To be ignorant
of what happened before you were born is to be ever a child. For what is
man's lifetime unless the memory of past events is woven with those of earlier
times?). *Orator*, 34, 120.

of England. Both these books, along with many others, were revised and reprinted as the century went on, but they were far more popular with adults than with children.[2] Miss Yonge is simply the best-known and most prolific of these later writers, who also diversified into this fertile field, with efforts such as *Aunt Charlotte's Stories of English History for the Little Ones*.[3]

These textbooks were not particularly sophisticated in their analysis of history, but they aimed to be accurate with respect to date and place, and they had their place and importance, just as the simpler juvenile 'character-building' novels did. Their role was largely that of providing the reader with the basic facts about English history, Scottish history and even Irish history, as well as a number of rather simplistic stereotypical descriptions of figures and periods in the past. Mrs Markham found herself able to sum up history for the benefit of her audience in a one paragraph answer; for instance:

> *Richard*: I shall be very glad, mamma, when you come to a good king. It is very disagreeable to hear about bad people.
> *Mrs Markham*: It is one of the great drawbacks to the pleasure of reading history, that it is such a painful record of human crimes. One cause of this is to be found in the nature of the human heart, which is so formed that rank, and power, and fortune all tend to incline it to what is wrong. Kings and statesmen and others, who from the greatness of their station are most prominent in history, are therefore more liable to err than people in a lower and happier condition of life. And, perhaps, there is another cause why history is so much fuller of wicked than of virtuous deeds: the virtuous deeds are passed over, as not affording so much to be said about them.[4]

Henry II fared little better at her hands:

---

[2] Mrs Markham (pseud. of Mrs Elizabeth Penrose), *A History of England* (John Murray, London, 1859); Lady Maria Callcott, *Little Arthur's History of England* (John Murray, London, 1860). The latter is still available in modern editions.

[3] Charlotte M. Yonge, *Aunt Charlotte's Stories from English History for the Little Ones* (Marcus Ward & Co., London, 1873).

[4] Mrs Markham, *A History of England*, pp. 55–6.

Richard: How shocking it was, mamma, that such a great and excellent king should have such wicked children!

Mrs Markham: I fear there must have been some latent fault, which we have now no means of finding out, in his conduct towards his sons. My own opinion is, that they acquired habits of disobedience to their father by seeing how little harmony subsisted between him and their mother. When children see their parents disagree, they seldom learn to treat them with duty or respect ... If we could know Henry's secret thoughts, I dare say he often, in the bitterness of his heart, thought he had paid a heavy price for the rich provinces [Queen Eleanor] brought him.[5]

However, texts of this nature were not really suited to the transmission of more complex and powerful messages to an adolescent readership; particularly ones with subtle gender implications. Once again, it was to the novel that such authors looked as the medium for more sophisticated indoctrination, if only because the popular historical novel was no new phenomenon by the mid-century. Sir Walter Scott had first shown how impressive and exciting a fictional use of history could be in his books from the *Waverley* novels to other favourites like *Rob Roy*. His tales continued to be much beloved, especially by boys, and were presented as models of 'good' fiction. Good though they were, however, his novels were too general in their thrust to make the fullest use of the past in a setting designed to push contemporary messages to an adolescent market. Yet he showed how sound scholarship could be combined with vivid storytelling in an effective and compelling manner. Captain Marryat, in his perenially popular story *The Children of the New Forest*, revealed the potential in a moral story with a realistic historical background written specifically for a younger audience.[6] It was left to a writer for adolescent girls to develop

---

[5] Ibid., p. 93.

[6] Captain F. Marryat, *The Children of the New Forest* (Hurst, London, 1847). Though a number of earlier writers had produced moral tales for the young set in 'olden times' this was the first full-scale novel for non-adult readers with a firmly recognizable historical setting. From the start, the pace of the story was accepted as lending an agreeable aspect to the didactic content. It was, however, Marryat's last completed novel. Moreover it was not really a gender-based work.

the genre of the didactic historical novel further, however.

Taking up where Scott left off in many ways, and much inspired by him as her early literary hero, Charlotte Yonge pioneered the historical novel based on genuine efforts to re-create and interpret a realistic past in a way designed to appeal to a youthful middle-class readership at the same time as instructing. She complained that Scott had 'wilfully carved history to suit the purpose of his story' but that the mid-nineteenth-century spirit required 'a certain amount of credibility by being in keeping with established facts, even if striking events have to be sacrificed ... to keep within the bounds of historical veracity'.[7] However, she and her contemporaries were at least as guilty as Scott in carving history to suit their purposes: it was merely that their efforts needed to be less immediately obvious if their aims were to succeed.

Miss Yonge started modestly enough. A number of her earlier efforts, largely those that are still popular today, were simple stories aimed at a non-gender specific, pre-adolescent market, including her first historical work, *The Little Duke*. The basic (and largely timeless) thrust of this favourite concerns character development: essentially good but thoughtless, Richard learns through adversity to fear only dishonesty and wrong-doing as summed up in modern Christian terms.[8] Increasingly, though, she aimed her historical endeavours at the same market as the majority of her other books, producing stories with a much more complex array of messages with contemporary significance for a specifically girlish audience. Other writers in the genre, such as Mrs Emma Marshall, also saw the potential in this field for reinforcing the attitudes and stereotypes conveyed in their contemporary works. It would seem that the historical novel for adolescent girls increased in popularity as the century drew on: Evelyn Everett Green, for instance, found almost more demand for historical than for

[7] Charlotte M. Yonge, *The Chaplet of Pearls* (Macmillan, London, 1871), Preface, pp. viii–ix.

[8] Charlotte M. Yonge, *The Little Duke, or Richard the Fearless* (Macmillan, London, 1854). Set in tenth-century Normandy and dealing with a genuine historical character, deriving her story from ancient, largely French, chronicles etc. Despite the air of authenticity, Miss Yonge's insistence that his contemporaries would have interpreted Richard's actions as motivated by an essentially Victorian sense of right and wrong seems unlikely.

contemporary novels, while Emily S. Holt concentrated on this aspect of the genre to the exclusion, apart from two obscure publications, of any other.

Stories with a historical background were popular not only with girls, of course. Large numbers of historical adventures were produced for the adolescent male. However, there was a very discernible difference between the stories for young men and those written for young ladies. Writers for the boys' market, like Henty, looked more to the broad sweep of history as surveyed by Macaulay: to war and adventure on the grand scale within which to encapsulate their stirring message of enduring English manhood, with the domestic background playing little or no role.[9] Equally, as with modern adventure novels, little attention was paid to the deeper motivations or emotions of the historical characters. It was enough to say, for instance, that a hero was English and well-born; the corollary of his noble nature from start to finish of the novel was axiomatic, therefore, needing no exploration of self-doubt or distrust – the character stereotyping for this market was as usual far cruder.

It is not surprising: this was, after all, far more 'suited' to the larger, public sphere in which men were to operate and to the didactic needs of the masculine gender. History adventures provided a particularly happy setting for displaying the sound results of that unthinking and instinctive courage on the part of right-thinking and well-trained 'lads' that was so synonymous with male patriotism to the conventional middle-class Victorian mind. Aged 16, Walter Somers, in *St George for England*, overhears a plot laid by a powerful, if wicked, knight to drown two ladies. He promptly gathers round him a band of equally foolhardy youths, and sets out to thwart the plot without informing any adult. Naturally, however, as he is English and of noble birth, he succeeds, if narrowly, in rescuing the fair damsel and her mother from the Thames. The general

[9] For further discussions of historical writing for boys see Guy Arnold, *Held Fast for England: G.A. Henty, Imperialist Boys' Writer* (Hamish Hamilton, London, 1980); also J.S. Bratton, 'Of England, Home and Duty: The Image of England in Victorian and Edwardian Juvenile Fiction', in John M. Mackenzie (ed.), *Imperialism and Popular Culture* (Manchester University Press, Manchester, 1986).

response is that he had 'done well', and if he might have done better 'one cannot expect old heads on young shoulders' and it is understandable that he wanted to 'accomplish the adventure' without aid. Even the ladies accept this interpretation of their ducking, and the fair maiden ends up marrying Walter after he has fought in a few battles, thus restoring him to the family estates.[10]

The adventures in which girls took part, if set in equally turbulent periods, were usually less immediately stirring and battle-dominated, being as usual intended to illustrate character development as well as events. They also included consideration of prominent historical personages, frequently male, but were also more rounded in outlook because the scenario was generally viewed from a domestic stance, which equally suited the fundamentally 'private' nature of the feminine sphere, and the expectations of female comprehension and interest. Girls' historical novels were consciously used to demonstrate the long-term as well as the short-term impact of actions and attitudes. Consequently, writers spent time delineating the thinking behind masculine attitudes to an even greater extent than in 'modern' tales to demonstrate the reasons for the traditional role of women and their relations with men. As a result of all this, one particularly noticeable feature in these girls' novels, contrasting with the ethos of the boys' books quite strongly, is the lengths to which they went to recreate the historical past as accurately as possible in factual terms, via a weighty compilation of information concerning life in the period in which the tale is laid, often with a strong emphasis on the domestic aspects thereof.

These books also reveal the extent of the expectations of the authors for this feminine middle-class market. As has been said, they took great pains to produce information that was historically accurate, but equally, they clearly anticipated that their readership would have already a considerable grounding in the subject background, presumably as a result of reading the history textbooks designed for them at a younger age or other required reading such as Foxe's *Book of English Martyrs*. Most adolescent stories do centre on reasonably well-known

[10] G.A. Henty, *Saint George for England: A Tale of Cressy and Poitiers* (Blackie, Glasgow, 1885), p. 34; p. 36.

periods or events, such as the Crusades, the Reformation or the Glorious Revolution: but such stories usually plunge *in medias res*, taking for granted familiarity with the setting up of the Crusader Kingdoms, the personalities involved in Henry VIII's divorce, or the abdication of James II. Some, like Charlotte Yonge, even endowed their audience with a capacity to read or to research old French with a reasonable degree of fluency, by giving verses or comments in the original.[11] In other words, these books were not intended to act as channels through which historical fact would be painlessly imbued by a novice in the field. They could only be read intelligibly and enjoyably, to say nothing about profitably, if a large degree of knowledge was already present. Historical novels did indeed provide extra knowledge, but of a much more recondite kind.

It had become possible for such women writers to produce such stories with the background wealth of authentic domestic detail and minutiae allied to wider considerations and messages in the general format that was considered suitable for a feminine readership because, to a very considerable extent, of the work of a number of professional women historians. Agnes Strickland and her sister were in the van, but there was a growing band of women working in this field, such as Mary Anne Everett Green (née Wood), mother of Evelyn Everett Green, with her work on the State Papers of the early modern period and also Kate Norgate.[12] Their scholarship won considerable contemporary respect for its authenticity and careful survey of sources, if not for its overall contribution to the discipline. Such work was usually described as being suited only to women with their talent for the petty and the painstaking: it focussed on careful and detailed accumulation of knowledge in areas then generally overlooked as being too trivial to influence interpretations of great events by the male historians in the Whig tradition, such as Lord Macaulay. Equally, the interpretations of history by such women, frequently in the form of the less acceptable biographical studies, were considered to be of 'little real value to [male] students'.[13]

[11] Charlotte M. Yonge, *The Little Duke*.

[12] Both these women were noted and meticulous scholars, with a considerable scholarly output, largely concentrating on the Middle Ages.

[13] William Cates, *The Treasury of Biography* (Longman, London, 1882), entry for Norgate.

Yet if such works were not the sources of background material that a Henty might use, it is not difficult to see why so many women authors of didactic fiction felt able to draw on this kind of source for their own work. Ready to their hand was a type of scholarship that was generally considered suited to female talents and comprehension, and based on the view of history most suitable to the feminine novel. In these historical books authenticity did not depend primarily on depicting a recognizable lifestyle, but on the air of authority conveyed by the apparent dependence on historical sources. Stories made much use of detailed historical anecdote in this respect. Evelyn Everett Green, drawing on her mother's work in *The Church and the King*, recounted that when a black-clad and grief-struck Henry VIII, went to visit Anne Boleyn after receiving news of the death of Katherine of Aragon, he found her dressed in yellow, rejoicing with her similarly-decked ladies. There was, however, one exception – Jane Seymour had defied Anne to dress herself suitably.[14] Twentieth-century scholarly opinion that the pedigree of this anecdote is dubious overlooks the credence likely to have been given to such by youthful, and even adult readers of these tales in the previous century. References were often made in the text to contemporary material: Charlotte Yonge made frequent use of Froissart in her string of novels concerning French history and made sure that her readers knew it. Quotations from surviving documents or diaries, from pipe rolls to Pepys, also made appearances in a variety of books. Such interventions were not then held to interrupt or detract from the story, but to add to it by making it more believable. It was for this reason, for instance, that writers of historical novels from Charlotte Yonge to Emily Holt also made use of lengthy factual appendices and even footnotes to reinforce elements in their texts.

These performed a variety of functions from giving the original sources from which they had taken ideas or quotations; to explaining the historical usage of a term or the economic base of a period. For instance, in *One Snowy Night* by Emily Holt a chapter beginning with a discussion on the historical usage of surnames, carefully linked with character identification and

[14] Evelyn Everett Green, *The Church and the King: A Tale of England in the Days of Henry VIII* (Nelson, Walton-on-Thames, 1892), pp. 364–5.

personal mobility in twelfth-century England, has the following footnote amplifying a reference to the son of a priest, John Fitz-al-Prester:

> [1] 'William, son of the fat priest,' occurs on the Pipe Roll for 1176, unless 'Grossus' is to be taken as a Christian name.[15]

Later in the same book the mother of the household, Isel, goes shopping for her household at the great annual St Frideswide Fair in Oxford, buying a pig (19d); half an ox (17d); cloth (1s 5½d per ell); a cloak 'for a mark' and capes for 6s 8d each; slippers were 'laid in' at 6d per pair and boots for a shilling. Cheese cost her a halfpenny each, a load of flour 14d and of meal 2d; beans were 1s 8d; cabbage is 2d; herrings 2s. She bought a coffer and nails at 5s and 2s 4d, and a rug for a coverlet at 2¼ marks. The relevant footnote gave the modern apprentice *Household Angel* the contemporary value:

> [1] Modern value of above prices: Pig, £1, 19s 7d; half ox £1, 15s 5d; cloth, £1, 16s 5½d per ell; cloak £13, 6s 8d; cape, £6, 13s 4d; pair of slippers, 12s. 6d; boots, per pair 25s; cheeses, 2s 1d each; flour and cabbage, each £1, 9s 2d; meal and herrings, each £2, 10s; beans, £2, 1s 8d; coffer £6, 5s; nails £2, 18s 4d; rug £50. It will be seen that money was far cheaper than now, and living much more expensive.[16]

It was clearly expected that the recipient of this information would find their enjoyment increased by such apparent interruptions of the narrative flow. However, the fictional element of the story was the channel through which the message was worked out to a satisfactory and profitable conclusion.

The dramatis personae of the books were thus of considerable importance. The purpose of the historical novel was to show the 'real' long-term consequences of actions and attitudes undertaken by characters, good or bad, so those characters had to be as authentic as possible. In the interests of authenticity, therefore, the historical novel for girls generally contained a cast made up to a considerable extent of genuine characters

[15] Emily S. Holt, *One Snowy Night, or Long Ago at Oxford* (Shaw, London, 1893), p. 40.
[16] Ibid., pp. 97–9.

from the past, with the heroine and hero and perhaps some others carefully worked into the tapestry. Evelyn Everett Green used legends and papers of her own family in tales such as *Maud Melville's Marriage*, a tale based around the events of the Glorious Revolution and a child bride's successful efforts to free from Newgate and win a pardon for her husband from Queen Mary.[17] Emily Holt used real personages to such an extent, especially in her medieval and early modern stories, that she found it necessary to point out in her appendices or footnotes those people in her story who were *not* vouched for in primary sources.

Often she would take a name with little or nothing known about the personality lying behind it and endow that name with a suitable persona, as she did in *Lady Sybil's Choice*, the story of Guy de Lusignan and his path to the kingship of Jerusalem in his wife's right. In this case, only two names cannot be referred to historical authority, and they play a background role in the working out of the plot.[18] She took 'accuracy' so far in this respect that where possible, she used contemporary portraits as the basis for her physical descriptions – as she consistently informed her readers. She was consequently able to give a greater air of authenticity to her character interpretations by linking such descriptions to personality. It was generally accepted that, with very few exceptions, a pleasing appearance was an indication of moral soundness; while physical facial distortion, especially around the eyes, conveyed a spiritual villainy. In a story about the Wars of the Roses, Anne Neville was delineated as a 'mixture of gentleness and dignity. Very queenly she was . . . in the true sense of that innate kingliness of soul which can tolerate nothing evil . . . a lily among thorns' on the basis of a contemporary portrait.[19]

[17] Evelyn Everett Green, *Maud Melville's Marriage* Nelson, Walton-on-Thames, 1893), introduction.

[18] Emily S. Holt, *Lady Sybil's Choice: A Tale of the Crusades* (Shaw, London, 1879). As well as copious footnotes giving character authenticity, this contains an exhaustive appendix giving the history of the de Lusignan family in the thirteenth century and of the dynasties associated with the Kingdom of Jerusalem.

[19] Emily S. Holt, *Red and White: A Tale of the Wars of the Roses* (Shaw, London, 1882), p. 40, fn. 1 assured the reader that 'all personal descriptions were taken as far as practical from contemporary portraits', especially those of the Warwicks and royal family; p. 44.

Charlotte Yonge made an equivalent use of history in this respect. She took the name of that de Ribaumont family whose representative had been awarded a chaplet of pearls as a token of bravery by Edward III of England, and wove the subsequent 'history' of the family into a series of convincing tales such as *The Chaplet of Pearls*, where the fortunes of the family were bound up with that of the French Hugenots in the 1560s and 1570s.[20] On another occasion she reviewed the romantic story of Mary, Queen of Scots in *Unknown to History* – a title with a certain irony unlikely to have been appreciated by the author. Her tale was based on speculation by Agnes Strickland, and presented in a very convincing fictional guise.[21] Brought up by the Talbot family who found her as a baby, Cecily eventually discovers herself to be in reality Princess Bride of Scotland, daughter of Mary and Bothwell. The discovery puts her life and her future happiness in danger, but by constant practice of daughterly duty to her real and her adopted family (despite the obvious conflict of interest) she is enabled to marry the man she loves, her foster brother, after Mary's execution. They then retire to Holland to live, refusing the blandishments of Elizabeth I to make Bride her heir instead of James Stuart. Consequently in exile they live and die together happily, if childless, thus making it easier for them to remain 'unknown to history'.[22]

In the additional interests of veracity, the dialogue of these books was almost invariably archaic: by Shakespeare out of Malory for those set in pre-seventeenth-century times; and by Gibbon out of Milton for the subsequent periods. Certain authors, notably Emily Holt, were more assiduous than others in writing in such a style. For instance, the arrival of a new lady of the bedchamber to the Countess of Warwick in *Red and White: A Tale of the Wars of the Roses*, is announced in distinctly tortuous form:

[20] Charlotte M. Yonge, *The Chaplet of Pearls*. The story of Edward III's gift to Sir Eustace de Ribaumont as a result of his bravery in the field is well documented and formed a favourite incident in tales of this period.

[21] Charlotte M. Yonge, *Unknown to History: A Story of the Captivity of Mary of Scotland* (Macmillan, London, 1882).

[22] Ibid., p. 589.

An't like you, Madam, your new chamberer that shall be, is now come.
The Lord Marnell, his daughter?
She, Madam.[23]

Thee's and thou's were almost invariably used in more intimate discussions by all authors writing stories set before 1750. Laboured though dialogue like this may sound, the very consistency of style in these novels means that, with the addition of the footnotes and glossaries for unusual words, the prose is relatively easy to follow. Adult reviewers were sometimes a little amused, but concurred that the language made a valuable contribution towards the impact of these novels.[24]

The books, it must be remembered, were written for a purpose where historical veracity was not an end in itself, but simply a medium through which a message was passed and given greater conviction. History was seen as a continuous process of improvement. Thus it was admitted that in earlier times, different attitudes were taken towards certain issues. Evelyn Everett Green, for instance, commented that the laxity of 'olden times' in their merry-making was 'scarcely edifying to our modern notions'.[25] Equally, entered a cloistered life was acceptable in pre-Reformation times when the exigencies of everyday life were different. Emily Holt, for instance, claimed that before 1533, it was not possible for a girl to remain unmarried outside the cloister.[26]

However, this latitude did not include the basic standards of humanity. The general consensus in the nineteenth century was to view people from earlier times in purely modern terms; and nor was this considered to distort or misrepresent history in any way. It was both valid and justifiable to judge figures from earlier periods by standards current in Victorian England, and the incongruity in this apparent to twentieth-century readers was not seen then, even by most professional historians.

[23] Emily S. Holt, *Red and White*, p. 38.
[24] See the extract from a review in *The Spectator* quoted in the front of Emily S. Holt, *Red and White*.
[25] Evelyn Everett Green, *The Church and the King*, pp. 110–11.
[26] Emily S. Holt, *Red and White*: 'an old maid, out of the cloister, was unknown before the Reformation', p. 513.

Thus without sacrificing her professional reputation, Emily Holt could write of, for instance, Elizabeth Woodville that 'it is true that few women have known more crushing sorrow than she. But I think it is too commonly forgotten how much she had deserved it' – by stepping outside the bounds of a good Victorian matron.[27] Evelyn Everett Green could write of Edward I and his Welsh policy that 'He was too keen a statesman and too just a man to desire anything but a conciliatory policy so far as it was possible'. It was largely the fault of the Welsh 'a very wild race . . . barely civilised' and with 'a vein of fierce treachery' that Edward was roused to anger and stern action against them.[28]

Any reader of novels in this genre would have found it possible to recite at considerable lengths such definite judgements on a range of monarchs and prominent men or women and their actions from most periods of history. Examples range from the dismissal of George I as 'a man of little intellect and less morality' and fundamentally unkingly: to the approval of Mary II as 'capable of great kindness and consideration' despite an outward coldness and haughtiness.[29] Consequently, it is not surprising that all of the characters depicted in these novels, if historical in name, were purely nineteenth-century in nature. The criteria by which such personages, real or fictional, major or minor, were judged as being satisfactory or unsatisfactory were firmly founded on modern mores, with no attempt to evaluate those of their own period.

This lack of any feeling of historical constraint in character interpretation was particularly noticeable in the case of heroines. Beyond the terms of speech or descriptions of dress, there was no intrinsic difference made between a damsel of the thirteenth century and one of the nineteenth. Edith Peynton, Elizabeth Alford's seventeenth-century *Fair Maid of Taunton*, is an older Ellen Montgomery in fancy dress:

in the rich bloom of her complexion, in the golden tinge of her

[27] Ibid., p. 327.

[28] Evelyn Everett Green, *The Lord of Dynevor: A Tale of the Time of Edward the First* (Nelson, Walton-on-Thames, 1892), p. 128.

[29] Emily S. Holt, *Ashcliffe Hall: A Tale of the Last Century* (Shaw, London, 1870), p. 347; Evelyn Everett Green, *Maud Melville's Marriage*, p. 320.

abundant coils of hair, in the fearless brightness of her deep blue eyes, Edith might have her rivals; but in the poise of her shapely head, in the dignity of her carriage, in the graceful ease of her every movement she distanced all competitors. And yet so unmindful was she of her beauty, so free from all craving for admiration, that there was not a fair maid ... who begrudged her the homage she received.

By the end of the tale, the suffering and self-sacrifice involved in the Civil War 'brought out the depths of her character and changed her from the bright loving girl, into the tender, sympathizing, heroic woman'.[30] She acquired this status as a result of her nursing the sick and wounded of both sides, without fear or favour, and was rewarded by the love of a gallant and sober-thinking young gentleman of royalist tendencies but sound religious training and well-tended estates. In other words, Edith is, in appearance and in mentality, a stereotypical model maiden of the basic type. She conformed in other respects also, being religious, a good and conscientious housewife and a dutiful daughter. As Miss Alford makes plain, she will thus make an ideal wife in the right social station.

Increasingly, however, the stereotypical heroine of this type of fiction conformed to the more robust, *Home Goddess* stereotype. Both Emily Holt's and Evelyn Everett Green's young ladies, for example, displayed that capacity and resilience combined with the usual feminine attributes found in the majority of the modern fictional heroines of the post-1880s. They might be slight in stature, but never in personality or resource. In Emily Holt's tale of the St Batholomew's Day Massacre, 16-year-old Rose Perier, aided only by divine inspiration and protection, gets her young brother and sister out of Paris and eventually to safety in England. She disguises her sister and herself as humble vegetable sellers and hides her little brother under the cabbages in a donkey panier. On the long and dangerous journey only her wit and resource, as well as her courage, help them out of a number of perilous situations, though one feels that the cabbages must have been

[30] Elizabeth M. Alford, *The Fair Maid of Taunton: A Tale of the Siege* (Shaw, London, 1878), p. 3.
[31] Emily S. Holt, *Sister Rose, or The Eve of St. Bartholomew* (Shaw, London, 1870), p. 231.

rather the worse for wear by the time they reached Boulogne: but throughout she herself is suitably 'unaware of the extent, and of the full risk, of her own heroic act'. Instead, she settles down in her new country to keep her reduced family by turning her unaccustomed hands to the production of quantities of fine lace until her brother is old enough to make a living for his family, losing neither status nor approval as a result of her actions.[31]

Of course, the men, particularly the heroes, are equally nineteenth-century in outline and motivation – necessarily so if they are to form fitting mates for the heroines. Thus the heroes are courageous, physically prepossessing, if not absolutely handsome; high-principled and noble-natured, good-mannered and family-minded. In the days of their youth they may be a little rash and impetous, like Rupert Lorimer in Evelyn Everett Green's *Ruth Ravelstan*. But in required fashion, Rupert learns by experience and the example of a good woman, so when he requests Ruth's hand from her puritan father, General Lorimer sees a face that is 'Not handsome only – that beauty is but skin-deep'. Instead it bears:

> the impress of strenuous purpose, self-restraint, strong will kept in bounds. It was the face of a man to be trusted already, to be honoured and revered as the years passed by, were this promise of early manhood to be fulfilled. And who could better help him to fulfil it than a woman loved and loving, in whose heart was implanted the fear of the Lord?[32]

Such a man could be relied on to appreciate a *Home Angel* when he is entrusted with her. Still more important, the result of such a combination will be the creation of a soundly based family unit, with much promise for the future.

The much-cherished middle-class ideal of the Family featured prominently in stories with a modern setting. However, the attributes of historical fiction were seen as making that genre also a suitable vehicle for discussing the role and value of the family. The combination of fact and fiction permitted a firm focus on a particular idea or moral and a discussion of the

[32] Evelyn Everett Green, *Ruth Ravelstan, the Puritan's Daughter* (Nelson, Walton-on-Thames, 1907), 1st edn (1901), p. 410.

long-term consequences of behaviour, good or bad, that was not always possible in a modern tale if an air of realism was to be sustained. Yet at the same time, the reliance on genuine and respected historical sources enabled any story using such a background to carry the air of veracity necessary to carry conviction in putting across its message. It is in this context first and foremost that the boom in the writing of historical fiction for the feminine market, which, after all, largely predates that for the masculine market, must be placed.

Using tales of the past, it was possible to create a convincingly authentic pedigree by which the nineteenth-century conception of the ideal nuclear family, linked with its rightful traditional setting of the home, could be presented as hallowed by age and experience, thus safeguarding its present and guaranteeing its future. It was presented as the social unit which had been responsible to a great extent for advancing England to its nineteenth-century peak of civilization. No matter what the period, good men and women at least were shown to have played the same types of role in the pattern of society: women the centre of a private, domestic circle and men the upholders of the external, public world. Together, such a combination was invincible, enduring and unquestionably beneficial. The 'realistic' surveys provided by such novels, backed up by 'facts', showed that heroes and heroines of historical fiction almost always came from sound family backgrounds themselves, and aimed to secure their own happiness by recreating them in their own adult domestic life – and, of course, passing them on to their progeny. Misery was equally convincingly shown to result from attempts to distort the 'natural' rules of society. As a result, it was important that these rules be shown as having the potential to operate at all levels of society, and during all periods of history.

Edward I was shown in a series of novels by various authors to have been a kind and affectionate father as well as a model husband, if occasionally a little stern – an interpretation which might surprise some scholars now. This aspect of his nature was emphasized in Evelyn Everett Green's *Lord of Dynevor*: 'The stern soldier-king was a particularly tender and loving father', while the gentle Queen Eleanor has the truly womanly knack of making simple domestic comfort the keynote of life in any royal castle. It is as a result of the example set by this domestic bliss and Edward's paternal indulgence to his son, the delicate Prince Alphonso, that the Welsh rebel, Wendot Res Vychan, is reconciled to English rule over Wales. Wendot repents of his deeds against the English crown, marries an English heiress, is forgiven by the King and settles down to bring up his son in a fit manner to cope with his mixed English and Welsh estates:

> The experience of the past has taught me that in the English alliance is Wales's only hope of tranquility and true independence and civilisation ... methinks there is no humiliation in owning as sovereign lord the lion-hearted King of England ... We will rally round the standard of father and son and trust that in the future a brighter day will dawn for our long-distracted country.

Wendot is even able to prove to his Welsh vassals 'to their own satisfaction that the royal Edward is their best friend'.[33]

Emily S. Holt, by contrast, in *One Snowy Night*, showed the family ideal against a humbler background, that of the townspeople of twelfth-century Oxford and London. A major theme is that genuine affection, respect and trust between husband and wife leads to parental affection and the abiding happiness and confidence that binds families together despite difficulties and oppression. When some of these families are thrown out of their homes and into the snowy night for heresy, they help each other cheerfully and die together joyfully. Others who survive recreate their families in new homes, with every hope and confidence in the future thereby. This family-based security is pointed up by the nagging wife, Ananias, who makes her husband's life a misery by her tongue while her children are ungovernable and she herself bitterly unhappy:

> But it did not occur to her to inquire of what the woman was made who habitually tormented that easy-tempered man [her husband], nor how much happier her home might have been had she learned to bridle her own irritating tongue.[34]

These authors were using the 'facts' of history to demonstrate

---

[33] Evelyn Everett Green, *The Lord of Dynevor*, pp. 93–4; p. 253; p. 257.
[34] Emily S. Holt, *One Snowy Night*, p. 350.

the complementary importance of men and women in building a secure and desirable society.

This meant that, as in the nineteenth century, family loyalty had necessarily to be based on the correct ground. Love, in the Victorian understanding of the term, was the only secure basis on which to ensure a sound marriage and the consequent prosperous continuance of the family. As Mistress Corbet, in *Lady Betty's Governess*, comments 'the trials of temper which come in the happiest marriage would be too much' without it. In furtherance of this theme, heroines were generally able to remain unmarried because of parental indulgence of this 'natural' womanly desire to see marriage as a question of love rather than worldly policy. It is partly for this reason that the majority of historical heroines marry at ages of nineteenth-century discretion, when they could be expected to have the maturity, acknowledged by their parents, to judge their own emotions and those of their suitors and to understand 'the true nature of a wedded love'.[35] In addition, it was believed that empathy between the modern girl and a child-wife of an earlier century was less likely. In novels like *Maud Melville's Marriage*, where such a match is made for a heroine, the child is old beyond her years and there is no question of a youthful couple setting up together until they are both older and have learned to love and trust each other in adult terms.[36] It was also acceptable to have two children as childish sweethearts with this emotion developing in time into mature affection. It was, however, quite common for fictional heroines to remain unwed and waiting for their destined mates into their twenties despite the pressure of rank, beauty, possessions and suitors, as did the twelfth-century Elaine de Lusignan in *Lady Sybil's Choice*, or the sixteenth-century Beatrice Fane in *The Church and the King*.

Even when there was parental pressure in this respect it would be overcome in the wider interests of society. Evelyn Everett Green's Alys de Knaston, daughter of the Constable of Oxford during the reign of Henry III, is faced with two suitors. One is Leofric Wyvill, the rising scholar with 'a singularly attractive face'. His:

---

[35] L.E. Guernsey, *Lady Betty's Governess, or The Corbet Chronicles* (Shaw, London, 1878), p. 180; Evelyn Everett Green, *Maud Melville's Marriage*, p. 27.
[36] Ibid., p. 34; p. 40.

brow was broad and massive, indicating intellectual power. The blue eyes ... looked out upon the world with a singular directness and purity of expression. The features were finely cut, and there were strength and sweetness both.

The other is Amalric de Montfort, a younger son of Simon de Montfort, a goodly youth of 'knightly aspect' and a particularly good prospect in material terms.[37] Amalric, however, is not so high-minded and the fair Alys, being a typical example of the discerning damsel, prefers Leofric. Worried that her father might betroth her against her will, she is comforted by Eleanor de Montfort. None would:

> urge thee to act against which thy heart rebels. We cannot give our love as if it were a toy. Our hearts will speak, and they discourse eloquent music ... It shall never be said of the house of De Montford that its sons wooed unwilling brides!

In the event, Amalric very conveniently dies of wounds after the Battle of Evesham, leaving the field to Leofric, by this time a rich and popular – and pioneering – Master at Oxford.[38] Providence in some form always intervenes to prevent a mistaken adult from diverting the course of true love in this way, giving the modern maiden no excuse for any weakness in this respect.

Historical fiction was also presumed to act as a corrective and a reassurance for girls, by showing the long-term rewards accruing to women for faithfully and professionally performing their allotted role within the traditional domestic circle. Evelyn Everett Green's Deborah Ravelstan was a near paragon of good wifehood. Though personally opposed to many of her husband's ideas and actions during the Civil War and the Interregnum, she remembered that she had married him for love. By the time of the Restoration, her husband had gained a truer appreciation of the situation.

[37] Evelyn Everett Green, *A Clerk of Oxford, and His Adventures in the Barons' War* (Nelson, Walton-on-Thames, 1898), pp. 9–10; p. 193.
[38] Ibid., p. 383. The author apologizes in a footnote on p. 438 for discovering that in fact Amalric was only captured, not killed, She also insists that, contrary to modern scholarly opinion, secular masters were beginning to make an appearance at Oxford at this time.

Sad though her spirit had been in those days, her lips framed no word of reproach for her husband or those he trusted. Now was she reaping her reward. Her gentle, silent patience, this sweet saintliness of life, had been more eloquent than the words of many preachers, and had taught truer lessons.[39]

When, as with Charlotte Yonge's series on the de Ribaumonts or L.E. Guernsey's *Corbet Chronicles* series, it was possible to trace the story of a family through a number of generations, the continuance of a family virtue was even more apparent. In such cases, both men and women played a significant part: frequently the inspiration was feminine if the active role was masculine. For instance, the de Ribaumonts were a truthful and fearless family, willing to brave any peril for their principles, so in Charlotte Yonge's interpretation, it was natural that they became Huguenots. The married cousins, Berenger and Eustacie de Ribaumont in *The Chaplet of Pearls*, go through various perils, but throughout both display the true family spirit, typified by courage and constancy to their beliefs, and so are united finally to bring up their children as worthy successors.[40]

It was not just the tradition of the family that was seen as being enhanced by historical fiction. The Anglican religion also received a propaganda boost in these stories; to the extent that it is very difficult to find any historical novel for this market where the Anglican tradition is not emphasized in some way. The nature of that boost depends to a considerable extent on the religious tone of the author: Charlotte Yonge took a distinctly high Church tone, finding Calvinist-style beliefs distasteful and a little irreverent.[41] Evelyn Everett Green used the experience of history to warn against 'stripping away from worship too much of the beauty and reverence which is God-given'. The Wesleyan movement had begun because the Church of England was not 'doing its duty', but its sparse doctrine had encouraged the evils of social rebellion amongst its listeners, evils which were being combatted by the Oxford Movement and the return to worshipping God in the beauty of

[39] Evelyn Everett Green, *Ruth Ravelstan*, pp. 412–13.
[40] Charlotte M. Yonge, *The Chaplet of Pearls*, p. 338. See also the sequel, Charlotte M. Yonge, *Stray Pearls* (Macmillan, London, 1888).
[41] Ibid., p. 19.

holiness.[42] By contrast, Emily Holt displayed much more of a low Church, evangelical bent in her works, with stern warnings against the eternal machinations of Rome, seeing the Oxford Movement as succumbing to the wiles of the Roman Jezebel.[43] Others, like Mrs Emma Marshall and L.E. Guernsey trod the broad middle path of general satisfaction with Protestant doctrine. However, there is throughout, even in the works of high Church authors, a strongly anti-Roman Catholic strain in these books.

As a result, despite all the apparent, sectarian-inspired differences, there is one common strand running through the high-profile presentation of English Christianity in historical fiction: the patriotic element. Adolescent girls were presented with a tradition where to a very important extent, nationalism was an aspect and a consequence of Anglicanism and *vice versa*. Emphasis is laid in these books on the appearance of English national characteristics from a very early period. These characteristics are shown as developing and strengthening as time passes, to reach their highest level, of course, in the nineteenth century – though with the promise of yet higher standards in the future.

Evelyn Everett Green, among others, discerned factors which by the Middle Ages set the English and those willingly associated with them apart from (and above) other European nations. Englishmen were generally taller, braver and more honest, and the only true lovers of liberty. They fought only for the sake of personal and national honour, when necessary. Edward III spent the night before Crecy according to Evelyn Everett Green in prayer 'less for victory than that England's honour might be upheld, and that whatever the issue of the day, this might be preserved stainless in the sight of God and man'.[44] Thus while Englishmen were 'always ready to fight if

[42] Evelyn Everett Green, *Arnold Inglehurst, the Preacher: A Story of the Fen Country* (Shaw, London, 1896), p. 55.

[43] Emily S. Holt, *Clare Avery: A Story of the Spanish Armada* (Shaw, London, 1876), Preface: 'England stands now in as much peril of having Popery insidiously infused into her, as she did in 1588 of having it rudely forced upon her.

[44] Evelyn Everett Green, *In the Days of Chivalry: A Tale of the Times of the Black Prince* (Nelson, Walton-on-Thames, 1893), p. 218.

they could find an enemy to meet them', when they would fight 'shoulder to shoulder, fearless and dauntless'; they preferred to fight a foe that was at least equal. This explained the English dislike of sieges, as they had no wish to prove themselves against 'half-starved men'. Once victorious, though, it was 'England's pride' that Englishmen did not 'torture our prisoners': because 'in this land men may obtain justice better than in any other' – witness Magna Carta.[45]

Moreover, English women were equally outstanding in nurturing such values in themselves and their menfolk from a very early period. In one typical example, Elaine de Lusignan in *Lady Sybil's Choice* established her credit as an honorary Englishwoman, being a native of Poitou and therefore willingly subject to Henry II of England, by declaring her love of noble deeds. She admired men who saved 'their country at the risk of their own lives' and women who emulated them as far as possible in their own sphere: 'a mother who sacrificed herself for a child ... a lady who was ready to see her true knight die rather than stain his honour'.[46] Thus also Joan in *Days of Chivalry*, saved from the proverbial direst of fates, writes to her anguished lover bidding him stay with the English army: 'it were better he should do his duty nobly by the Prince ... than hasten to her side. In days to come it would grieve them to feel that they had ... thought first of themselves when King and country should have taken the foremost place'. Meanwhile, she saves her would-be ravisher from torture and humiliation, and settles down to await her marriage, which is delayed a mere two years: 'such love as theirs was not for time alone; it would last on and on through the boundless cycles of eternity'.[47] With women like this at their sides, how could English men fail to be superior.

Authors universally agreed that it was divine inspiration that had helped English men and women to maintain their high standard. The same divine guidance had opened English eyes to 'the monstrous evil of Rome' and encouraged England to throw off that 'accursed yoke'.[48] It is in this respect that it becomes a little unfair to continue to voice the dismissive

[45] Ibid., p. 76; p. 222; p. 248; p. 502; p. 518.
[46] Emily S. Holt, *Lady Sybil's Choice*, p. 3; p. 10.
[47] Evelyn Everett Green, *Days of Chivalry*, p. 501; p. 551; p. 558.
[48] Evelyn Everett Green, *Arnold Inglehurst*, p. 56.

PLATE 7   THE CAPTIVE FREED

The model maiden in history. From *In the Days of Chivalry: A Tale of the Times of the Black Prince* (1893)

criticism of women historians and historical novelists of this
period. The usual complaint is that, unlike the Macaulays,
Lyttons and Scotts, even Hentys, women were incapable of
grasping the wider issues of history. Georgina Battiscombe, in
her biography of Charlotte Yonge, commented that 'Her
accuracy in small matters is only equalled by her incomprehen-
sion of large issues.'[49] The work of professional historians like
Agnes Strickland is already being re-evaluated. It is also possible to reassess the historical grasp of authors like Emily Holt
by identifying the theoretical stance from which they operated.
Emily Holt in particular was concerned to demonstrate the
lengthy pedigree of 'English Catholicism'. In her series of over
20 titles of tales of England in 'olden times', she argued for a
neatly worked out interpretation based initially on ideas put
forward by Foxe in his *Book of English Martyrs*.

Foxe had argued that the English Catholic Church had
always been separate from the Roman Catholic Church: tracing
its inception to pre-Augustinian days and justifying Henry
VIII's break with Rome as a return to English orthodox
traditions. Emily Holt took up this theme and amplified it
considerably, both in detail and in extent. Starting with *Imogen*,
her tale of the Augustine mission to England, she depicted the
history of Christianity in England into the nineteenth century.
She said that its purity aroused the hatred and envy of Rome,
whose business it was constantly to assail and attempt to corrupt
the stalwart English faith, which gave rise to the peculiarly
English character. In *Imogen* she argued that the English
Church was firmly established by the time that Augustine
arrived, and that his mission of conversion started the corruption and misdirection of English Christianity which continued
for centuries after. She accepted in later novels that the Roman
Church was not as evil in early days as she had become by the
Middle Ages. In particular, transubstantiation did not become
dogma until the end of the twelfth century. Much of the blame
for the downward spiral in the Roman Church was placed on
the shoulders of Robert Curthose, son of William the Con-
queror, who despite his acquaintance with a pure English faith,
refused to accept the divine intention that he take the throne of

[49] Georgina Battiscombe, *Charlotte Mary Yonge: The Story of an Uneventful
Life* (Constable, London, 1943), p. 43.

Jerusalem, bringing that holy Kingdom under the kings of England and their faith. Encouraged by this, the evil powers at work in Rome spread their power, resulting in the fall of Jerusalem to the infidel, with all the deleterious effect this had on even the pure stronghold of English faith.[50]

One result of this dereliction of duty by the Norman monarchs was the spreading of Roman Catholic-style religious persecution to England, something that was displayed in all books as being innately unEnglish. Thus the mission of Gerhardt the German and his band of Paulicans in the mid-twelfth century to bring the true teaching of Christ back to England resulted in their persecution; but the heart of England remained true, and the doctrines re-awakened by Gerhardt survived as a subliminal stream in English Christianity, resurfacing as 'heresies' such as Lollardy and eventually, as the separate Anglican Church.[51] She commented of the thirteenth century that:

> Perhaps in this nineteenth century we scarcely realize the gallant fight made by the Church of England to retain her independence of Rome . . . some of her clergy were perpetually trying to force . . . the chains of Rome upon her, but the body of the laity, who are really the Church resisted this attempt almost to the death. There was a perpetual struggle between the King of England and the Papacy.[52]

It is a somewhat unorthodox interpretation, perhaps, but Emily Holt backed it up with a welter of fact. It is interesting to note as part of that struggle the people that she describes as clinging to this purer faith, including Henry VI and his subject, the Duke of Suffolk. Both these men were, if not overt heretics, supposedly influenced in childhood by Lollard nurses.[53]

For all his faults, especially his promiscuity, Henry VIII receives forgiveness for acting as a tool of divine will in

[50] Emily S. Holt, *Imogen: A Tale of the Early British Church* (Shaw, London, 1886); *Lady Sybil's Choice*, p. 143, fn. 1; pp. 66–7.

[51] Emily S. Holt, *One Snowy Night*, pp. 383–4.

[52] Emily S. Holt, *Earl Hubert's Daughter, or The Polishing of the Pearl* (Shaw, London, 1880), pp. 18–19.

[53] Emily S. Holt, *Red and White*. She does admit that it is speculation rather than outright proof in her historical appendix.

breaking away from Rome. In this respect, Mary Tudor was described in the darkest of terms for her attempt to return her country and sacred charge to the outer darkness of popery, resulting in the most tragic persecution of innocent martyrs. Thus her death was greeted with suitable rejoicing:

> It is not often that the old British Lion is so moved by anything as to roar and dance in his inexpressible delight. But now and then he does it; and never did he dance and roar as he did on that eighteenth of November, 1558. All over England, men went wild with joy . . . and were like children in their frantic glee that day. . . . It was seen that day that however she had been oppressed, compelled to silence, or tortured into apparent submission, England was Protestant.[54]

But Miss Holt was not content to leave Foxe's hypothesis there: she saw in succeeding years a continuing threat to England from Rome and was determined to use the facts of history to expose it.

She laid a great deal of the burden of protecting the English Church on the monarchy – the head of the secular and the spiritual government of the nation. Those who failed to live up to the demands made on them thus betrayed more, in her view, than the material interests of their subjects. In this way, despite her reverence for the monarchical office, she was able to justify the rebellions of the seventeenth century and the eventual growth of parliamentary power. Her argument was that the linked incidents of Mary Tudor's reign and the threat of Spanish invasion in the sixteenth century had taught England lasting lessons:

> There are two things that England has come to value above even her throne and her peace. These are her Protestantism and her liberties. For these, and these alone, she will fight to the death.

Thus James II, though the rightful king, deserved deposition:

> It was not that King James, being a papist, was made King out of his turn, but that being heir to the throne he became a Papist. I

[54] Emily S. Holt, *The King's Daughters, or How Two Girls Kept the Faith* (Shaw, London, 1888), p. 243.

see an immense difference between the two. God, not we, made him our King.[55]

It was necessary to dispense with the Stuart line, but it was a lasting shame to that dynasty that it should be so necessary.

The succeeding Hanoverian line was redeemed only by its allegiance to Protestantism: George I was a lax king who surrendered his divinely-given prerogative. He was 'the first who resigned to a mere official the grandest act of the royal prerogative': that of initiating legislation. The resulting growth of parliamentary power had a great danger: that of growing liberalism which handed to the mob the power to order the government of the nation.[56] If England was not careful, Rome might yet triumph. Miss Holt pointed to the French Revolution as being an example of liberalism taken to its extremes. It was also a warning of the future scope of divine power: the mills of God might grind slow but they ground exceedingly small. Thus the French Revolution of 1789 was a divine response to the St Bartholomew's Eve massacre of Huguenots in 1572.[57]

By the nineteenth century, Rome had again put herself in the position where she could infect the national virtue and the potential consequences were dire indeed. So 'England stands now in as much peril of having Popery insidiously infused into her, as she did in 1588 of having it rudely forced upon her'. But whereas in 1588, patriots rallied to the Protestant standard, where in 1888 was the necessary 'noble, unanimous, self-forgetting patriotism' to combat the danger?[58] It is very easy to dismiss such an interpretation as amusing or crackpot and totally without credibility at any time, but then few things appear more ridiculous than an out-dated or unfashionable scholarly theory. It should not be overlooked in evaluating her work, that Emily Holt intended her ideas to be taken very seriously, a factor that her reviewers were well aware of. In general, her reception was favourable and at times laudatory, particularly on the grounds of her scholarship and the factual

---

[55] Emily S. Holt, *Ashcliffe Hall: A Tale of the Last Century* (Shaw, London, 1870), p. 69; p. 366.

[56] Ibid., p. 366; p. 382, fn. 1.

[57] Emily S. Holt, *Sister Rose*, p. 97.

[58] Emily S. Holt, *Clare Avery*. Preface: 'Who shall save England now?'

basis of her work.[59] Moreover, Emily Holt was not alone in her interpretation: she had merely worked it out in more comprehensive detail than authors like Evelyn Everett Green or Charlotte Yonge, who made equally harsh and rigid comments on the role of Rome in the evolution of the English national character. It was widely agreed that of all nations, 'England could not rest beneath the yoke of Rome'.[60] Nor was such an interpretation out of keeping with the place accorded to religion in nationalist ideas and philosophies of the time.

Religion also played a role in the modernizing of another strand in the creation of a well-established English nationalism: the up-dating of chivalry. To a considerable extent, the popularity of stories set in the Middle Ages and the Civil War period depended on the gloss given to adventure in those periods by the idea of chivalry. Nostalgia and attempts at a nineteenth-century chivalric revival were popular in art and in adult literature. Its impact in turn on the middle-class youth of the nineteenth century can partly be gauged by the importance of the chivalric scene on the popular Victorian entertainment of *tableaux vivants*. Such spectacles avoided many of the disagreeable elements associated in the conventional middle-class mind with amateur dramatics, such as lack of true talent and professionalism, while furthering knowledge of art and history at the same time as allowing young people the pleasure of dressing up and taking on the impersonation of a favourite character. Magazines often gave hints on historical scenes or works of art which were suited to staging in this way.[61]

As didactic tales for girls additionally emphasize, chivalry provided a constant inspiration: fictional *tableaux vivants*, invariably feature several scenes depicting famous chivalric incidents such as Queen Philippa begging the lives of the Calais burghers from Edward III or Lancelot and the Fair Elaine from Arthurian legend via Tennyson.[62] Even the lavish example of the

[59] She was widely praised for her use of available printed primary source material, and for her references to contemporary works of comment on events. From *The Spectator* to *The Christian* her books received universally favourable reviews for the soundness of her teaching and her facts.

[60] Evelyn Everett Green, *The Church and the King*, p. 480.

[61] 'Tableaux Vivants', *The Strand Magazine* II, July–Dec., 1891, pp. 2–8.

[62] See, for example, Evelyn Everett Green, *Olive Roscoe, or The New Sister* (Nelson, Walton-on-Thames, 1896), pp. 289–90.

Tournament at Eglinton in 1838 was seen to be followed. The wealthy Earl of Easterby decided to celebrate his heir's coming of age in the 'pseudo-medieval fashion that is dear to the hearts of young people'. The young men of the neighbourhood practised their jousting, while their sisters made sham suits of armour and fancy dress for themselves – with detachable ribbons to give to the 'knights' of their choice. Titles of books such as L.T. Meade's *A Knight of Today* also indicate the prevalence of chivalric ideas in contemporary Victorian language.[63]

This harking back to the days of chivalry stems partly from Scott, particularly his poetry such as *Marmion* or *The Lay of the Last Minstrel*, and continued by men like Tennyson. By the mid-century, enthusiasm in poetry and prose, to say nothing of art and architecture, for subjects such as Arthur and his Knights of the Round Table was well-established, as Mark Girouard has demonstrated.[64] It was, however, an enthusiasm that had become increasingly middle class and based on the modification of the ideals of chivalry to suit nineteenth-century notions of ideal behaviour, especially for men. Chivalry gave middle-class men as well as men from the upper classes a moral code which they found acceptable. Kenelm Digby, a member of the Anglo-Irish gentry, was one of the first to demonstrate that a modern relevance for the chivalric code could be constructed within the limits of nineteenth-century social understanding. *The Broad Stone of Honour*, his *magnum opus* of 1823, was subtitled in the first editions 'Rules for the Gentlemen of England'.[65]

The initial thrust of such efforts was undoubtedly directed at a receptive aristocracy and gentry: but before long, this idea of contemporary relevance was taken up with enthusiasm by diverse groups of men, particularly those members of the Protestant middle-classes eager for social advancement and the accolade of 'gentleman'. Not surprisingly, it soon became

[63] Evelyn Everett Green, *Greyfriars: A Story for Girls* (Leisure Hour Monthly Library, London, 1905), 1st edn (1890), pp. 193–202; L.T. Meade, *A Knight of Today* (Shaw, London, 1877).

[64] Mark Girouard, *The Return to Camelot: Chivalry and the English Gentleman* (Yale University Press, New Haven, 1981), pp. 178–81.

[65] Ibid., pp. 56–7.

apparent that one obvious contemporary application of the
chivalric code was in stories for boys with aspirations to become
gentlemen. Girouard places a considerable emphasis on the
role of an Anglocentric, Christian-inspired chivalry in schoolboy tales such as *Tom Brown's Schooldays*, first published in 1857
and a constant favourite for teaching boys the 'right' code of
conduct throughout this period.[66] It may seem logical that
women's role in even this modern chivalry should be passive
rather than active: it is the men who are the knights, the
protectors of women and the guardians of the Grail. However,
such a simplistic interpretation of chivalry grossly underesti-
mates the pivotal role played by women, certainly in the
nineteenth century.

Tennyson pointed to the role of good women as inspirers of
the chivalrous impulse in men, and the guardians of male
purity in the carrying out of their tasks as noble knights. In the
Idylls of the King, Arthur fails to establish his perfect earthly
kingdom in England not because of his own failings, but
because of Guinivere's and the ruin she brought to him, to his
dreams, and even to other men like Lancelot:

> . . . till the loathsome opposite
> That all my heart had destined did obtain,
> And all through thee. . . .[67]

By contrast, of course, good women like Enid or Lynette make
and keep their lovers good men, true to their ideals and their
country's interest. Women were the professional arbiters of
society's spiritual health and indirectly therefore, its actual
success. Tennyson's Guinivere was well aware of the greatness
of her fault, of the way it extended beyond her personal
relationships with betrayed husband and guilty lover to the
state of the kingdom. Twentieth-century experience also
emphasizes the necessity for the willing participation of women
in that process. Without feminine acquiescence in and proper
reaction to chivalry's codes it has proved difficult, if not
impossible, for most men to retain dignity and self-confidence
in behaviour and beliefs motivated by such rules. It was, by the

[66] Ibid., pp. 166–9.
[67] Tennyson, *Guinivere*, II, 1. 486–8.

1850s, agreed by conventional middle-class society that chivalrous, or gentlemanly, behaviour on the part of individuals was one of the foundations on which collective English greatness rested. Thus it was equally seen as essential that women be as well, if not better informed, than men about the rules of modern chivalry and how they applied to nineteenth-century English society if that chivalry was to continue and flourish.

Adolescent girls thus became as much a target for information in this respect as boys. Didactic fiction abounded in coded information about the ways in which it was possible to recognize a true chivalrous knight in Victorian trappings, while avoiding the counterfeit or less perfect model – for instance, many a model maiden referred to her lover as her Galahad.[68] Given the established role of women as educators of future generations of model males, as mothers or teachers in some form, they too needed to be shown the pedigree and the efficacy of such behaviour in historical terms, as well as the role that women traditionally played in instituting and maintaining it.

In order to modify the medieval forms of chivalry to suit nineteenth-century England, it was seen as necessary to use Anglican Christianity. From its beginnings, chivalry had claimed to depend on, among others, the primary virtues of piety, temperance, chastity, fidelity, truthfulness – all of which could be approved by the modern middle-class establishment as having a modern application and a part to play in maintaining their ideal society in England. It could not be denied, however, that despite the respect given to these attributes, previous ages even in England had been far from perfect, and the further back in time towards the Dark Ages, the greater the discernible faults. Nor was it possible to put all the blame on monarchs or aristocracy and their government, though it was undeniable that the 'irresponsible power they too often held' in the past had been a 'crying evil' only remedied by 'the growing independence of the middle-classes'.[69]

One obvious problem was the 'wonderful hereditary fighting instinct' that was seen on the one hand as an indispensible part of the English character. Hymned in poetry and prose, that

---

[68] See, for instance, Evelyn Everett Green, *Days of Chivalry*, p. 559; Mrs George de Horne Vaizey, *More About Peggy* (RTS, London, 1901), p. 292.
[69] Evelyn Everett Green, *Days of Chivalry*, p. 31.

instinct had played a very substantial role in preserving England's independence against foreign aggressors, and ultimately helped to advance her power in the European and world arena. Yet associated with that bravery in times when civilization was at a more primitive level was bloodlust and cruelty, manifesting itself as a love of war and combat for its own sake that was frequently linked with the practice of chivalry. In earlier times, too many paid only lip-service to the essential chivalric virtues, putting aggression at the head of their list of indispensible qualities for a practitioner. Men and women of this disposition, distorted the code into 'a code of barbarity'. Some individuals, real and fictional, were 'bright exceptions': though willing to fight when necessary they eschewed cruelty for its own sake as being inherently opposed to the code of chivalry.[70] It is along these rather obvious lines that the division into hero and heroine, villain and villainess was made by authors dealing with this theme in its historical setting. Of those historical personages who were seen as doing their best to preserve and enhance the true spirit of chivalry, and in the process drawing to them a long list of fictional good men and women, Edward III and the Black Prince were always quoted, despite occasional lapses caused by the stress of the more primitive times or the lack of a Protestant religion.

Both these men were shown as realizing that the national as well as the individual interest lay in the preservation of chivalry. Edward, for instance, was given a foresight not always recognized in him by twentieth-century historians. He understood that as civilization advanced, 'warlike chivalry declined' but he wanted to give 'impetus to retaining the spirit' of real chivalry by emphasizing elements such as true piety and the protection of the weak and helpless. As the Black Prince was made to comment, 'Let chivalry once die out and so goes England's glory'.[71] These two paragons were depicted as facing a dilemma which they shared with heroes like Henry V and Henry VIII and with the numerous fictional characters in the genre. This was shown to be a question of how to encourage the development of a more 'civilized' version of chivalry without sacrificing necessary levels of fighting ardour: something that was ex-

[70] Ibid., p. 107; pp. 302–3.
[71] Ibid., pp. 79–80; p. 82.

pected in a modern period to be of interest to any right-minded girl who might have to guide and encourage a man destined to serve on the frontiers of empire.

Such interested individuals could be reassured by the events of English history. This provided the 'proof' that it was 'not chivalry but a true and living Christianity' that 'could alone withhold the natural man from deeds of cruelty and rapacity'. This linking of Christianity with chivalry was put forward as being the means by which chivalry retained a relevance for the modern age. Indeed, in *In The Days of Chivalry*, Evelyn Everett Green wrote that in real terms, 'the highest chivalry was that of our Lord himself, when He laid down His life for sinners'. It also brought chivalry very much within the feminine province.[72]

The plot of *In The Days of Chivalry* concerns the journey of its hero, Raymond de Brocas, to a state as near perfection as the cause of realism would allow in a human; so the heroine, Joan, can say of him: 'Methinks I have found my Galahad at last'. He achieves this state by examining the real meaning of chivalry, which inevitably means an interpretation of chivalry fully consistent with the requirements of the nineteenth century, the English middle class and the Empire. Discussing the matter with an equally introspective brother-in-arms they conclude that:

> there was more in the truest and deepest chivalry than the mere feats of arms and acts of dauntless daring that so often went by that name ... in self-denial, self-sacrifice, the subservience of selfish ambition to the service of the oppressed and the needy, chivalry in its highest form was to be found.

This chivalry would 'rise upon the ashes of what had gone before, and lead men to higher and better things' in a period 'when battle and bloodshed should be no longer men's favourite pastime'. No longer would chivalry be the province of the aristocracy: like Christianity it would have a meaning for men at all levels of society, especially the middle ranks who were already appearing as the best guardians of the nation's health and interests. This was an idea 'vastly in advance of the

[72] Ibid., p. 199; p. 290.

spirit of the day', but by no means impossible for Englishmen of a future, happier or Victorian age.[73]

English history was interpreted in such a way that readers were shown how the aid of women and the development of the Church of England combined to advance the development of this ideal and its more universal application in society. Joan acts as the significant confidante and sounding-board, combining her 'great sympathy' with the ideas of Raymond gave 'new impulse and zest to his plans', and her 'ready woman's wit' acting to broaden and deepen them. The story ends with Joan and Raymond settling down at his manor at Basildene, where the former soon creates the necessary home atmosphere in which their family can be trained up to revere their parents' beliefs. It is, of course, a traditional interpretation, to say nothing of justification, of the role of women and their capacity for professional spiritual expertise in the development of human thought, found time and again in didactic fiction throughout this period.[74]

The Church played a significant role. It was considered axiomatic that the Protestant forms of Christianity were better suited to the development of the higher chivalry. This advanced chivalry had to be more discriminating than the more aggressive, primitive version. It would thus only be achieved by individuals and the nation as a whole when it became a thinking chivalry: where adherence to the code became a matter of choice, demanded by a good active conscience. Roman Catholicism, it was argued, was inherently opposed to the free exercise of the individual conscience: men and women were expected to dull their minds and accept dictats without question, which had dangerous implications for the advance of mankind.

The independent-natured English, as a nation, were shown to be instinctively opposed to this and to the persecution that tended to result from attempts to thwart individual thought. There was 'something repellent to the instincts of the nation in the thought of persecution for conscience' sake'; which explained why religious persecution in England before the Reformation came in fits and starts, and why, after it, persecution

[73] Ibid., p. 599; p. 130; pp. 119–20.
[74] Ibid., p. 158.

was the weapon of those who were traitors to their country, such as Mary Tudor:

> It seemeth to me a fearsome thing for any man to bind himself over to blind obedience to any power ... and reserve not to himself the use of his own reason, his own conscience, his own interpretation of God's all wise and all-merciful laws.[75]

A good Englishman's interpretation was bound to lead to moral chivalry.

All the authors in this genre portrayed the guardians of national liberty and true chivalry in history, real or fictional, also including less obvious candidates like Henry II and Henry VII, as engaging in a constant struggle with the papacy because of their understanding of England's interests as well as the path of true religion. That well-known bastion of chivalry, Henry VIII, for instance, had a conviction of the need for 'religious reform and for the limitation of papal aggrandisement' long before he saw Anne Boleyn, and the 'episode of the divorce formed only a feature and not an integral part' of a great national revolt against the continuing operation of papal tyranny. Henry VIII might as an individual have failed to live up to the chivalric code, but he knew its importance, and as he also had 'the good of the nation at heart', he promoted a national church.[76]

In this respect, authors were putting forward the accepted scholarly belief that one of the most important long-term results of the Reformation was an increase in the positive influence of women in everyday life. Before the Reformation, it was argued, this had been restricted because too many good women had been absorbed into conventional life and removed from effective participation in the life of the community, leaving secular leadership to their faultier sisters. As Emily Holt explained to her readers, a single woman outside the cloister

[75] Evelyn Everett Green, *The Church and the King*, p. 36.

[76] I am indebted to Dr Maria Dowling for first pointing out to me that this argument has also been used by modern scholars as being one of the factors giving a new status to family life in the post-Reformation period. Ibid., p. 350; p. 27. Emily S. Holt, for instance, argued that monarchs like John and Richard II were only classed as bad kings by most historians because they relied on the biased view of them given by monks, who took the side of the Papacy in the struggle between the kings of England and Rome. She even argues that Henry II was right in his dispute with Becket because he was only standing out for 'the liberties of England': *Earl Hubert's Daughter*, pp. 18–19.

was unknown before the Reformation. One of Evelyn Everett Green's heroines, the good but initially rather misguided Ermengarde, wishes to become a nun because she wants to do good to people. She learns that it is in reality a 'selfish and hollow life', and luckily, is freed by the dissolution of the monasteries to find real usefulness in life as a wife and mother.[77] It was not necessary to wed to do this: Emily Holt sniffed that it was 'a man's notion that a woman must marry', but it was wrong for women to remove themselves from the world.[78] It was all very well to be 'a saint on earth' but:

> 'Methinks the time has come when we need these saints in our own homes to help us [men] in our battle with sin and temptation. Surely a woman . . . does more for us by living amongst us, and helping us with the trials and burdens of life than she can accomplish' [as a nun].

There was great truth in the words 'Laborare est orare' if mistranslated as work is the best form of prayer. While Rome 'set itself against the ties and cares of family life' on the grounds that they were 'a snare', divine wisdom emphasized the central role of family life in the struggle for the Holy Grail. Evelyn Everett Green commented that Galahad would not be nearly as effective as a pattern for modern life if he had been a monk.[79]

It has to be admitted that the motivation was not always so high-minded. Authors in the genre of girls' didactic fiction responded pragmatically to the situation of their audience. As girls grew more independent, by the 1880s for instance, significant numbers found the more limited tales of earlier writers less interesting and less relevant. Thus they demanded more exciting books to read, and it became necessary to tailor the output of fiction for this market to take account of this, while not encouraging readers to become unwomanly. Historical tales hedged about with the usual limitations in active feminine involvement unless under very unusual circumstances, proved to be an ideal vehicle in this respect. It provided a useful way of fulfilling feminine desires for adventure vicariously without, it was hoped, creating a desire for emulating

---

[77] Evelyn Everett Green, *The Church and the King*, pp. 171–2.
[78] Emily S. Holt, *Clare Avery*, p. 62.
[79] Evelyn Everett Green, *The Church and the King*, pp. 180–1; p. 248; Evelyn Everett Green, *Days of Chivalry*, p. 125.

more than the spirit of the various adventurous enterprises of times past. After all, the opportunities for adventure, within England at least, were decidedly fewer: marauding barons no longer inhabited the countryside; there were no serious threats of invasion and Victoria was secure on her throne. Only people like Emily Holt considered that the continuation of the Anglican supremacy was in jeopardy, and even she expected that threat to be combated more peacefully in the nineteenth century and not via actual martyrdom at the stake. 'Alarums' and excursions and tales of feminine heroism in cases of national or individual peril could, effectively and convincingly, be wrapped safely in an historical setting with the essentially modern qualities that developed such bravery carefully portrayed for the girlish reader.

Historical tales for girls, moreover, were careful to show the unusual context in which such adventures took place. L.E. Guernsey's Winifred, aged 17, provides a good example of a Victorian model maiden in a period setting. She saves the life of Lord Arthur Carew after Monmouth's rebellion, taking him food and tending his wounds under cover of darkness, and risking her life even further in helping to smuggle him away. Once he has been got safely out of the country, Winifred's life returns to its previous humdrum state and after the excitement it 'seemed hard to return to the little common duties of everyday life'. Being a good girl, she applied herself to her allotted tasks, including the nursing of a household through a dangerous fever. By 1688, and Carew's return in the train of William of Orange, she had learned a central lesson for her sex; one that:

> all women must learn, sooner or later, that it often requires as much courage, though of a somewhat different kind, to live one's common every-day life as it does to risk that life in some great danger or adventure.

As a man and a soldier, Carew inevitably led a more exciting life, but that did not degrade the courage that it had taken Winifred to accept a quieter and more traditionally womanly lot. In addition, without the inspiration of her behaviour, Carew's own bravery might have been tarnished. He tells Winifred that he has been amidst scenes of 'temptation and trial, among wild and dissolute men, and women still worse; but your face has always come between me and harm'.[80] Winifred's happiness and ultimate reward, therefore, came from accepting that her life could not be one long adventure, unlike that of a man: a message intended to strike a chord in the mind of a girl pining for more than a placid home-life was likely to give her.

History provided a useful tool for the author in this genre. It was intended to be educational; but not primarily to convey factual information about the past. Its major aim was to provide additional information about the present and the future, which is why so many of the areas which gave concern to established opinion in the nineteenth century made their appearance in historical fiction, from class to social unrest.[81] It was agreed that by placing such issues in an historical context, authors were able to bestow a greater authority on many essential nineteenth-century middle-class priorities for society as a whole, and women in particular, by portraying as traditions evolved and tested over time, matters such as the role of the family. Moreover, the air of authenticity evoked by the weaving of stories into historical fact, plus the excitement and glamour associated with incidents from England's past made it easier for authors to give fuller rein to their didactic tendencies than in contemporary stories. A historical setting enabled authors to take a long- as well as a short-term view of the consequences of actions, on both an individual and a general level. Yet the historical good girl, whatever her setting, remained intrinsically English, and middle-class and Victorian, in all aspects and in all circumstances.

It would, however, be a mistake to think that these stories provided the only arena in which girls could read of a wider sphere of action than was possible for them in the modern domestic sphere. In contemporary terms, the British Empire provided the action absent from the security of daily life in

[80] L.E. Guernsey, *Winifred, or An English Maiden in the Seventeenth Century* (Shaw, London, 1878), pp. 157–8; p. 327.

[81] Discussions of class, and the importance of keeping to one's divinely appointed station, or social unrest, and the individual duty of remedying discontent by means of philanthropy and exhortation differ little from the modern settings in this historical fiction. Thus the chapter has concentrated on elements more unique to this aspect of the genre.

England; and it is not coincidence that, as Josephine Bratton has also noted, justification for the existence of that Empire is implicit in tales of England's history.[82]

[82] J.S. Bratton, 'England, Home, and Duty', in John M. Mackenzie (ed.), *Imperialism and Popular Culture* (Manchester University Press, Manchester, 1986).

5

Imperial Responsibilities and England's Daughters

Winds of the world give answer: they are whispering to and fro, and what should they know of England who only England know?[1]

If history, as demonstrated in the historical novels for the adolescent girl, played a significant part in creating a pedigree and an authoritative weight for the ideas that established society in England had about the national character, so also did imperialism. It was, to some extent, a case of making a virtue out of a necessity. By the middle of the nineteenth century the British Empire was already part of the consciousness of middle-class society in England, featuring in its cultural artefacts from art to literature and considered by that class to involve all levels of society. In 1810, for instance, Ann Taylor wrote *A Child's Hymn of Praise*, which was to become a classic for the rest of the century, learned by most children at their mother's knee. Its first verse in particular was beloved and so quoted that it became almost hackneyed.[2]

> I thank the goodness and the grace
> Which on my birth have smiled

[1] Rudyard Kipling, 'The English Flag', *Verse*, Definitive edition (Hodder and Stoughton, London, 1940).

[2] See, for instance, C.C. Eldridge, *England's Mission: The Imperial Idea in the Age of Gladstone and Disraeli* (Macmillan, London, 1973); R. Hyam and G.W. Martin, *Reappraisals in British Imperial History* (Macmillan, London, 1975); R. Hyam, *Britain's Imperial Century 1815–1914: A Study of Empire and Expansion* (Methuen, London, 1976).

And made me, in these Christian days
A happy English child.[3]

This opening statement was expanded in subsequent verses, explaining that the English child was happy because he or she was not born 'as thousands are' in Asian lands 'where God is never known', and forced to cope with the disadvantages of life under those conditions. These lines, as well as establishing that an English passport was the best qualification for Heaven, reveal the extent to which patriotic Christian sentiment was already conscious of a wider English interest overseas. It is easy to see how children brought up on these sentiments could become early imbued with a certain Anglomania: it also helps to explain why these sentiments were so readily expanded to form an equally religious, imperialist nationalism by the middle of the century.

From the start this imperialist style of nationalism was grounded in class faith in the nation's destiny, and the responsibility for fulfilling it, as well as more mundane considerations of profit and prestige. If it was a faith that in the 1850s and 1860s was often taken for granted, by the 1880s nationalism in its imperial aspect had become sufficiently self-conscious with regard to motivation and justification for poets like Newbolt and Kipling to be able to define its qualities and merits. The Empire, and consciousness of its existence, was presumed to evoke the noblest qualities of human nature from all sorts of people in all sorts of jobs, regardless of gender, thereby reinforcing and broadening the individual's love and understanding of England and all that it stood for in the eyes of middle-class society. Kipling understood this. The core of his imperialism was his love of England itself, his sense of personal responsibility towards it, and his faith in its people and 'national character'. Hence he insisted on the historical 'pedigree' of Englishness, going back to Roman times and before in books like *Puck of Pook's Hill*: and believed, for example, that Anglican Christianity was the true rock on which the Empire as well as

[3] Ann Taylor, 'A Child's Hymn of Praise', in Ann and Jane Taylor, *The Poetical Works* (Ward Lock and Tyler, London, 1877).

England herself rested, as expressed in *Recessional*.[4]

Kipling, like so many of his peers in the nineteenth century, conceived of patriotism in terms of a wider imperial nationalism. The monarchy played a considerable part in all this. The British Empire existed as a symbol in the great heights to which the nation had raised itself, as a result of her virtues. The Queen, the symbol of her lifestyle and beliefs of so many of those virtues was thus a personification of the Empire and all it meant. As one of Evelyn Everett Green's young heroes comments: 'We've got the best sovereign reigning over us that the world has ever seen, it's for us to try and make ourselves the very finest set of subjects that a sovereign can have.'[5] How better to do that than to go out and spread English ideals around the globe? The opening quotation thus operates in a wider sense than the obvious advocacy of physical encounter with overseas English possessions. It points also to the middle-class belief that information about the Empire helped to inform the recipient about England and its people in a way that reinforced the basis of patriotism and sustained them in their imperial role. It was largely in response to this that faith in the God-given imperial destiny of England, earned and sustained by individual effort and sense of duty was developed.

That role was not a light one to bear. Until 1914 at least the Empire's impact on the middle-class sector of English society grew and broadened. It can, however, be difficult to assess that impact quantitatively. The British Empire was, by the 1840s, an extremely complex affair, a mixture on the one hand of long-held territories such as Jamaica and the Bahamas and more recently acquired ones like Australia, and the acquisition of territories was a continuing process throughout the period. It was also an Empire held for a mixture of pragmatic reasons, including financial ones and those concerning imperial security. Some parts of the Empire were colonies of permanent

[4] The constant refrain in Rudyard Kipling, 'Recessional', *Verse*, is a plea to God to help the English remember that it is to God that they owe their Empire and that it is evanescent unless they remain in His grace! For instance 'The Captains and the Kings depart,/ The shouting and the tumult dies' but 'Still stands thine ancient sacrifice/ An humble and a contrite heart./ Lord of Hosts, be with us yet/ Lest we forget, lest we forget.'

[5] Evelyn Everett Green, *For the Queen's Sake* (Nelson, Walton-on-Thames, 1898), p. 23.

settlement; others were areas with native populations with a hierarchy of professional British administrators. There were also those who went to try to exploit the financial promise of a region, while others hoped to proselytize a race to Christianity. Others found themselves defending the imperial interests by military means on land or sea.

In coping with the demands of maintaining these overseas possessions both men and women were affected, and not necessarily to their personal advantage. In this respect it was the members of the middle classes who took most of the burden of Empire on themselves.[6] They provided a substantial portion of the emigrants to areas like Australia and Canada. Most of the administrators in the service of the British government came from their ranks, especially after the introduction of competition into the colonial civil service,[7] as did the majority of missionaries. In addition, army and naval officers serving overseas were largely drawn from those belonging to the middle classes. Not surprisingly, just as the middle classes had come to dominate the social mores of the period, they also played the most conscious role in developing a distinctive imperial ethos to the national character.

An important element in this was the link that was perceived between Empire and the armed services. It was axiomatic that the British Empire was constantly threatened from a variety of sources, and that its continuance therefore depended on eternal military vigilance. As a result, over 50 per cent of British army officers could expect to spend a significant portion of their service overseas as a normal part of their duties; a figure that could rise in times of conflict such as the Boer War.[8] Only

[6] It is not intended to claim that members of the working classes were either uninvolved in Empire or that, where involved, their experiences were likely to be harsher than the common middle-class experience: but that proportionally more of the middle-classes were involved in Empire. See A.P. Thornton, *The Imperial Idea and Its Enemies* (Macmillan, London, 1959).

[7] Entry to the colonial civil service, including the Indian civil service, was via competitive examination after 1865. This had the effect of increasing the numbers of successful aspirants from the middle classes quite considerably, as well as ensuring a generally high calibre among those in the colonial administration.

[8] I am indebted to Douglas Peers for information and advice in this respect. See also the Army Lists for the relevant period.

the Guards regiments stayed regularly in England in peace time, and members of those noble bands of men tended anyway to be socially exclusive as well as expensive. For other regiments in the British army service overseas, even after the Cardwell army reforms, was an inescapable part of their duties, though it was possible for the wealthiest officers to avoid overseas duty.[9] However, no ambitious officer was likely to take that opportunity as it was service overseas that offered the chances of glory and honour via involvement in the numerous small colonial campaigns that disturbed the peace of Victoria's Empire.

It was also possible, by joining the Indian army, to spend one's entire active service overseas – a route often taken by those without the financial resources to maintain a good showing in a regiment in England. As one character in an Evelyn Everett Green novel said dismissively 'Indian army. . . . Show's they're poor, you know – good pay but no prestige' compared with a British regiment.[10] Naturally naval officers could also expect periods of active service on stations outside Europe as part of their normal duties, with the navy charged with the responsibility of 'showing the flag' as a reminder of England's interest and might from the 1870s in areas as disparate as West Africa and New Zealand.

If military service provided the most obviously glamorous way for men to serve Queen and country overseas it was certainly not the only way fraught with peril and difficulty. Most forms of service and most regions provided that to some extent. Even the medical advances of the later nineteenth century did not remove the threat of death or disablement

[9] The 1867 Cardwell army reforms had a far-reaching effect on the organization of the army. Instead of small contingents of troops being scattered around the Empire, Cardwell concentrated the overseas sectors of the army in a number of stategically chosen depots such as Halifax, Nova Scotia and Mauritius so that useful numbers of troops could be swiftly sent to trouble spots. See R. Hyam, *Britain's Imperial Century*.

[10] When Sir Garnet Wolseley was organizing an expedition against the Ashante in autumn 1873, he was overwhelmed by the numbers of applications from officers wanting to join him, especially those stationed at home and longing for action. See J.D. Rowbotham, 'Edward Knatchbull Hugessen, 1st Lord Brabourne, and the British Empire 1871–1893', unpublished Ph.D. thesis, University of Wales, 1982, pp. 73–4. Evelyn Everett Green, *Miss Greyshott's Girls* (Melrose, Ely, 1905), p. 59.

from tropical disease. For instance, the missionary hero of H. Louisa Bedford's *The Twins that Did Not Pair*, Harold Braba-zon, does noble work until laid low by 'the deadly fever which so often proved fatal to Europeans'; and even in death he does not shirk his duty, waiting so long at his African mission that he is too ill to live to see England again. His heartbroken father is told not to 'grudge the sacrifice'. He has died in battle as surely as if he had been shot.[11] West and East Africa were seen as notoriously risky in this respect, but India and the West Indies were by no means free from danger. Those men who emi-grated to Canada, Australia or New Zealand were less at risk from unknown disease but for many carving out a new life was risky in other ways, including isolation and financial ruin.

Inevitably, therefore, the Empire drew heavily upon the resources of those in England involved in its maintenance. It was largely in response to this that the faith in the God-given imperial destiny of England, earned and sustained by indi-vidual effort and sense of duty, was developed. The qualities Empire required were fundamentally those that were already established as the ideals of character and behaviour. For instance, the qualities of essentially middle-class masculinity were already laid down by writers of prose and poetry in an English setting, for adults and young boys. Picking up where Tennyson left off, Newbolt extolled the virtues of 'playing the game' and doing one's duty in approved public school manner in far-flung lands; while novelists like Rider Haggard ex-panded on Trollopian virtues to display the happy results of applying the effects of English self-sacrifice and manly virtue to an African context in tales like *King Solomon's Mines* that enthralled many a boyish imagination.[12] In the midst of all the emphasis on the male role in serving the Empire, it is currently all too easy to overlook an equally significant role played by women and the feminine concepts of duty and self-sacrifice in maintaining the welfare and security of the English community as a whole.

[11] H. Louisa Bedford, *The Twins that Did Not Pair* (RTS, London, 1898), pp. 204–7.

[12] Sir Henry Newbolt, 'Vitae Lampada', *Collected Poems, 1897–1907* (Nel-son, Walton-on-Thames, 1908), Sir Henry Rider Haggard, *King Solomon's Mines* (Cassell, London, 1885).

This was one reason why the Empire became a popular theme in the didactic fiction for English youth of both sexes. The growing popularity of the imperial theme also indicates the increasing imperative felt by adult society to ensure that their faith in the Empire and its destiny was passed on to a future generation of guardians. By the 1880s, too many members of the middle classes had an important stake in the British Empire to let it pass away lightly. In many ways the Empire was seen as an institution whose real profit would be in the future, and for the benefit of future generations, at home and abroad. Thus men who had invested their present energies and dreams in it, far more than money, and women who had done the same, or who sought a justification for the loss of loved ones in its service all provided a powerful pressure group for its continuance as a matter of faith rather than economic or political necessity.

It is this sense of essentially religious conviction about the continuing role of the English and their civilizing mission in these far-flung places, far more than the business aspect of Empire, that was presented to youthful readers as the real raison d'être of overseas possessions. This is epitomized in Evelyn Everett Green's story for early adolescents, *For the Queen's Sake*. Young Caspar Adair was left an orphan because his mother died of the Indian climate and his father 'toiled on through the sweltering Indian heat, putting things in order before he departed' on his overdue leave and was struck down by cholera as a consequence. Far from being put off the Empire and its service, Caspar is shown as revering his father's memory and doing his best to equip himself to follow the parental path in due course. Hilda Charteris, similary orphaned in *One Summer By the Sea*, reminds her brothers of all that their father 'a distinguished officer in the Indian service' has done, to prepare them all for a continuation of this self-sacrificing family tradition.[13]

The imperial fiction for adolescent boys has remained the most accessible to modern readers, with novels by G.A. Henty, its most popular exponent, being reprinted (suitably purged for modern taste) to this day. The imperial fiction written for

---

[13] Evelyn Everett Green, *For the Queen's Sake*, pp. 11–12; pp. 23–5.

boys by men like Henty, George Manville Fenn and Gordon Stables consists of rip-roaring adventures which demonstrate very explicitly the attributes necessary to produce a new generation of men able to build and guard an empire: courage, patriotism, honesty etc. The list is wide-ranging and comprehensive. It is certainly possible to glean a great deal of information about the public school ethos involved in Empire from such a source and much is to be learned about the developing notion of the English imperial gentleman and details of how to administer an Empire justly.[14]

Yet the fiction written for the adolescent girl is equally, if not more, informative about middle-class attitudes towards and reasoning about the Empire between 1840 and 1905, and the changing ways in which it contributed towards that society; particularly from the women's aspect. As a general rule, for example, it can be said that the role played by Empire in this genre of fiction was not as unquestioningly self-glorifying as that designed for the adolescent male market. Moreover, in boys' books little consideration is given to the role of women: Henty's heroines, for instance, are two-dimensional in the extreme. The only contribution they make to the action is to give unquestioning support and admiration to the efforts of their heroes, and to point them, if necessary, to the Christian way.

The usual impression of girls' fiction is that it is generally less overtly imperialist in tone, as girls were largely excluded from active participation in the great colonial adventure until well into the twentieth century, if then. However, it is not possible to discern a spirit of anti-imperialism or even any outright lack of concern or interest in the Empire in any book aimed at this market, even in the earliest period. Writers such as Charlotte Yonge may not have made such extensive play of England's imperial status as later writers, but it was present as an intrinsic and significant part of their consciousness in their depictions of

[14] For further information on G.A. Henty see Guy Arnold, *Held Fast for England: G.A. Henty, Imperialist Boys' Writer* (Hamish Hamilton, London, 1980). For further discussion on Imperialism in boys' fiction see, J.S. Bratton, 'For England, Home and Duty: The Image of England in Victorian and Edwardian Juvenile Fiction', in John M. Mackenzie (ed.), *Imperialism and Popular Culture* (Manchester University Press, Manchester, 1986).

society, if only because of the necessity to reconcile readers to the problems it might well present to them. When linked up with the historical novels described in the previous chapter, the pro-imperial tone in the genre becomes even more noticeable. Coded discussions of present-day implications for English responsibilities in the imperial field are presented through historical justifications of the English takeover of Wales.[15] Possibly commentators have tended to overlook the pervasive imperial consciousness in writers for the adolescent girls' market because in the contemporary sense, such emphasis was given to the apparently 'negative' aspects of Empire such as pain and parting.

In writing on an imperial theme for adolescent girls, the most general requirement of society was that the apprentice *Fireside Angel* should be encouraged to accept the drawbacks of Empire before the advantages. This emphasis is not surprising. For the majority of the middle-class readership of these novels, even at the start of the twentieth century, the negative aspects of Empire must have been far more real to them, personally, than any other. Boys, after all, were provided with a compensation for their risks via the action and excitement it promised to provide – even if this did pall in reality.[16] Middle-class English girls could only expect to wait, with Kingsley's words ringing in their ears 'Men must work and Women must weep' and seek compensation for the strain; largely in religion and 'the gratifying feeling that our duty has been done'.[17]

Feminine abnegation in the face of imperial duty took an ever more prominent profile in fiction during the period after the mid-1870s, as the drawbacks of Empire spread wider in their effects on society and as girls, many already dissatisfied with the restricted expectations of their domestic role, became

[15] It is worth noting that numbers of authors like Charlotte Yonge and Evelyn Everett Green wrote books dealing with both historical and imperial themes. See ch. 4.

[16] That too much adventure can lead to a surfeit was frequently brought out in girls' novels when characters seek the restfulness of home to recover their shattered spirits and health etc. For instance, Evelyn Everett Green, *The Head of the House: The Story of a Victory over Passion and Pride* (RTS, London, 1886).

[17] C. Kingsley, 'The Three Fishers', *The Poems* (Dent, London, 1927); W.S. Gilbert, *The Gondoliers*, Act II.

increasingly conscious of the more obviously attractive careers open to their brothers or friends with the proliferation of adventure stories in colonial settings etc. While it was possible to point out ways in which the individual might share in the glory and profit, writers in this genre were deeply aware that it was at a cost for both sexes. However, the boys' authors were able without sacrificing realism to gloss over the price paid by men for Empire by stressing the excitement and thrill of the enterprise, to say nothing of possible kudos.

This is not a channel open to writers for the feminine market. It was hardly realistic to show the majority of women as facing anything other than the fate of Evelyn Everett Green's Dorothy Ewing waiting for news of her brother on an expedition to Tibet or Mrs George de Horne Vaizey's Norah Bertrand waiting for her lover's return from making his fortune in India. Dorothy's heart-felt cry is 'If only I could be with him and share the peril, I should not mind', but that is practically impossible. She is well aware that if she were present she would only be a hindrance to a soldier. Equally there is no question that Norah could be permitted to accompany Rex on his peripatetic adventure in remotest India. She will have to wait years until he finds a more civilized base.[18] The separation between the jobs doled out to the public world of men and the private world of women necessitated a different approach to the question of participation in the imperial enterprise, and one that, in view of the 'Woman question', had to be handled tactfully.

Many writers for this market, like Mrs Juliana Ewing, had personal experience of the darker side of involvement in Empire, a type of experience which was by no means outside that of other middle-class women at the time. She drew on that experience in writing her books for both the juvenile and adolescent market; most notably in the latter case *Six to Sixteen*, the tale of an Indian army officer's orphan daughter.[19] How-

[18] Evelyn Everett Green, *Miss Greyshott's Girls*, p. 171.

[19] Mrs Juliana Ewing, *Six to Sixteen*, Queens Treasures Series (Bell, London, 1908), 1st edn (1875). It was supposedly an autobiographical tale, written from an adolescent standpoint. Mrs Ewing was married to an army major and went with him not only around England but also to Canada. She lost friends to wounds and disease in India and Africa, notably as a result of the Zulu War which prompted her to write her famous juvenile tale *Jackanapes* (Christian Knowledge Society, London, 1884).

ever, her aim is by no means anti-imperialist. It is, instead, an exercise intended to reconcile her readership to the continuance of Empire without falsifying its likely effects on their lives, and in so doing, to reconcile her readers to the conventional view of the role that women could play therein: to raise false expectations in didactic fiction would run the risk of creating a spirit of disenchantment with the adult reality that could lead to destabilizing opposition to imperial demands in the feminine sector. Equally it was a *sine qua non* that women had to be involved in the workings of the British Empire if it was to survive, just as women were an essential in the survival of British society as a whole.

The reason for this was that one of the most significant social impacts of Empire was on the family. English responsibility overseas on an imperial scale meant that the domestic circle had to accept that increasingly, separation would be an almost inevitable element in its development. This factor accounts for a constant two-fold theme in adolescent girls' fiction: the ways in which it was possible to maintain the family circle despite the absence of some members, and the need to accept cheerfully the burden of sacrifice entailed by involvement in Empire. The responsibility here as so often fell very heavily on women; they too were in the imperial service, if not on its official lists. Good girls thus had to be trained to deal with it professionally. Separations might take a variety of forms – parting from parents, from siblings or from friends and fiancés and even from one's children.

However hard, the true woman was expected to accept and make the best of such events without adding to the sorrow of others by useless complaint or by inability to cope. More than that, it was necessary for women to take the lead in teaching men how to cope with their stresses. It has been seen that women were expected to teach men, from boyhood, the qualities necessary for moral and spiritual development: one aspect of this learning was the development of an imperial patriotism, ideally first imbued at a mother's knee. It was believed that this early association would ground this patriotism in the necessary spiritual character which would enable later development of the public school ethos, with its concomitant qualities of 'playing the game' and unquestioning heroism in the face of all odds. Essentially it was women who were entrusted with the task of passing on the concept which Kipling immortalized as 'The White Man's Burden'. Grumbling because Miles is about to go off and seek adventure overseas, Mrs George de Horne Vaizey's Cynthia Alliot is rebuked by him 'And who makes the men?' – a salutary reminder for a discontented maiden.[20]

Maintaining the bounds of Empire during the nineteenth century involved numerous small campaigns and wars in various parts of the world. Mrs George de Horne Vaizey commented to her female readers that 'It's the Border Wars which keep the Empire together ... which entail the most self-sacrificing and thankless work'. To die or become incapacitated in the service of Queen and Empire was a very genuine likelihood for a young man joining the army: balanced by the opportunities presented to earn promotion and honour as a result of action. Yet that alone might not be enough to keep a man to his post in time of trial. As Colonel Digby in *Betty Trevor* told an aspiring soldier:

'I have been afraid ... many times over. ... To camp with a handful of men among the great lonely mountains ... never knowing when or how the attack may fall – an attack of devils rather than men . . . that shakes the nerves of the strongest man.'[21]

It was necessary to convince the soldier, therefore, that he was not alone in such circumstances. A soldier in the English army should always consider himself also enlisted in Christ's army and to that end, women had to help present Christianity as 'a fine and manly' thing, because they have the 'faculty born in them' of understanding that. For this reason girls' books placed nearly as much emphasis as boys' books on military matters, if from a slightly different perspective. The old soldier Colonel Digby, for instance, sees his service in terms of 'Christ, the Captain! I am here to obey His orders' as well as those of a commanding officer. The good officer in fiction was always a Christian English gentleman. It is not, for example, until Amy Le Feuvre's young lieutenant, Jack Tracy, becomes a genuine Christian that he develops the qualities of leadership that enable him to become a good officer and eventually, during the Boer War, a hero. Equally, Alick Keith in Charlotte Yonge's

[20] Mrs George de Horne Vaizey, *Betty Trevor* (RTS, London, 1907), 1st edn (1905), p. 164.
[21] Ibid., pp. 97–8.

Clever Woman of the Family is devout as well as a holder of the Victoria Cross. Not all soldiers, however, had the chance of such visible heroism, and needed to be prepared to carry on without. A soldier joined the army and fought not for personal glory, but for 'his King', which was 'enough for him', ideally at least.[22]

In practical terms however it was feared that even a Christian soldier might well slacken in his zeal without the additional support of human love: patriotism, after all, became personal through the family unit. The returning hero from the Sudan in *Three Bright Girls*, an 1892 novel, tells his tearful beloved that it was thoughts of her that kept him to his duty when it was hard, and her parting gift of a rose, kept in a silver box, that turned the tribesmen's otherwise fatal bullet. It is thus no accident that the ideal soldier was seen as coming from a sound family background, where he would have learned to revere women. He would also have been well taught by his mother or some other female the early character lessons of patriotism and conformity that would fit him for military service: duty to those in authority over him; loyalty and a desire to please through prompt, cheerful and unquestioning obedience those for whom he cared. In the army, he would be sustained and kept up to the correct high standards in the performance of his role by the loving support and encouragement of his family, and in particular the women, because it was they who maintained the moral and Christian tone of that family.[23]

Girls thus needed to know the qualities that made a good soldier, and there was considerable discussion in didactic fiction for girls, more or less skilfully introduced, intended to inform them in this respect. There was more that had to be judged than the physical appearance, though as always a man's bearing was presumed to give a clue to his character just as dress did for a woman. Much, therefore, was made of an upright, alert or 'soldierly' bearing (frequently associated with a well-cultivated

---

[22] Ibid., p. 98; pp. 107–8; Amy Le Feuvre, *Olive Tracy* (RTS, London, 1902); Charlotte M. Yonge, *The Clever Woman of the Family* (Virago Press, London, 1983), 1st edn (1865), pp. 342–3.

[23] H. Louisa Bedford, *The Twins That Did Not Pair*, p. 97; Annie E. Armstrong, *Three Bright Girls: A story of Chance and Mischance* (Blackie, Glasgow, 1892).

moustache) hinting at long hours doing drill in preparation for conflict. Captain Raphael Everard in Evelyn Everett Green's *Two Enthusiasts* indicated his inner nature by the lines of his face and his deportment. The good soldier, being the obvious modern knight and guardian of chivalry, was inevitably presumed to possess a large portion of 'the noble instinct of self-sacrifice that seems born and bred in the British race' in physical terms at least. This led in turn to a self-effacing modesty with regard to his own exploits. Deeds of daring were cheerfully done for the 'honour of their country and for the upholding of that country's integrity and empire in the sight of the world', not the individual's glory; hence the 'soldier-like modesty' of the heroic Captain Ewing when faced with an admiring circle in *Miss Greyshott's Girls*. As his destined bride comments 'He won't talk about the things he's done, only what other men did, but that's just like all really brave men'.[24]

Courage was essential in the soldier, but the British army, charged with defence of a large Empire needed more than that, a point that needed to be put forcibly to girls who might otherwise be blinded by military glamour. *Sister's* Colonel Clarence understood that the professional officer, like the professional *Household Fairy* or *Home Goddess*, needed first to know his job properly.

> No man is fit, in my opinion, to be a commanding officer who does not know every detail of a private's work. I only wish our present system consisted of less book cram and a great deal more good, hard, practical work! We don't want bookworms to lead our men in battle; we want *men*!

It was axiomatic that success in the military sphere would come to men of action, but such men should never mistake courage for foolhardiness, a particularly serious crime for any officer in charge of a useful body of men. Girls were thus encouraged to deprecate deeds done without forethought or real need, whatever the provocation. The sagacious Colonel Clarence provided a fine example of the right type of officer: 'I never saw a man so cool under fire and in deadly peril as he. Always in the front of

---

[24] Evelyn Everett Green, *Two Enthusiasts* (RTS, London, 1888), p. 82; p. 216; *Miss Greyshott's Girls* pp. 225–6; p. 209; p. 223.

everything. . . . Recklessly? Well it almost amounted to recklessness sometimes; and yet he never actually crossed the boundary line which transformed courage into foolhardiness.'[25]

It was essential to train women to regard it as a pivotal part of their responsibility as women to be proud of their military menfolk, and to be ready to dispatch them to their duty, even if it meant worse than temporary separation. Tears, for instance, might weaken a soldier at a crucial point and make him too conscious of the value of his own life. Thus Eugenia Darley, the young orphaned wife, in *Her Husband's Home*, parting with her husband to go to the Afghan War in 1879, weeps alone but swiftly pulls herself together: 'with a hasty movement [her tears] were wiped away. Her husband might return at any moment, and he must not find her in tears. She – a soldier's wife – a soldier's daughter – she must never be a hindrance to him in the path of duty.'[26] This fortitude must plainly have been less rigid in reality but the frequent fictional illustration of such scenes does indicate the perceived need to continue sympathy for this supremely self-sacrificing tradition. Even those who could not reach such heights of resigned self-abnegation were shown as being conscious of their failure like Evelyn Everett Green's Lois Everard and also conscious of a need to keep striving for it. After all, it would have been disastrous for Empire had women refused to try at least to acquiesce meekly in such expectations, to continue blaming themselves and not the system for any failure.[27]

Showing women that their background role was by no means totally passive or devoid of practical use was also of considerable importance, not only in reconciling women to their comparative inactivity, but also out of genuine conviction that prayer was an active force. Waiting for news of Captain Everard, wounded in the Zulu War, Beatrice complains that: 'We poor women have much the harder task, I think, in sitting still at home, whilst they have all the danger and all the glory. . . . I

[25] Evelyn Everett Green, *Sister: A Chronicle of Fair Haven* (Nelson, Walton-on-Thames, 1898), p. 397; p. 91.

[26] Evelyn Everett Green, *Her Husband's Home, or The Durleys of Linley Castle* (Shaw, London, 1887), pp. 18–19.

[27] Evelyn Everett Green, *Two Enthusiasts*, p. 133, Lois describes herself as 'unworthy' to be a soldier's daughter, and a coward.

hate to sit here by my comfortable fireside while our brave men are in danger facing the enemy. . . . I dislike the feeling of being quite helpless.' The clearer-sighted Erica replies, meaningfully, 'Are we quite helpless?' – and goes away to pray; prayers, naturally, that are rewarded by the recovery of the gallant Captain: his proposal of marriage is merely an extra benefit.[28]

Even where there was no such reunion, there was still a reward to be gleaned by those who waited and prayed. Such monuments were honoured and envied by other women for the unflinching performance of this duty. Moreover, girls were reminded, as Evelyn Everett Green's bereaved young Mrs Durley was, that death was sometimes kinder than life, and the harsh reality was that to wish for a soldier's return at all costs was selfishness in the extreme.

> 'It is sometimes better to be a widow than a wife. . . . Suppose he had come home to you maimed, helpless, shattered – many soldiers do, you know – would that not be worse?'
> 'For him perhaps,' answered Eugenie, after a brief pause, 'but not for me'.
> 'Ah!' he remarked after a significant pause, 'I always did say that for selfish cruelty there was no match for a woman – a woman of gentle birth and breeding'.
> Eugenie's eyes were raised to his, with a look of startled inquiry. 'I do not understand'.
> 'You must be slow of comprehension. You would rather have your husband back, to linger out a useless life of suffering and helplessness, than feel that all his troubles are over, and he safe and at rest somewhere. . . .'
> 'It would be my life's work to nurse and tend and relieve him. He would understand – he would know what I mean'.
> 'I know what you mean well enough . . . but I should have thought experience would have taught you wisdom . . . do not quarrel with Providence . . . When you go home just take your Bible and read the story of Elisha and the Shunnamitish woman . . .'[28]

A grave in a foreign land might deprive a woman of the consolation of visiting it, but it certainly was presumed to give

---

[28] Ibid., pp. 133–4.

her a very concrete stake in the imperial future.

It is also interesting too to trace the growing importance of Empire to the middle classes through the domestic and maternal theme. Writers from the earlier period, such as Charlotte Yonge and Elizabeth Sewell had a consciousness of Empire almost solely through this particular question and the problems Empire brought, and it was an aspect that never disappeared from the fiction. If involvement with Empire for most girls was primarily presented throughout the nineteenth century as a question of self-sacrifice in various ways, it was a self-sacrifice that was seen as being absolutely central to the continuance of England and its Empire. Without women, the middle-class ideal of family would collapse; without the family unit England could not continue to hold the position of moral pre-eminence on which her wordly success was founded. It is not accident that many political commentators on Empire used the family as a metaphor in describing it. If England was the Mother Country, the pivot on which the welfare of her offspring colonies depended, then the professional mother, or her substitute was the pivot on which England herself depended.[30] Moreover, with even many conventional young women asking for a challenge or even for greater responsibility within their sphere, one reply was to point to the Empire and the existing challenge that the modern extension of national burdens entailed on the female participants therein.

Thus that the maintenance of links between family members, especially parents and children, and siblings, over long distances and times was a constant concern to established society for a mixture of reasons is seen both by the wide range of books which deal with the theme, and the range of remedies they offered to help and profit women. From Charlotte Yonge to Mrs George de Horne Vaizey and Bessie Marchant, writers depicted the problem and the variety of acceptable solutions. The separation between parent and child was presumed to be the most acute. All too often the inexorable and inescapable exigencies of overseas service temporarily broke the family circle when the children were around six or seven, possibly younger if they were sickly. A major question was how this was

---

[29] Evelyn Everett Green, *Her Husband's Home*, pp. 214–15.
[30] See, for instance, E. Knatchbull Hugessen, *Hansard* CCVI, 12 May 1871.

to be most successfully accomplished. A woman could either leave her husband and return to England to bring up their children there; or she could stay with him while her children were returned to England, to relatives, friends or schools to be brought up.

There are fictional examples of the former, largely from the early period before the 1860s or authors continuing to write in that earlier tradition, when the presence of memsahibs in dependent colonies such as India was rarer, but it was always seen as posing enormous problems especially for the women. In both Elizabeth Sewell's *Amy Herbert* and Mrs Marshall's *Over the Down*, for instance, the plot develops around the problems that result from the absence of father and husband for a delicate mother with a young family. As was typical of such a stereotype, both wives suffered 'the hard fate of Indian service': Colonel Herbert was in India, serving with credit in the 1844 Sikh Wars, while Mr Temple was in the Indian Civil Service. The burden of absence falls very heavily on both wives: letters are long in arriving, there is the constant fear for their husbands of death, through disease or native insurgency. Mrs Herbert, being a good and Godly woman, bears up nobly, and maintains the domestic circle suitably. She teaches her daughter 'all she needs to know at her mother's knee',[31] while performing all her household duties and writing encouraging letters to her husband; doing it all in such a way that when the Colonel does return on leave, he is able to take up his role as head of the family without any more upheaval than results from the delight felt by his wife and daughter at seeing him again.

By contrast, Mrs Temple is a less resolute woman and her husband faces a less happy return: his headstrong daughter Christabel, unrestrained by her mother, damages her spine in a fall and adds another invalid to the home to which the long-suffering man returns. In both books, great stress is laid on the importance of maintaining family ties despite time and distance. Both girls shirk their duties to their parents in this respect because 'I know him so little and he scarcely knows me,

[31] Mrs Emma Marshall, *Over the Down, or A Chapter of Accidents* (Nelson, Walton-on-Thames, 1885); Elizabeth M. Sewell, *Amy Herbert*, 2 vols (Longman, London, 1844), p. 30.

except by my photograph', while their mothers 'tell papa everything'. While mamma does indeed do this so that neither father is unacquainted with the true nature of his daughter on his return, the girls themselves have missed the point of the exercise. They need to learn to sustain affection and duty over such obstacles in case of future need in adult life, and such letters would provide sound early training and experience.[32]

Eleanor Hawkescroft in *Scenes and Characters*, also facing family separation due to imperial responsibilities followed the pattern that was to become increasingly the norm in accompanying her husband, leaving her child to be trained and educated by relatives in England; a theme that plays an important role in the working out of the story's moral. In settling on a suitable place in which to leave their baby son they must discern the best available mother substitute among the options open to them. Eleanor's unmarried sisters initially hope that their nephew will be left with them, but they have not attained the proper standards required of good *Household Fairies*. Regretfully, Eleanor thus leaves young Henry to her better regulated sister-in-law, where the child can be sure of correct training in a family environment, growing up to be a credit to his family and his country.[33]

By the post-1870 period separations between husband and wife took place much more infrequently, usually only if the husband was posted to a campaign or a generally dangerous area and the wife herself was in fragile health. However, such scenarios were unusual, partly because of the obvious strains that any lengthy partings would put on any marital relationship, endangering therefore the fabric of family life. There were, to contemporary eyes, other pressing reasons behind this fictional emphasis: in the individual case, the problems in his profession social circle that being left without a wife would bring to any man. Thus Lady Merrifield in *Two Sides of the Shield* only returns to England with her youngest children when her two oldest daughters are adult enough to deputise for her in the General's establishment in India. In the wider sphere there was a perceived growing need to establish English civilization,

[32] Mrs Emma Marshall, *Over the Down*, pp. 17–18.
[33] Charlotte M. Yonge, *Scenes and Characters, or Eighteen Months at Beechcroft* (Macmillan, London, 1885).

which required the presence of women to act as the professional arbiters of social conduct in these frontier areas. During the
last 30 years of the century, the numbers of English women in
colonies such as India increased significantly.[34]

It was admitted that this course was by no means easy for the
woman. Not only were social circles generally more limited in
the colonies, even in India, but also the climate in many
imperial outposts was not often conducive to energetic supervision of a household, even if the resources were to hand to
make it practicable to try to maintain the 'professional' standards of an English home. Most serious of all, the duty of
remaining with one's husband entailed the corresponding duty
of parting with one's children. In *About Peggy Saville*, one of her
most popular and critically acclaimed books, Mrs George de
Horne Vaizey depicted the plight of such women very graphically. Mrs Saville needs to find a suitable home for Peggy, who
has not been happy at school. In desperation, she turns to an
old schoolfriend, married to a parson, and pleads, successfully,
with Mrs Asplin to give Peggy a home. Looking at Mrs Asplin
with her husband and family around her, Mrs Saville bursts
into tears:

> Oh, how happy you are! How I envy you! Husband, children, –
> all beside you. Oh, never, never let one of your girls marry a
> man who lives abroad. My heart is torn in two; I have no rest. I
> am always longing for the one who is not there. I must go back, –
> the major needs me; but Peggy, – my own little girl! It is like
> death to leave her behind.[35]

It is a vision she will remember as she lies 'panting under the
swing of the punkah'. When she comes to say goodbye to Peggy
the grief of both is acute, and intended to strike a chord,
prophetic or reminiscent, with many readers:

> There was much they wanted to say to each other, yet for the
> most part they were silent.
> If I were ill, mother – a long illness – would you come?

[34] Charlotte M. Yonge, *The Two Sides of the Shield* (Macmillan, London,
1885), p. 22.
[35] Mrs George de Horne Vaizey, *About Peggy Saville* (RTS, London, 1900),
p. 33.

On wings, darling! As fast as boat and train could bring me . . .
You must write often . . . You will be almost a woman when we
meet again. Don't grow up a stranger to me, darling . . . Don't
fret, dearie. I shall be with father, and the time will pass.
Peggy shivered, and was silent . . . This was the last time, the very
last time when she would be a child in her mother's arms. The
new relationship might be nearer, sweeter, but it could never be
the same, and the very sound of the words 'the last time' sends a
pang to the heart.[36]

It is the call of duty and the remembrance of their Christian
faith that helps to reconcile both the Savilles to the parting.
Certainly Peggy is shown as learning her lesson dutifully: in the
sequel, Peggy is prepared to become engaged to Robert Darcy,
who intends to spend his life as an explorer and botanist.
Painful separation, from husband as well as children, would
thus be likely to be her lot: but she accepts the prospect
willingly and enthusiastically. Making a virtue of necessity, duty
has become her pleasure.[37]

As the increasing pace of imperial expansion brought
heavier demands in its wake from the mid-1870s, it became
necessary to expound more fully on this imperial theme in
fiction. As a result, the Empire played an increasingly visible
role in stories. More and more heroines had family or friends
involved in the imperial service in some form, as soldiers,
administrators, settlers, missionaries and even traders and
more and more detailed information was given about the facts
of such enterprises. In *The Twins that Did Not Pair*, for instance,
considerable information is given about mechanics through
which Harold Brabazon went out to Africa as a missionary; and
in Evelyn Everett Green's *Half-A-Dozen Sisters*, similar information is given on the route taken by Gypsy in becoming an
Indian senana missionary.[38] Pride in the imperial achievement

[36] Ibid., pp. 40–1.

[37] Mrs George de Horne Vaizey, *More About Peggy* (RTS, London, 1901),
p. 170.

[38] H. Louisa Bedford, *The Twins That Did Not Pair*, pp. 145–8; Evelyn
Everett Green, *Half-A-Dozen Sisters* (RTS, London, 1910), 1st edn (1905). It
became unnecessary, however, to give 'elementary' geographical or historical
details, because it was assumed that any moderately educated girl would know
where, for instance, Hyderabad was and why it was important!

became more conscious and more explicit, accompanied by the evocation of a spirit of nostalgic 'homesickness' which was shown to be an inescapable corollary to overseas life. This not only mirrored the developments in the adult world, but was also, in this genre, an attempt to justify continuance of Empire and to reassure those left behind in England that they were not lightly forgotten and that in this respect at least, the 'stay-at-home' was most likely to achieve an early reward. Gypsy, going out to a wide sphere of service in India, was most likely to wait until heaven to receive her due recompense; while her sisters settled down to married domesticity, with its attendant trials and happinesses, in predictable England.

These stories reflect also the fact that by this time, going overseas meant taking a weighty, if invisible baggage of national character and behaviour with one. In darkest Brazil, for instance, L.T. Meade's Mr Frazer is 'English to the backbone, and liked to keep up all the names and customs of his native land as far as possible'. This involves ignoring as far as possible the difficulties of pursuing an English lifestyle in a tropical climate, to the extent of feeding his unfortunate children on porridge for breakfast and going to the lengths of growing his own oats to ensure a regular supply, in order to build 'backbone' in them. A diet of local fruits was clearly a recipe for moral and physical laziness.[39] As Mrs Bessie Parkes Belloc put it so authoritatively in her survey of the peoples of the world, the 'traditional' diet of the English, with its emphasis on red meat, 'well-digested' was, along with the invigorating English climate, responsible for the superiority of the English character.[40] They provided an unmatchable environment. Pride in England and all things English was presumed to grow automatically in a foreign setting, along with the consequent homesickness. As one emigrant to the charming town and salubrious climate of Melbourne regretted, the colonies had a 'want . . . of all that is old', sighing nostalgically for Norman cathedrals and other tangible monuments to long-standing English greatness.[41]

[39] L.T. Meade, *Four on an Island: A Story of Adventure* (Chambers, Edinburgh, 1892), pp. 8–10.
[40] Mrs Bessie Parkes-Belloc, *Peoples of the World* (Cassell, London, 1870). this was a well-known and popular text for children.
[41] Emily Brodie, *Jean Lindsay, the Vicar's Daughter* (Shaw, London, 1878), p. 67.

This pride and nostalgia was presumed to remain even when Englishmen and women had emigrated to take up permanent residence in colonies like Australia or Canada and subsequent generations had been born on these distant shores. In Evelyn Everett Green's *My Cousin from Australia*, for instance, the model English maiden, Evangeline asks her Australian visitor, Griffeth Colquhoun:

Have you been in England before?
Never, This is my first visit – although, of course, I always speak of it as 'home'.
Do you? Why?
Oh, we all do that – everyone out there does. It does not matter whether we have any stake in the old country, whether we have ever been or ever mean to go. It is always 'home' to all of us, and I suppose it is the dream of everyone of us to see it.

Griffeth Colquhoun then goes on to expound on the great beauty of England, its greenness and freshness to eyes used to the dryer, hotter Australian landscape. He will be a better person on his return to Australia for his visit to the Mother Country, nor is it unexpected when he falls in love with the fair cousin who is an embodiment of the freshness of English virtue and maidenhood. The result is a marriage that will strengthen the bonds of Empire, as with landed responsibilities on both sides of the globe, the happy pair will have to travel between Australia and England frequently, reinforcing the weight of the English pedigree in the colony, while importing a certain colonial vigour into 'olde' England.[42]

However, there was also a due appreciation that the nostalgic love of England was not always prominent, and that it did not preclude a genuine commitment to the future of the land of emigration. It was agreed that the English character, while the ideal foundation, would modify and adapt to suit the requirements and opportunities of a country very different to the Mother Country. It was even admitted that natures which did not flourish in the cosier surroundings of England might flower

[42] Evelyn Everett Green, *My Cousin From Australia* (Hutchinson, London, 1894), pp. 27–36.

and expand in the face of colonial rigour. Bessie Marchant was one who laid great emphasis on the 'honest pride in the land of his adoption which most Colonials feel when success is crowning their efforts'.[43] Having once emigrated, few of her characters return to the land of their birth, or even want to do so for more than a visit, though they retain a love of England and a respect for things English in nature, if colonial in practice. She stressed instead the salutary effects on men and women of being put in a position where it was necessary to rely on one's independent efforts and test one's limitations in a way that it was not possible to do in England.[44]

For those men who had failed in England to maintain the standards of honesty, diligence and decency, the colonies could provide a chance to redeem themselves. In a new land a fresh start could be made, and possibly a status achieved that could make atonement, even restore pride to a shamed man's family in England. In *Temple's Trial*, for instance, Percy succumbs to temptation to squander his and his brother's money on gambling and drinking. Found out, he confesses his guilt and his consciousness of ruin. He sees his only course as to 'get away somewhere, and make a fresh start. I should like to go to the colonies, if my uncle approves'. He ends up in Australia, which is admitted to be a place in which his past sins can be overlooked so long as he 'buckles to' and develops physical and spiritual muscle.[45] It is an interesting reflection on the way in which colonial life was viewed as being, for all its English connections, essentially less civilized and rougher at the edges. There is never any suggestion that a colonial rogue should come to England to 'make good'.

For those who went out and returned, in fiction as in reality a life of service in the colonies was not always considered a good foundation for a happy retirement in England. For instance, a stereotype evolved in fiction of many variations of the returned old India hand unable to settle easily in the country of his birth,

[43] Bessie Marchant, *Cicely Frome: The Captain's Daughter* (Nimmo, Hay & Mitchell, London, 1900), p. 69.

[44] Bessie Marchant, *Three Girls on a Ranch: A Story of New Mexico* (Blackie, Glasgow, 1901), pp. 236–7.

[45] Evelyn Everett Green, *Temple's Trial, or For Life or Death* (Nelson, Walton-on-Thames, 1887), pp. 316–18.

no matter how beloved. This brought even more problems for any female members of his household circle, be they wife, daughter or sister, in trying to ensure that domestic priority, male comfort. Some, like Mrs Marshall's Mr Temple, could not stand the English climate – understandably perhaps. Others like Mrs George de Horne Vaizey's Colonel Saville returned happily enough to the climate after the blinding heat of India, but could not happily accustom themselves to the drop in living standards that living in England entailed. Colonel Saville was used to a large household, smoothly run by experienced servants and, in retirement, found himself in comparatively reduced circumstances.[46] He had, however, the good fortune to have survived in India and to be able to return, with his family, to his native shores in a state of sufficient fitness to make the most of his retirement. His fortune was not always shared in reality, and fiction needed to reflect this darker aspect of military life, and attempt to do it in such a way that women would accept the risks to their happiness with resignation if not with joy.

The regional element to the question of familial separation became stronger and more significant from the 1870s on, despite improvements in communications and transport. This may seem too obvious to need stating, but it was a factor of considerable importance to English society. The area of Empire involved largely dictated the nature and duration of any parting. Colonies of white settlement, from New South Wales to British Columbia, were generally peaceful: there was less likelihood of military service in such regions. Also, the environment in such places was considered to be sufficiently similar to that of England as to pose no threat to the development of an English character there. Thus in general members of a family circle going to regions like these could expect a lifetime gap in their numbers.

Some colonial families might, if financially successful enough, return to England for visits or even permanently. If lucky, brides might be collected in person by a fiancé before returning overseas: more had to travel out by themselves as their bridegrooms could not leave their posts without damage

[46] Mrs Emma Marshall, *Over the Down*, p. 119; Mrs George de Horne Vaizey, *More About Peggy Saville*, pp. 180–6.

to their prospects there.[47] Some parents might, if sufficiently well-off, decide for educational or family reasons, that some at least of their children should go back to England for some of their schooling.[48] There was rarely any question of returning to England for reasons of health – frequently the climates of such regions were considered to be healthier than that of England. For instance, in *Three Girls on a Ranch* the fragile near-invalid father becomes much more physically vigorous as a result of living in the New Mexican climate.[49]

By contrast the majority of African and Asian colonies were regions where the English went to administer, fight, convert or trade for a limited duration. Experience of such regions came as a result of employment not emigration. Also, most of these colonies were considered to be dangerous in a number of ways, including environment and native unrest. In this respect, India took a particularly visible and central role: it demanded the greatest sacrifice from those involved with her. As that offspring of soldier stock, Lady Myrtle Goodacre, exclaimed in *Robin Redbreast*: 'Ah, yes, our Indian possessions cost us dear in some ways'.[50] This was partly due to scale. India provided greater and more pressing problems than anywhere else, for a number of reasons. For one thing, the enormous native population needed a considerable investment in terms of manpower to administer and guard. A considerable military presence was an essential, with small-scale skirmishes commonplace and more major campaigns occurring regularly. Major demands were also made on civil servants, and on various branches of auxiliary personnel, including civil engineers, missionaries and doctors.

In addition, not only did India make these very considerable demands on personnel, both service and civilian, but it possessed a climate generally agreed to be risky for adults, and in

---

[47] For instance, Emily Brodie, *Jean Lindsay*, where the bride only knows her husband through his photograph and his family; accepts him on their recommendation and the character of his correspondence; and travels to join him escorted by his sister, p. 101.

[48] Eg. E.L. Haverfield, *Queensland Cousins* (Nelson, Walton-on-Thames, 1903), p. 219.

[49] Bessie Marchant, *Three Girls on a Ranch*.

[50] Mrs Mary Molesworth, *Robin Redbreast: A Story for Girls* (Chambers, Edinburgh, 1892), p. 185.

particular, unsuitable for bringing up healthy children. There the danger to physical well-being, and also the environment, was held to be invidious to the development of English qualities. This aspect of India was accepted by serious writers like Kipling in books such as *Kim* as much as by writers for the didactic genre. Frances Hodgson Burnett was responsible for the best-known examples in this latter respect: Sara Crewe in *A Little Princess* and Mary Lennox in *The Secret Garden*, but there were many more.[51] It is interesting to note that I have found no example of a book intended for the adolescent market which advocates children staying beyond about six or seven with their parents in Indian conditions. The question of survival seems to have been accepted as being too acute.

There was another element involved with the growth of the Empire which had an impact on women, particularly those who found themselves actively involved in its maintenance outside England. Life in such areas meant some contact with native races, and this contact tended to be presented to a female reading public in domestic terms. It might be expected by twentieth-century women that the sense of restriction felt by so many English women would lead to a certain sympathy for the restricted lot of non-English subjects of the Empire. The bald truth is that, despite the efforts of some extraordinary women, the majority of nineteenth-century English ladies, whether in England or overseas, did not generally develop a real sensitivity towards the native races they read about or came into contact with. Women like Mary Kingsley, with her opposition to the activities of the Colonial Office, were unusual and their interest frequently considered unfeminine and even unhelpful in this respect, and even potentially unpatriotic.[52] It was far more general for women to accept that the benefits such as Christianity brought by English imperialism to indigenous races were too obvious to need questioning.

Examination of the makeup of the racial components of the United Kingdom and the historical background to their incorporation as a 'single element' sheds a very interesting light on

[51] R. Kipling, *Kim* (Macmillan, London, 1901); Frances Hodgson Burnett, *A Little Princess: The Story of Sarah Crewe* (Warne, London, 1905).

[52] Dea Birkett, *Spinsters Abroad: Victorian Lady Explorers* (Basil Blackwell, Oxford, 1989).

English conventional nineteenth-century racial attitudes. Little or no difference is made, in modern fictional terms, between the English and the Scots or the English and the Welsh. Both these Celtic races had certain national characteristics which were considered to be practically complementary to the English character: Scots independence and physical sturdiness, for instance, or Welsh musicality and loyalty. In times past Scotland and Wales had both been separate nations, but they had been absorbed into a greater whole with England for their own greater good. England might be the dominant partner, but that was because of her inborn ability to rule other nationalities wisely and well. An enlightened former Welsh rebel of the thirteenth century, for instance, told his fellows that 'in the English alliance is Wales's only hope of tranquility and true independence and civilisation'.[53] Acceptance had brought Wales and Scotland prosperity and stability, and therefore placed them in England's debt.

This theme of mutual advantage to regions and people brought under English sway was pursued in a number of tales dealing with the Angevin British Empire with a sense of very conscious comparison and justification. Evelyn Everett Green commented that 'the shrewd Gascons . . . knew when they were well off', and that was under an English monarch. 'It is plain to the reader of the history of those days that Gascony could never have remained for three hundred years a fief of the English Crown, had it not been to the advantage of her people that she should so remain . . . it was to their own advancement and welfare thus to accord this homage and fealty.'[54] The implications for the modern Empire were intended to be obvious to the most naive reader. Nor was Miss Everett Green the only one to make comparisons between the stout Gascon race of the Middle Ages and the modern Scot, and the place of Scotland in the British Empire. Both counted as honorary and honoured Englishmen in their period, and did not, therefore, need to be separately distinguished.

Ireland, however, came under a different category. There

[53] Evelyn Everett Green, *Lord of Dynever: A Tale of the Time of Edward the First* (Nelson, Walton-on-Thames, 1892), p. 253.

[54] Evelyn Everett Green, *In the Days of Chivalry* (Nelson, Walton-on-Thames, 1893), pp. 26–8.

was great affection for the Irish in most of these works of fiction. Irish characters were merrier, more amusing, more charming than many of English origin, like many of L.T. Meade's or Mrs George de Horne Vaizey's heroines, in particular the latter's Pixie O'Shaughnessy. They were also, however, more careless, more idle and more spendthrift. Those of the Anglo-Irish gentry class were usually admitted to the equivalent English confraternity – but it cannot be denied that to twentieth-century commentators the tone taken towards the Irish in these works verges on the patronizing. Unlike the Scots, the Irish had signally failed to take advantage of the opportunities offered them by association with England; her people, less farsighted and ambitious, were content to muddle along in a state of civilization markedly behind that of the rest of Great Britain. The Irish peasantry, in particular, were frequently seen as an inferior and less capable race. For instance, Paul Rutland in Evelyn Everett Green's *The Percivals*, tells his prospective bride that:

> 'I feel more and more convinced that my life's work lies here, amongst these poor, ignorant, misguided people, whose capacity both for good and evil is so great, and who may be led anywhere by a little kindness, but cannot and will not be driven.'[55]

It is shown to be a measure of the greatness of nature of men like Paul Rutland that despite the ingratitude of so many among the Irish people, even leading to acute physical danger, that they were willing to continue their mission, secure in the knowledge of divine approval. Paul Rutland is shot and wounded, but like a true imperialist he stays, and Judith Perceval comes out to join him and add that necessary woman's touch to his work. It may be noted that much of the blame for the Irish condition was laid at the door of the Roman Catholic Church, for hindering the development of family life etc.[56]

[55] Mrs George de Horne Vaizey, *Pixie O'Shaughnessy* (RTS, London, 1903); Evelyn Everett Green, *The Percivals, or A Houseful of Girls* (RTS, London, 1903), 1st edn (1890), p. 169.
[56] J.M. Callwell, *One Summer by the Sea* (Nelson, Walton-on-Thames, 1893); Laura Barter Snow, *Honour's Quest or How They Came Home* (RTS, London, 1903), p. 48; 'The secret of Ireland's failures is not the blunders of an English government . . . it is because she is under the iron heel of Rome, and cannot get free. The teachings of that corrupt Church have eaten into her very heart's core.'

This, of course, was the spirit that was expected to imbue those men and women involved in maintaining the Empire via contact with a variety of native races. In the expectation that growing numbers of girls would have to face this in their adult life, numbers of racial stereotypes were presented to them for their information. Such stereotypes would enable the English-woman to deal appropriately with those natives with whom she came into contact, in the course of her domestic round or through the men in her life. It is possible in all this, after the 1880s, to see the impact of Social Darwinism, giving a scientific gloss and justification to the hierarchical ranking of non-English races. It is worth noting, though, that the theories of evolution were used simply to confirm an existing hierarchy as regards other races, rather than to encourage any serious re-evaluation in this species of fiction. In practical terms it may have encouraged increasing numbers of Englishwomen to cut their households off, as far as possible, from any meaningful contact with indigenous populations. There was a necessity to maintain the standards of a civilization at a higher evolutionary level in order to preserve the principles of that civilization uncontaminated by less advanced influences on the one hand. There was also the necessity of providing an example to the 'lesser breeds' at all times, even within the household, for the sake of native servants.

At the top of the scale for non-European races were those who displayed a military spirit that could be admitted by the English. Most notable in this respect were the more warlike Indian tribes such as the Sikhs, who had fought bravely against the British, and subsequently provided troops for the Indian Army of British India. Elizabeth Sewell's Colonel Herbert, for instance, referred to the Sikh race as 'a worthy foe, with little of the treachery and mean-spiritedness of other Indian races'.[57] Other native races granted a certain status for their prowess in arms were the Zulus and the Maoris – if somewhat reluctantly in both cases. While it was impossible to dismiss as totally degenerate races which had proved capable of inflicting not-able defeats on British armies, neither race could be trusted even to fight fairly if they came too near alcohol. Equally, while

---

[57] Elizabeth M. Sewell, *Amy Herbert*, p. 283.

Maoris could fight, they would not work as Martin Leveridge in *A Girl of the Fortunate Isles* discovered. According to him it is 'ruin' to try to run a farm with Maori labour. Apart from the Zulus, the majority of other African races received scant justice, being usually dismissed as both idle and untrustworthy 'Kaffirs'.[58] Idleness was generally taken in didactic fiction to be an indication of a lowly position on the evolutionary scale. Races such as the Mexican, despite the likelihood of European blood, were thus regarded as being on a very similar level to the African races. However, the lowest of the low on this scale was undoubtedly the 'homeless and lawless' Australian aboriginal: 'They are treacherous and savage, and most repulsive in appearance. Though spoken of as black, they are really choco-late-brown, but so covered with hair as to be very dusky. Being very cunning in their movements, it it always difficult to know where they are.' Unlike most other native races, 'the Australian black-fellow cannot be tamed and trained' because his 'nature is too wild and fierce to be kept within bounds except by fear and crushing'. Certainly this latter course was vigorously followed by a considerable number of settlers.[59]

All this is, in some ways, very much the obvious presentation of the British Empire to a particular audience: a presentation orientated around a desire to ensure the continuance of a series of values, for the ultimate goal of national and imperial preservation. From the 1880s on, another aspect developed which can be described as being less predictable, and certainly as more individually profitable from the feminine viewpoint. The reports of the less limited sphere of action available to women in many areas of the British interest overseas helped to provide young women in England with a working model of ways in which it was possible for women to reconcile the constraints of domestic duty with a more personally fulfilling lifestyle.

This was partly the result of knowledge about imperial pioneering women of varying types. The majority of these were linked with exercises in advancing essentially domestic values in

---

[58] Bessie Marchant, *A Girl of the Fortunate Isles* (Blackie, Glasgow, 1907), pp. 34–5; p. 47; Edith M. Green, *The Cape Cousins* (Wells, Gardner, Darton, London, 1902), pp. 14–18.

[59] E.L. Haverfield, *Queensland Cousins*, p. 23.

PLATE 8   'NELL FOUND THAT SHE WAS BY FAR THE MORE EXPERT
ON SNOWSHOES'

Competence and Empire. From *Daughters of the Dominion*
by Bessie Marchant

a foreign setting, working as missionaries, nurses and even doctors. Women such as Charlotte Tucker spent a lifetime working to improve the lot of Indian native women in the Zenanas. Others, like Mary Kingsley with her explorations in Africa, worked more for self-fulfillment and, ironically, were frequently less complacent about the impact of English civilization on areas which they visited than those who saw themselves as partaking in a vast imperial, civilizing mission.[60] But whatever the motive behind their departure, the female imperial pioneers stepped outside the narrow limits conventionally allotted to women in England; something which presented a considerable difficulty for realistically inclined authors of fiction.

Adventures beyond the everyday round of life in the historical context could be explained away with relative ease: conditions of civil war, for instance, no longer obtained in England. Such excuses did not hold good for the imperial frontiers. It was necessary, therefore, to produce a set of criteria that would on the one hand defuse the radical nature of womanly exploits there, while avoiding devaluing the Empire as a whole and the contribution made by women to its continuance.

In practice, this meant that contemporary reporting aimed at the women's market, particularly the adolescent sector, stressed the continuing femininity and apparent conformity to established social mores (at least while in England) of women like Mary Kingsley. In addition, the undoubted contribution of such women in fields such as scientific study enabled their public presentation as professional though unusual, women. Fortunately, Miss Kingsley for example also retained a modesty about her work that was considered characteristically feminine and English: this helped considerably in retaining the goodwill of society on her behalf. Yet inevitably this meant that women like her were adopting a higher profile, which was socially acceptable, if not encouraged. It is not surprising, therefore, that these women provided adolescent girls with real female models for imperial iconography that were by no means universally approved by established opinion.

However, the more desirable role models were the women

---

[60] Agnes Giberne, *A Lady of England: The Life and Letters of Charlotte Maria Tucker* (Hodder, Sevenoaks, 1895).

who dedicated their lives to the spreading of the Christian message and the improving of living conditions of the native races incorporated in the Empire. This brand of imperial philanthropy, though dominated by men, was taken up by growing numbers of dedicated women with a sense of mission. The mission field in general was one that any good English girl had to be proud of. In *The Twins That Did Not Pair*, the youthful Brabazon children are told that when a 'black man asked why England was strong, and governed so many people', the Queen 'handed him a Bible, and told him that as long as Englishmen loved the God that Book taught them about they would keep happy and good and strong'. It was no light task being a missionary, and those who entered the field needed to feel a genuine 'call' in order to sustain their efforts in the face of 'the fight with languages, with climate . . . with repeated failures in so-called converts'. However, the definition of a missionary as 'a soldier of the Cross' meant that joining such a dedicated band was one way in which an ardent and patriotic girl could fight for her country and her God.[61]

There was a growing consciousness that if lasting effects were to be gained by missionary efforts, the women of a tribe or nation needed to be touched, so that succeeding generations would be brought up in a proper belief. Yet the local customs in places such as India meant that male missionaries often had the utmost difficulty in reaching those important people. Nor was the job of missionary just to improve the spiritual health of those to whom he ministered. As in England the work also involved ministering to bodily conditions. Here again women could be essential in ensuring that medical aid, for instance, reached local women. Finally, the potential impact of a Christian feminine influence on all members of even primitive tribes was not to be underestimated. The loyal Indian servant in *Douglas Archdale* tells his spiritual mentor, Edith Ryan, that she has 'shown me that your faith made women angels'. Thus properly trained, dedicated and devout women could justifiably be shown to have a major role to play in preserving and improving the Empire.[62]

[61] H. Louisa Bedford, *The Twins That Did Not Pair*, p. 21; p. 47.
[62] C.M.K. Phipps, *Douglas Archdale: A Tale of Lucknow* (London Literary Society, London, 1885), p. 101.

Frank Prochaska has shown that the nature of philanthropy in England encouraged an early interest in overseas missions. Fiction abounds in bazaars and fêtes organized by enterprising good girls to raise money for deserving causes abroad as well as at home. The Rendall girls in *A Houseful of Girls* raise their yearly mission subscription by means of a sale of work showing thereby their interest in their 'poor brothers and sisters' overseas as well as their capacity for enjoyment. They raise 'Forty-three pounds seven and twopence . . . in solid coin of the realm' by their sterling efforts. Nor do such girls miss the chance to go to hear missionaries on home visits. Madge Elwyn in *Her Next-Door Neighbour*, for instance, is the niece of a missionary who has been killed by 'the black heathen people' that he went to teach. She goes eagerly to hear a mission talk by 'Lady Robert Waterford', accompanied by a notable African convert 'King Khama, chief of the Bamangwatos', and inspired by their eloquence (a silent testimony in the case of Khama), organizes a 'Missionary Society Working Party' to make suitable garments for 'poor Hindoo girls that have had a famine'.[63]

Initially in fictional terms, those women who work in the mission field were involved because of their husbands. Norman May in *The Daisy Chain*, for instance, takes his young wife out to New Zealand because he has felt the call to go to 'those Southern seas' and takes with him his wife Meta, who has 'a brave enterprising temper' and 'between them they will make a noble missionary'. By the turn of the century, however, single fictional women were offering themselves up to the mission field, particularly in India. On hearing of the need for a good Christian lady to go and teach in a Woman's College in up-country India, Florence Witts's Ethel Lester, in a voice 'which trembled with emotion', says 'I can give nothing but service. If you see fit to send me, I will go'. Gypsy in *Half-A-Dozen Sisters*, for instance, hears the call of the 'poor, suffering heathen women' in India, and undergoes a three-year medical training to fit her for a life-time of work as a medical missionary in the zenanas. It is worth noting, however, that women like

---

[63] F.K. Prochaska, *Women and Philanthropy in Nineteenth-Century England* (Oxford University Press, Oxford, 1980), pp. 73–94; Mrs George de Horne Vaizey, *A Houseful of Girls* (RTS, London, 1902), p. 14; p. 217; M.S. Comrie, *Her Next Door Neighbour* (Shaw, London, 1900), p. 28; p. 31; p. 129.

Evelyn Everett Green who applaud the bravery and dedication of such women, also warn of the hardships and the need to have a resilient brand of faith. When Gypsy undergoes a period of religious doubt, for instance, she believes that until it is overcome she will have to abandon her plan because it would be worse than useless to go out to minister to her Hindu sisters without a secure faith.[64]

Plainly, this imperial philanthropy was, in practice, a channel through which good girls were enabled legitimately to expand their sphere of activity. Another, more secular, fictional factor also appeared at this time which presented a less lofty but equally adventurous role model for English girls. For the first time, books were appearing in significant numbers that were actually set entirely in the colonies, written by authors like Ethel Turner who were themselves colonials, thus guaranteeing unquestionable accuracy of background as well as message. Inevitably, perhaps, there was an initial reserve on the part of English authors with respect to the feminine qualities of the girls depicted by such authors. Emily Brodie, for instance, referred to the unfavourable impact made on those arbiters of feminine quality, the recent emigrants, by colonial women. They lacked 'the retiring manners we Englishmen like to see'; while not requiring 'dolls' emigrants did not approve of women who needed 'no support' from men.[65]

Despite such reservations on the part of conventional adult society in England, the books written by colonial women depicting a more self-sufficient stereotype became so popular with girls seeking more variety in their reading that a number of English writers, most notably Bessie Marchant, began to fill this market need by writing their own versions of the colonial adventure story for girls. Though not colonial themselves, their work was based partly on personal travel and partly on very careful research.[66] Their stories were intended to demonstrate

---

[64] Charlotte M. Yonge, *The Daisy Chain*, pp. 459–62; p. 548; p. 557; Evelyn Everett Green, *Half-A-Dozen Sisters*; Florence Witts, *In the Days of His Power: A Story of Christian Endeavour* (Sunday School Union, London, 1902).

[65] Emily Brodie, *Jean Lindsay*, pp. 103–4.

[66] Bessie Marchant and similar writers relied heavily on travel books for facts, which is one reason why so many of their descriptions of scenery read so lyrically, and why they so often put in population figures, etc!

that in places like Australia it was possible for girls to live a far more active life, but that this was most happily to be achieved without sacrificing their essential femininity or their national character, and without moving too far into the public, male sphere.

In fiction, these girls helped to create a society that was recognizably English in format and values. The areas of white English settlement were becoming more civilized, in English terms, by those men and women who had made it their mission to go out and tame the wilderness. Towns and cities were growing, taking a generally British pattern if not name: communications and resources were improving, and there was the additional attractiveness of such communities being less 'stiff and shut in' than in England, particularly urban England. Above all, women frequently seemed to have lifestyles which permitted a more active participation in a variety of ways. The colonial fictional female farmer is one instance: never afraid to seek male help and advice, but equally competent to run a successful agricultural enterprise requiring an input of hard physical labour. Juanita Kennard in Bessie Marchant's *No Ordinary Girl* runs a large estate in the wilds of Panama almost totally unaided.[67]

Professionalism remained the keynote as colonial girls demonstrated the way to develop a lady-like capacity for business and practical management under even adverse circumstances in books such as *Three Girls on a Ranch*. Faced with ruin unless she does something practical, Clementina researches the type of crops that will grow easily and will also sell for a good price, she organizes the planting of an alfalfa crop. The invalid father tells her that: 'if we ever make the ranch pay, Clem, [and they do] it will be owing more to your enterprise than mine, for I am beginning to find out that farmers, like other geniuses, are born, not made'. Yet Clem is essentially the good girl of the *Home Goddess* type, a genius with a duster as well as an alfalfa crop, and is thus a good marriage prospect for a canny male pioneer. It can be fairly argued that this parallels the more independent version of the good girl found in books with an English background from the 1880s and it is true, in so far as English and colonial good girls both display a sound manage-

[67] Bessie Marchant, *No Ordinary Girl* (Blackie, Glasgow, 1905).

rial capacity. The difference is that women like Floy Rivers in Evelyn Everett Green's *Bruce Heriot* merely oversee the work done by their employees. Clementina goes out and indulges in physical hard work alongside her male Mexican ranch hands, and, with nationality able to overcome gender, doing her work better all round and yet remaining an unmistakable English lady.[68]

Other tales with colonial settings like *A Brave Little Cousin* pioneered a fictional ability to 'make the best of it' through inventive ingenuity and resource in the face of limited incomes and considerable odds without losing either caste or gender status. Ursula Giffard displayed her mettle in tasks as diverse as darning her male cousins' socks to saving the sheep from a flood when her cousins were absent thus earning the tribute of 'a downright plucky' lady.[69] Her reward is marriage to the best of the cousins, Ralph, to whom she has been a constant inspiration.

One aspect of this which had particular importance for girls in England wanting work was that the colonial experience revealed good girls performing menial manual tasks in a professional and competent manner, and doing so without either losing caste or marking themselves as apart from the usages of everyday society by becoming missionaries, for instance. These heroines are all unquestionably ladies. That the class system was alive and well in all the colonies was firmly emphasized by such novels. In *Family at Misrule*, her sequel to *Seven Little Australians*, Ethel Turner's fictional family suffers greatly when one of the brothers falls in love with a local butcher's daughter, who is automatically considered as being as lacking in refinement as any vulgar English tradesman's daughter could be. Equally, the reaction of a colonial cousin to suggestions of colonial equality in one of E.L. Haverfield's tales is 'What rot ... I don't know how you could believe it. Our friends were all gentlemen and ladies. Australians are as particular as you are whom they have for friends'.[70]

[68] Evelyn Everett Green, *The Jilting of Bruce Heriot* (RTS, London, 1904), pp. 27–8; Bessie Marchant, *Three Girls on a Ranch*, p. 236.

[69] Bessie Marchant, *A Brave Little Cousin* (Society for Promoting Christian Knowledge, London, 1902).

[70] Ethel S. Turner, *The Family at Misrule* (Ward Lock and Bowden, London, 1895), p. 30; E.L. Haverfield, *Queensland Cousins*, p. 179.

Of course, the publication of such stories was initially more an attempt to fill a gap in the market for the female adolescent reader which had resulted from the popularity amongst both sexes of the contemporary Henty-esque adventure in the fiction presented for boys' delight and edification. However the efforts to emphasize that the girls involved in such adventure remained ladies and that they never lost their sense of feminine fitness even while demonstrating a capacity for coping with a situation that turned them into heroines had important implications for the domestic arena. It was axiomatic in these books that these energetic, competent young ladies were English in nature, dealing with crises and native races with all the aplomb of their male counterparts. Therefore, why was it so unreasonable for the restricted middle-class girl living in England to dream of a life that would provide more opportunity to exercise her talents without moving down the social scale so long as she was still prepared, as the colonial girls apparently were, to act as the centre of a domestic circle and sustainer of menfolk?

Books like this began to make an impact on the female adolescent reading market at a time when life for many young women in England was changing. There was a growing band of middle-class women workers, for instance. The sturdier womanly stereotype in English fiction had become well-established, and the capable colonial girl thus formed an elaboration on a theme, and one that was particularly attractive to girls looking for more excitement in their reading, as well as their lives. As a result, the story that relied on teaching a narrow feminine message solely within a limited domestic setting had a good chance of looking outdated and irrelevant. In order to produce books, therefore, with a social and moral message that would still be read, it was necessary to reflect in fiction the wider opportunities open to women by the turn of the century. There are few popular books published for this middle-class feminine market with an English setting after that date which do not show their girls from everyday life displaying a wider competence and independence in areas outside the home.

Thus the need to inform an adolescent girls' readership about the Empire and the role it should play in their lives provided yet another channel through which women were able to modify and expand their limited role as *Household Angels*. It was often essential in depicting a realistic colonial setting to develop to their logical conclusion the feminine attributes which were emphasized so strongly in the ideal of the *Home Goddess*: such as the woman's ability, founded on moral purity, to detect a bad character, or the woman's adaptability and professionalism in organizing her domestic circle. To women was accorded the pivotal role in determining membership of the various strata of society. In a colonial situation, quite simply, the controls that existed in a more regulated English situation were not possible. In addition, it was, in practical terms, impossible to condemn as unfeminine the women who played increasingly active parts in helping to sustain the British Empire without condemning the Empire itself – which was, of course, unthinkable.

It was impossible to ignore the Empire in tales for girls. It was too much a part of daily life, and ideologically too important, to be played down. The themes of professionalism and appeals to feminine emotions were, of course, used to try to ensure that good girls were trained to take a proper attitude towards the demands that the Empire increasingly made on them. The complex nature of that Empire demanded consideration of a wide variety of scenarios, including reactions to native races and long-term separations of family members. However, the aspect that increasingly dominated was the growing need for a greater degree of feminine self-sufficiency as a result of Empire, especially overseas. The major concern then became to ensure that women did not become too independent and desert their traditional role without denigrating the imperial daughters of England.

Established middle-class opinion in England was forced to make concessions towards recognizing as socially acceptable new talents and powers in women, so often first tried in a colonial setting. This resulted in new codes of behaviour in England itself that permitted girls and women a freer scope to find self-fulfilment within their womanly sphere. The physically sturdier womanly stereotype of the post-1880 era matched that bodily vigour with a mental resilience and capability that could be shown not to undermine the basic *mores* of earlier conventional thinking in England. In the didactic fiction designed for young women, therefore, the British Empire

220 Imperial Responsibilities and England's Daughters

undoubtedly required conformity from young women to many middle-class beliefs. But it also acted as a medium through which women could discover more about themselves and the ways in which they could serve their country – if in ways that the established society of that country had not always predicted. By the end of the century, it was possible for middle-class girls to find outlets even within England that would have been socially inconceivable in 1840, as will be discussed in the next chapter.

6
Vocations and Fit Work for Ladies

Do the work that's nearest,
Though its dull at whiles,[1]

The work that was obviously nearest, and thus most conventionally desirable, for the stereotypical *Household Fairy* was and remained that associated with running her home and her family. As was said in chapter 1, the domestic associations of the feminine stereotype implied that being a woman should be a career in its own right. Yet from the start there were a significant number of women who could not, let alone those who would not, occupy their waking hours in this fashion. In the didactic fiction of the era up to the 1870s, single women only had a fully acceptable role within middle-class society when they could, in some way, operate as a substitute for or deputy to the career function of wife and mother. Ideally, unmarried daughters or sisters aided their mothers more and more as the latter grew less capable, or housekept for bachelor brothers in order to bring the comfort of a feminine touch to their lives.

Such an ideal, however, did not cover a large number of contingencies. It ignored the plight of single girls without finance or a family to turn to and with no immediate prospect, for whatever reason, of marriage. It overlooked the problem of families without the financial resources to support unmarried girls within the household. It took no account of those girls who, with or without financial pressure, increasingly actually desired to find a useful role for themselves outside the domestic circle. As Helen Brooke in *The Mountain Path* commented,

[1] C. Kingsley, 'The Invitation', *The Poems* (Dent, London, 1927).

'Even supposing it were the right thing ... that every woman should be maintained by some man ... there are not men enough. There are far too many of us [women]'.[2]

It is tempting to the modern observer to place most emphasis on the feminine desire to find a useful career outside the home, but it is a more accurate assessment of the reality to say that a combination of all three factors, particularly the two latter, forced a reassessment of the limits of the feminine stereotypes by the end of the century. The Victorian middle classes disapproved of waste and idleness, and it was becoming plain that it was not possible to cater for the large numbers of surplus, unmarried women within a dependent domestic role without a considerable amount of both. There was thus a growing consciousness that it was necessary to provide additional and useful outlets for feminine energies, which meant that the period between 1860 and 1905 saw an increasing acceptance by society of the existence of women with an amount of independence in their lives and activities, an acceptance that quickened in pace during the last decades of the nineteenth century.

Definitions of the kinds of work that women were capable of performing while retaining their essential womanliness developed throughout the last half of that century, but the restraining factor remained the constant perceived need for a division of spheres of competence between the sexes, and for women to shoulder the burdens of sustaining the domestic sphere before anything else. Questions of feminine competence were thus deeply affected by presumptions about the need for women to continue to be dependent to some extent and the beneficial personal effects of feminine self-sacrifice. While the need of some women to exert themselves to earn a living were admitted, it was seen as important to remind those undriven by such a financial need that the outside world was all too often harsh and unwelcoming to the toiler. It was a case of 'You ladies are sheltered, in your homes, from a lot of awfully hard knocks that fall to our share'.[3]

Nor was tradition the only factor behind such masculine-inspired attempts to limit the scope of feminine ambition.

[2] Lily Watson, *The Mountain Path* (RTS, London, 1888), p. 33.
[3] Ellen Louisa Davis, *Asceline's Ladder* (RTS, London, 1892), p. 21.

Rising male unemployment by the end of the century in both urban and rural areas enabled conventional wisdom to point out to women seeking 'absolute emancipation from the house of bondage' that there was not 'enough remunerative work in the world to employ everybody'. If ladies with 'husbands, fathers or brothers, willing to provide' for them insisted 'on turning bread-winners' for themselves, it would not only 're-verse the old order of things', but also since women were usually worth, and thus paid, smaller wages for their contribu-tions, they would selfishly help to throw men out of work, with the consequent effect on the families. So far from helping the cause of womankind, they would in real terms, retard it.[4] The constancy of this theme in didactic fiction indicates the central-ity of the concern on these two counts – that of possible feminine revolution, and that of genuine worry about the levels of unemployment amongst the existing workforce.

Despite the existence of significant numbers of women in need of salaries, in the years up to the 1860s few opportunities for paid employment were open to women, as has been noted by most commentators on women in this field.[5] The essence was that respectable employment had, in some way, to mirror the normal dependent state of women, and competence to do the job was essentially based on supposition of an innate feminine talent moulded by training received during childhood in the home in the various aspects of being a good woman. Thus governessing dominated the market, followed by acting as a companion. For those denied these outlets, the only other possible outlets in the eyes of most were being a seamstress or acting, usually for relatives or family friends, as a paid house-keeper. In all of these occupations, women were enabled to act still within their 'natural', essentially private domestic sphere, and thus retained their title to respectability and womanliness, even if they were no longer considered as forming an active part of the social circle.

Essentially, in this early period, a woman who was forced, or who desired, to earn her own living was considered to have

[4] Ibid., pp. 21–2.
[5] Martha Vicinus, *Independent Women: Work and Community for Single Women 1850–1920* (Virago Press, London, 1985); F.K. Prochaska, *Women and Philan-thropy in Nineteenth-Century England* (Oxford University Press, Oxford, 1980).

opted out of normal social usages.[6] Though they may have retained a claim to respectability, the status of such women was equivocal in the extreme and fraught with considerable practical difficulties. For instance, in the majority of cases the employed woman yielded up her right to be considered part of the social circle, to be eligible for marriage and motherhood. Thus they had to cease to expect to call and be called on, except as a matter of kindness by old friends or charitably inclined matriarchs and their daughters, or to receive invitations to entertainments of various kinds. Since they were not in a position to entertain on their own account, a single life of employment could be a frighteningly lonely prospect for a woman. These social rules were one factor behind the insistence that the only respectable jobs for single unemployed women regardless of age were those centred around the domestic sphere: it would at least permit some degree of social contact and prevent total isolation at the same time as providing a useful service for the more successful members of the feminine sex.

The fiction written by authors such as Charlotte Yonge and Elizabeth Sewell is clearly ambivalent about the role of employed women in middle-class society. It was, after all, necessary for some women to act as paid governesses, companions or seamstresses and there was, if unseen, some divine purpose behind the apparently arbitrary events which resulted in some single women being forced to look outside the shelter of their family circle to support themselves. As Emma Marshall commented, the reasons would be 'revealed by God' in due course, and in the meantime it should be seen as kindly 'divine discipline'.[7] That said, the dignity of such women needed to be supported since they did work that was commonly agreed to be essentially womanly. If ladies before they went into employment, the authors of didactic fiction were all unanimous in agreeing that they remained ladies. As Mrs Herbert and the governess Miss Morton in Elizabeth Sewell's *Amy Herbert*

[6] Elizabeth M. Sewell, *Principles of Education, Drawn from Nature and Revelation, and Applied to Female Education in the Upper Classes*, 2 vols (Longman, London, 1886), II, pp. 238–40.

[7] Mrs Emma Marshall, *Violet Douglas, or The Problems of Life* (Seeley, London, 1868), p. 22.

agreed, there was not 'anything vulgar in itself, but only when it is not befitting the rank and station of the person concerned'. So the argument was that to perform womanly duties for pay was not in itself demeaning, unless there was either no need for such a gesture or the person involved was not truly 'ladylike', in which case the job would be performed in an unsuitable manner.[8]

Didactic fiction also emphasizes the agreement felt that considerable spiritual fortitude was needed to bolster the spirits of the single middle-class woman forced to find work, especially when, as was so often the case, her employment involved residence at her place of work. She was required to work long and hard hours for her wage, but unlike her male counterparts or women of the working classes, she was debarred from seeking relaxation in her spare time on her own account in either a home atmosphere dedicated to providing comfort for a breadwinner, or in a place of public entertainment. The woman employed on a daily basis might be lucky enough to have a home to return to, and companionship there. Certainly she had some freedom to make friends amongst those of her own sex in a similar position. The best the resident woman could hope for was the friendship and forbearance of her employers in thinking of her outside the hours of work and catering for her in some way. For both categories, however, the path of the wage-earning woman was likely to be anxious and lonely, and a good woman in that position as Emma Marshall commented in *Violet Douglas* had to seek a hard-won contentment based on the principles of self-sacrifice and Christianity.[9]

Contentment could also be less easy to find for reasons apart from the conditions of employment, difficult though those might be, as fiction was also at pains to point out. Many women forced to earn a living during this initial period were also forced to take up work they were neither suited to nor found congenial. Women like Miss Gorman in *Frances Leslie* became governesses without any training let alone liking for the work and though 'faithful, painstaking' performers of their duty found their 'temper had been fretted' and their 'health impaired' by their distasteful and demanding work. As Evelyn

[8] Elizabeth M. Sewell, *Amy Herbert*, 2 vols (Longman, London, 1844), p. 40.
[9] Mrs Emma Marshall, *Violet Douglas*, p. 281.

Everett Green commented later 'a steady control over their won tempers. ... Very great patience and self-possession' were necessary in the governess, and all this was to be provided for small wages and frequently, scant consideration.[10]

Attempts were made to improve the lot of governesses through foundations such as the Governesses' Benevolent Institution and Queen's College, the first, London-based, organizations whose aim was to give a professional gloss to this type of work. As the century advanced more and more girls received some form of training before taking up a career governessing, thus increasing their value in their own eyes and that of their employers. The contrast between Miss Winter and Miss Bracy in *The Daisy Chain* is based on the fact that the latter has 'been qualifying herself for a governess' before taking up her position. Training was seen as important because of the consequent professionalism that it conferred, with all the consequent increase in status that entailed. The May sisters treat Miss Bracy with much greater respect and kindness than Miss Winter and do their utmost to make her 'feel at home – and like a friend – in her new position'.[11] Yet while professionalization of this sphere undoubtedly began to help the status of newcomers to the profession and those with the talent and resources to take advantage of training, the outlook remained far less inviting for the ill-qualified, unenthusiastic 'amateur' governess, forced by circumstances alone into this sphere.

Being a companion remained a chancy thing without even the small status accorded to the governess. There was no question of special training for that, and as fiction emphasized, large numbers of those who became companions to those who were not relatives did so because of lack of education or because they were so bad at being a governess they could not find jobs in that field. The governess at least had the schoolroom as her domain; the companion was unlikely to have any area in which she reigned supreme. Instead she was at the beck and call of a possibly capricious and probably exacting employer for a limitless variety of tasks not entrusted to the

[10] Miss E. Bickersteth, *Frances Leslie, or The Prayer Divinely Taught* (RTS, London, 1867), p. 83; Evelyn Everett Green, *Barbara's Brothers* (RTS, London, 1888), pp. 164–5.
[11] Charlotte M. Yonge, *The Daisy Chain* (Macmillan, London, 1856), p. 308.

servants, from reading aloud to washing fine linen, like Helen Brooke in *The Mountain Path*. With a need to support herself and no inclination to teach children, being a companion seems to her the only practical course, but for all her hopeful confidence, she soon finds it a difficult task, with the need to be constantly cheerful yet socially retiring, while being both competent and willing to undertake any task passed on to her. As a later companion, dignified by the name but not the status of 'secretary' finds, her job means that she has to 'mend her [employer's] stockings, and brush her dresses, and clean out her bird-cages, and exercise the dogs, as well as manage her accounts and write all her letters'.[12]

Equally there was little to be said for being a seamstress apart from its unquestionable fitness for feminine hands. It was poorly paid drudgery for the most part. Sometimes the seamstress found her employment entailed constant change of residence at houses where her services were required. In such houses she was likely to be poorly housed and, once again, treated with little consideration by staff unless given a very clear lead by the mistress. If working mainly from her own home the constant drudgery required of her gave her little time to enjoy its amenities. Faced with the realities of family ruin and a sick mother, Mabel Hampden in *Violet Douglas* does her best to add to the meagre family income by utilizing her talent with her needle. Emma Marshall lays indignant stress on the problems of such employment. Mabel, a 'graceful, ladylike girl', belongs to an Association through which reduced gentlewomen could sell their work without the shame of having to go out and seek orders. But the lady patrons of the Association are often guilty of a 'carelessness and thoughtless want of consideration' towards workers of such ambiguous status. All too often their attitude is tainted with charity rather than a businesslike attitude leading to prompt payment. The reality of this was a major drawback to reliance on stitchery as the sole source of income. At the same time, however, the existence of such Associations and bodies like the Royal School of Art Needlework, all founded to help indigent ladies sell their work gave a

[12] Lily Watson, *The Mountain Path*, p. 29; pp. 109–10. Raymond Jacberns, *Four Every-Day Girls* (Society for Promoting Christian Knowledge, London, 1903), pp. 41–2.

faint gloss of professionalism as well as gentility, and at least some protection from the complete exposure to exploitation which was the danger of being a companion.[13]

Yet so long as society insisted that women could only respectably perform work with a perceived direct link to the domestic duties normally assigned to the feminine sphere, there could be little practical remedy for such problems. The authors of didactic fiction acknowledged it, but could put forward no solution to it at this time. Their attitude was to appeal to the Christian compassion of readers and plead, like Charlotte Yonge in *The Daisy Chain* or Emma Marshall in *Violet Douglas*, for girls to treat the employed women they came across with kindness and forbearance where necessary, in case they themselves ever came to such a plight. Hints were also given to the unfortunates obliged to earn a wage on how to comport themselves and on the need for the common feminine experience of self-sacrifice. Charlotte Yonge's Miss Bracy is told by Ethel May that 'teaching takes a great deal out of one; and loneliness may cause tendencies to dwell on fancied slights in trifles. . . . But I think the thing is, to pass them over, and make a conscience to turning one's mind to something fresh'. The former then meekly agrees that 'referring all to one's own feelings and self is the way to be unhappy.[14]

The other consolatory attitude put forward by the didactic genre was the rather less realistic hope that being a governess or companion could, if fortune was kind, provide a good girl willing to make the best of her life with an alternative home which could even last a lifetime. It is made plain that neither Miss Morton in *Amy Herbert* nor Alison Williams in Charlotte Yonge's *The Clever Woman of the Family* will ever be forced to seek either fresh situations or fresh homes during the lifetimes of their employers and pupils. Lady Temple tells the latter that if she will only consent, Myrtlewood will be 'her home – her home always', a home she has earned by her thorough efforts.[15] Under such circumstances, the governess/companion became

[13] Mrs Emma Marshall, *Violet Douglas*, pp. 37–40; p. 60; pp. 91–3.

[14] Mrs Emma Marshall, *Violet Douglas*, p. 60; Charlotte M. Yonge, *The Daisy Chain*, pp. 551–2.

[15] Ibid., Charlotte M. Yonge, *The Clever Woman of the Family* (Virago Press, London, 1983), 1st edn (1865), p. 353.

almost sunk in the adopted daughter, a return to the domestic ideal and the best possible solution to the factors that drove a woman to seek employment.

Status was at the core of the problem, as M. Jeanne Peterson's essay on the subject of governesses in Martha Vicinus' *Suffer and Be Still* reveals so graphically. Social status depended on conformity to the stereotypes presented as traditions, particularly in the case of women because they were the moral guardians of the race. A woman, therefore, placed herself in an ambiguous position that conventional opinion could not easily resolve while maintaining strict standards for feminine behaviour when she stepped outside the desired boundaries of dependency on men as either wife and mother or alternatively unmarried family blessing, whatever the reason. Ruskin poured scorn on the habits of society for entrusting the education of precious children to a woman chosen for her character and attainments but treated by servants with scant respect.[16] Yet at the same time, didactic fiction could not ignore the feeling that, involuntarily or not, such a woman had, by conventional standards, failed and thus deserved less consideration. As Martha Vicinus has commented, 'Single women in fiction were not permitted to be single and happy outside a carefully defined set of family duties' – or at least not in the period up to the 1870s.[17] It required a change in attitude towards the capabilities of the feminine sex as a whole, based on an acceptance of greater feminine independence, to begin a change towards the ambiguous role of the wage-earning and thus independent middle-class woman, and for this to be reflected by fictional depictions of happy and contented working spinsters in the later stories.

Such a change is discernible in fiction from the mid-1870s, becoming firmly established during the 1880s, tending to indicate that the 1870s was the decade of change. What caused the change was not so much a sudden upsurge of surplus women in need of work at a time of economic difficulty as a

[16] M. Jeanne Petersen, 'The Victorian Governess: Status Incongruence in Family and Society', in Martha Vicinus (ed.), *Suffer and Be Still: Women in the Victorian Age* (Methuen, London, 1977), pp. 3–20.

[17] Martha Vicinus, *Independent Women, Work and Community for Single Women 1850–1920* (Virago Press, London, 1985), p. 11.

development in attitudes towards the feminine stereotype. Regardless of necessity, women were seen as being much more able to look after their own affairs and this had a widening effect on conventional opinion and its resistance to female enterprise. Though didactic fiction does not put forward many of the pioneering independent women of the 1850s and 1860s, like Frances Power Cobbe or Anna Jameson, as new role models for women, the impact of their ideas are increasingly plain in the writing of authors like L.T. Meade, Evelyn Everett Green or Mrs Molesworth.[18] Home remained the prime duty, but it was no longer the scene of the only acceptable career for women.

Much stress was laid by these later authors on developments like the Married Women's Property Acts of 1870 and 1882. Evelyn Everett Green reminded her readers how 'fortunate' they were to live in times which acknowledged the right of married women to own property.[19] Even the more limited 1870 Act was seen as having value in its effect on significant numbers of middle-class women who were given some rights in the conduct of their own affairs. The new state of affairs permitted those girls who had attained the age of legal majority to exercise control where appropriate over property, inherited and earned, without in any way harming their essential femininity.[20] Earlier heroines like Rachel Curtis in Charlotte Yonge's *The Clever Woman of the Family* had not seemed to feel specifically disadvantaged by their lack of legal status. Instead, they displayed an unbusinesslike foolishness in their attempts to organize large-scale schemes for the good of others. Rachel attempts to set up a training school for lacemakers on land she has at her disposal, but she cannot recognize that the man who

[18] P. Levine, *Victorian Feminism 1850–1900* (Hutchinson, London, 1987).

[19] 'The Married Women's Property Acts' by A Solicitor, *Girls Own Annual*, Oct. 1890–Sept. 1891, pp. 78–9; Lee Holcombe, 'Victorian Wives and Property: Reform of the Married Women's Property Law, 1857–1882', in Martha Vicinus (ed.), *A Widening Sphere: Changing Roles of Victorian Women* (Methuen, London, 1980), pp. 3–28. The new divorce laws also altered the legal status of women, but the social disapproval of divorce ensured it was largely ignored in didactic fiction, and was certainly not mentioned as a benefit!

[20] See, for instance, Evelyn Everett Green, *The Heiress of Wylmington* (Nelson, Walton-on-Thames, 1886).

offers to help her with the scheme is a villain because she does not understand the conduct of affairs. She does not even realize that she does not have possession of anything other than the copy of the title-deeds of the land of which she thinks she has let her family be defrauded.[21]

Yet the emphasis placed by the later writers on the importance of the Property Acts and their benefits for women indicate that a new generation of women had not shared the complacency of their predecessors about their anomalous status any more than they had been content to accept a more dependent stereotype for other areas of their lives. The unbusiness-like behaviour of the Charlotte Yonge type of heroines was replaced by an acknowledgement that feminine good sense and judgement could spread beyond the organization of her household accounts. Gwendolyn Maltby, Evelyn Everret Green's *Heiress of Wylmington*, refuses to give over to her first would-be husband 'the joint management' of both their properties, reserving to herself the right to judge what should be done with her inheritance, and is shown to have acted in a correct and thoroughly womanly fashion in declining to yield up her powers of decision over matters for which she has a responsibility. She is 'not fond of limited means' but understands that there are worse things, that 'wealth can do sadly little to ease an aching heart'. When coal is discovered on her estate, she decides to 'keep the land' instead of selling it and to take the trouble to open 'a great field of usefulness' with her second, worthy fiancé in looking after the people who will work in the mines.[22]

This new acknowledgement, enshrined in the law of the land, of a business capacity among women was also a considerable help in gaining acceptance of the idea that a significant body of women in England could have a vocation that would take them outside the home and permit them to find happiness in it. There was a considerable expansion in the range of occupations open to the unmarried womanly woman which could be included under such a heading, partly fuelled as has already been mentioned in the previous chapter, by the range

[21] Charlotte M. Yonge, *The Clever Woman of the Family*, pp. 284–5.
[22] Evelyn Everett Green, *The Heiress of Wylmington*, pp. 239–40; p. 417; pp. 459–61.

of occupations and tasks undertaken by Englishwomen in the colonies.[23] Yet fundamental assumptions about the feminine nature remained constant. It was still presumed that women were the emotional sex, even if it was agreed that they could channel these emotions in a way that was increasingly useful to the wider community. Thus all the role models and all the careers presented to girlish readers as being acceptable for them were based on the principle of helping others at cost to oneself. Careers outside the home were presented to good girls in the light of a vocation – an overwhelming divine calling backed up by a God-given talent in such a field, which justified the dedication of a lifetime's efforts to something outside the ideals of wedlock and maternity. To be convincing in this light, such careers for girls needed to concentrate on areas which could conform to such a stereotype. It was not just advances in medicine and a consequent demand for trained nursing staff that led to such widespread eventual approval of nursing as a vocation for girls, but also the potential for long-term denial and dedication within the field.

In addition, the class constraints of the time meant that it was impossible to describe as both womanly and ladylike areas of middle-class female employment that did not in some way approximate to the types of work that were considered suitable for middle-class and upper-class males. Yet at the same time, there was no wish to destabilize employment patterns by introducing female labour into important male professions. The flood of cheap women clerks, many belonging to the lower echelons of the middle classes, into the lower Post Office grades from the mid-1870s was adequate warning of the possible results of open competition between the sexes in areas where employers were keen to cut costs. The Post Office was happy, because women clerks enabled them to get employees who were better educated and of higher social status than most of the men willing to take such positions, and all for less money. At the same time, the entry of women into that field meant that fewer men were willing to take posts at a similar level: equal employment opportunities for both sexes in a job was seen as fundamentally reducing the professional status of that job and

[23] See ch. 5, pp. 217–19.

effectively, over a period of time, closing off to men an avenue of employment.[24] Thus increasing middle-class female employment was likely to have a major effect on the job market as well as on the social fabric, and thus the overall stability, of the nation. Neither male employers nor employees could be happy at the prospect. The compromise reached was to continue the idea of separate spheres, via the creation of new professions, such as nursing, which were to all intents and purposes, exclusively feminine in personnel and relationship to the 'traditional' womanly duties.

A reflection of this advance can be seen in the way that from the 1880s, didactic fiction began to add another important element to its guidebook aspect: that of careers adviser. For the first time role models appear in significant numbers who are not destined either for marriage or for a cheerfully resigned spinsterhood spent in helping the family ideal in some way. The tale of the single woman with a vocation that took her into professional work outside the home circle could now have a happy ending, if not the traditional one of marriage and motherhood. Thus using fiction of this genre, it is possible to gain indications of the relative importance and respectability of the variety of new professions that opened to women from the 1880s.

The impact made on fiction from the 1880s of nursing as a female vocation gives an indication both of its acquired importance in the eyes of conventional society and of the new status of the working middle-class spinster. Despite the efforts of Florence Nightingale in the 1850s, and the undoubted veneration given to her for her efforts, nursing did not appear as a widely acceptable outlet for the energies and talents of fictional young women until the end of the 1870s and the appearance of a new generation of writers, who reflected a wider sympathy for a more independent stereotype of womanly ideals. From that time on, nursing was portrayed as a real alternative career to marriage for girls. Its fictional depiction makes it plain that by the 1880s, nursing was established as the acceptable Protestant equivalent to taking vows for a good girl with either no wish or no prospect of marriage (there was considerable doubt about

24 P. Levine, *Victorian Feminism*, p. 44.

the existence of Anglican sisterhoods in such cases in the genre).[25] Becoming a nurse was seen as a lifetime choice, a matter of self-effacing self-dedication, not something that could fill in a few years before marriage.

Readers were thus warned that nursing was not a thing to be entered into lightly or for reasons of personal gratification – and it was known that authors like Evelyn Everett Green were speaking from experience.[26] Juliet Granby in the latter's *Barbara's Brothers* wishes that a European war 'might break out soon', because then she 'would go directly . . . to nurse the sick and wounded . . . like Florence Nightingale'. She believes she would 'learn directly [she] got there. 'One can do almost anything under the pressure of necessity and excitement'. She is firmly told, however, to forget her fantasies of being a second Crimean Angel, because: 'Those can do a great deal who know what should be done and how to do it . . . But the battle-field is not generally considered the place to learn the rudiments of nursing, nor do they fill the ambulances with untrained and enthusiastic girls.' Reiterating her wish to receive training, however, Juliet is warned that training is arduous and monotonous – 'The hours are long, early rising and punctuality are essential, as well as prompt obedience and strict attention to orders', to say nothing of the prospect of horrible sights.[27] Only a thoroughly disciplined good girl could cope with its demands successfully, and sadly, Juliet does not fall into that category. She did not expect to find things 'easy or pleasant', but she did expect to shine by acting on her own responsibility and thus to be placed on some kind of pedestal, instead of retiring into the background and letting her work speak for her, if necessary after her departure from a case. Inevitably her foolish desire for personal glory and praise in this sphere leads to a breakdown in health, and an ignominious return to home duties.[28]

Didactic fiction also reveals the mechanisms by which nursing arrived at its acceptable status. It was a process based partly on

[25] See pp. 175–6.
[26] Evelyn Everett Green was herself a trained nurse, who turned to writing under the impulsion of the message she wished to convey and the breakdown of her health.
[27] Evelyn Everett Green, *Barbara's Brothers*, pp. 166–9.
[28] Ibid., pp. 204–6; p. 292.

PLATE 9   '"GAVON," SHE SAID, "GAVON, I AM HERE! I HAVE COME"'

Vocations outside the home: a role model. From *A Sister of the Red Cross: A Tale of the South African War* by L.T. Meade (1901)

the belief that good women of all ranks had an instinctive talent for nursing. Indeed a wish to care for the sick and suffering within the domestic circle was considered an indispensable element in the womanly stereotype. From Ellen Montgomery's efforts as a child to care for her mother in *The Wide, Wide World* to the angelic demeanour in caring for the sick poet of L.T. Meade's Bel-Marjory, nursing was considered part of the gender attributes of the gentler sex.[29] The scientific advances and discoveries of the nineteenth century that raised the status of medicine generally also enabled the elevating of a previously essentially domestic pastime into a full-scale profession that was seen as eminently suited to the field of female endeavour. Nurses could remain essentially anonymous and private in their professional capacity, with their uniforms conveying both their femininity and their modesty. Nurse Anna in Emma Marshall's *Laurel Crowns* appears as 'the very picture of a nurse, with her pretty white apron with wide pockets and a close-fitting blue serge gown', to say nothing of an all-encompassing 'white cap'. Like all good nurses she has a 'sweet and musical voice', and her main aim is to find patients 'to whom I hope by God's blessing to be useful'. No other hint of her physical appearance is ever given.[30]

In addition, a nursing career could satisfy the emotional nature of a girl where necessary. All her natural instincts for affection could be sublimated in care for suffering humanity, as L.T. Meade suggested: 'Nursing! that seems to be the profession for a lonely girl, who has no mother to love, and no particular future to look forward to'. It is no coincidence that so many fictional women orphaned or disappointed in love are shown as turning to nursing from the 1880s on. It was considered a particularly useful way of utilizing a grief which might otherwise be destructive or inconvenient to society. It ensured a life of activity instead of morbid self-pity, for instance, because it 'took you so much out of yourself, and put you in touch with others'. Orphaned and apparently deserted

[29] Elizabeth Wetherell, *The Wide, Wide World* (Bliss Sands & Co., London, 1896), 1st edn (1852); L.T. Meade, *Bel-Marjory: A Story of Conquest* (Shaw, London, 1878).

[30] Mrs Emma Marshall, *Laurel Crowns, or Griselda's Aim: A Story for Brothers and Sisters* (Nisbet, Welwyn, 1889), pp. 151–2.

by her fiancé, Evelyn Everett Green's Miss Lucas turns to nursing where 'I was busy and I was content, if I could not be happy', and where her talents saved useful lives for the nation. Described in such terms and with role models like Florence Nightingale and Dora Pattison, all generally depicted in a halo of lifelong self-sacrifice, it is easy to see how society came to view nursing with such approval, even though it involved so much that was unpleasant.[31]

Moreover class had also a role to play in the defining of nursing as a ladylike profession. A demand for ladies to become nurses, whether in a private or a hospital capacity, was justified by the belief that the inborn womanly nursing talent was maximized in the middle and upper classes because of the habit of 'self-command and gentleness and quickness that belongs, in a greater degree, to the upper than the lower classes'. This ensured that the lady nurse did her duties with 'a capacity that quickly made them of value wherever they went', whereas a 'rougher' girl might take a long time to pick up the necessary qualities to enable her to learn her duties, and indeed might never acquire the quickness of mind and gentle refinement of touch necessary for more delicate or responsible jobs. It is worth noting that these books never suggest that the core of any such discernible difference might lie in educational differences rather than nature. A woman of humbler origins displaying such qualities would be described as one of 'Nature's Ladies', as in the case of the second Mrs Joliffe in Agnes Giberne's *Kathleen*. Mrs Joliffe is 'not a lady by birth' but she has an 'inner refinement' which makes her a splendid nurse when her stepdaughter falls ill. As the doctor confirms, Kathleen survives 'Thanks, under God, to your nursing, Mrs. Joliffe'.[32]

Consequently, nurses were divided into nurses and lady nurses, with the latter naturally being destined for the ranks of prestige, authority and power in the profession and only

[31] L.T. Meade, *Engaged to be Married: A Tale of Today* (Simpkin, Marshall, Hamilton, Kent & Co., 1890), p. 93; Evelyn Everett Green, *Sister: A Chronicle of Fair Haven* (Nelson, Walton-on-Thames, 1898), p. 188; p. 195; Eliza F. Pollard, *Florence Nightingale, the Wounded Soldier's Friend* (Partridge, London, 1981), for example.

[32] Evelyn Everett Green, *Barbara's Brothers*, p. 206; Agnes Giberne, *Kathleen: The Story of a Home* (Nisbet, Welwyn, 1883), p. 278; pp. 311–12.

occasionally being joined by women whose ultimate competence was deemed handicapped by their lack of inborn refinement. Nurse Bradley in Evelyn Everett Green's *Sister* is 'not a
lady, it is true', but being 'a thoroughly sensible . . . woman' she
might be 'a splendid person . . . for the management of the
cottage hospital' where she would deal only with the working
classes.[33]

Detailed information about the preliminary qualifications
needed for being a nurse, the training and where it could be
obtained, and the likely openings once training was completed,
to say nothing of the potential for a living wage, were revealed
to readers in novels by a wide range of authors. Evelyn Everett
Green's personal experience led her to speak with considerable
authority and frequency, but L.T. Meade and Emma Marshall,
for instance, were not backward in providing information and
their opinions on the matter of how a girl and her family or
friends could assess her suitability for such a profession. All
authors insisted that not all who wanted to be nurses were fitted
for the life. Much depended on character, and 'some people
are not fit for nurses', like Nurse Anna's sister who 'had not the
patience for it', as truly kind friends informed her. It was
relatively easy for any true woman to nurse a loved one in home
surroundings, but the dreadful sights that nurses had to
endure and the 'whims and fancies' of convalescent patients
who had no claim on the nurse beyond that of common
humanity was portrayed as a major hurdle, only to be overcome
by a true sense of mission.[34]

Yet those who did have the character to become 'capable and
experienced' nurses found themselves 'practically provided for,
for life'. Thus for those in need of such a provision, who could
be considered to have a vocation, details could be found in
didactic fiction of how to go about entering the profession. L.T.
Meade gave a comprehensive list of training schools in London
suitable for a lady: 'There is St Thomas's and Charing Cross,
and Guy's and the London Hospital'. Readers are informed
that to enter it is necessary to be recommended by a friend, or
failing that 'You must go to the hospitals . . . and state your
object, and then you will see one of the sisters or nurses'. One

[33] Evelyn Everett Green, *Sister*, p. 166.
[34] Mrs Emma Marshall, *Laurel Crowns*, pp. 211–12.

problem for a lady and her family or friends was that, as all authors stressed, 'to earn a living as a nurse requires a large present expenditure'. The penniless and friendless young lady was thus unlikely to be able to train for such a vocation unless willing to degrade herself by exposing herself to training in a common hospital where no proper provision was made for ladies. Yet there is no suggestion that this state of affairs might lead to a waste of natural talent: was there not always God's guiding hand and consequently a good, if unclear, reason for depriving a girl of such a training? The underlying assumption in male professionalism that training had to involve expenditure if it was to be worthwhile was clearly extended to the feminine sphere.[35]

There were few other paid occupations open to women which carried with them the vocational halo and the womanly suitability of nursing during this period. Yet there were far more women seeking work than could, for whatever reason, enter that hallowed profession. However, teaching also made its mark as a profession in these later novels, which, though not exclusively female and not so dedicated, was particularly suited to feminine talents. The new respect given to women teachers provides a mark of the growing importance of girls' education by the 1880s, and of the alteration that had come over teaching as a career from the feminine perspective. The development of institutions like Hughes Hall at Cambridge for the purpose of training and giving recognized qualifications to women intending to make education of other people's children their life's work was a major factor in achieving this. Fiction began to speak of 'certificated lady teachers', referring to those who had followed a university honours course, though not, with the exception of London graduates, awarded an actual degree.[36] Another factor was provided by the growing number of private girls' schools, both day and boarding, which enabled ladies to exercise the scholastic profession on a larger scale, but still in a private capacity and still on pupils of a middle-class background. This had a two-fold effect. Firstly, it raised the status of lady schoolteachers by providing them with a clearly defined

[35] L.T. Meade, *Engaged to be Married*, pp. 78–9.
[36] See, for example, Raymond Jacberns, *Four Every-Day Girls*, p. 60. For instance, Hughes Hall was founded in 1885.

gender-based sphere that could accord with ideals of womanliness and a life of dedication to the good of others. Secondly, it gave even the role of private governess a boost.

The availability of educational qualifications guaranteed by a certificate of some kind meant that parents increasingly expected to employ women with proven 'professional standards' as their governesses. This meant that ill-qualified women found it increasingly difficult to find employment in English middle-class families, and were driven to find alternative employment if they could, or starve or become objects of charity if they could not. At the same time, more and more trained young women found it preferable, on economic and professional grounds, to teach in a school rather than hiring themselves out in a private capacity. Teaching in a reputable school gave them greater personal freedom as well as good pay, more regular time to themselves during vacations at least, and often, the opportunity for taking their studies further. More and more fictional teachers, such as Miss Everett in Mrs George de Horne Vaizey's *Tom and Some Other Girls*, were Girton, Newnham or Somerville girls, reflecting a real-life trend amongst schools catering for a middle- and upper-class clientele. Priscilla Peel in L.T. Meade's *A Sweet Girl Graduate* is at St Benets because her friends consider it an essential step in order to qualify her to earn her living and support her family. As the vicar says 'when it becomes a question of a woman earning her bread, let her turn to that path where promise lies', and in Priscilla's case her promise lies in her bookish tastes. It is believed Priscilla 'could do brilliantly as a teacher' and by the 1880s this meant that she needed 'the advantages which a collegiate life alone could offer to her'.[37] As mentioned in chapter 3, the governess who left a family to set up a school or join an existing one became a fictional truism during the 1880s.[38] This tended to give those willing to continue teaching in a private capacity an increasing rarity value, reflected in their conditions and remuneration.

It is worth noting, however, that learning as a profession in

[37] Mrs George de Horne Vaizey, *Tom and Some Other Girls: A Public School Story* (Cassell, London, 1901), p. 164; p. 195; L.T. Meade, *A Sweet Girl Graduate* (Cassell, London, 1891), p. 51; Alice Stronach, *A Newnham Friendship* (Blackie, Glasgow, 1901).

[38] See pp. 132–3.

itself was not considered a suitable profession for girls. Attendance at fictional counterparts of the Oxford or Cambridge colleges or London University was generally depicted as a way of qualifying a girl for a future dedicated to teaching, or giving a higher cultural gloss to the intelligent wealthy girl which would enhance her home charms. As the intellectually ambitious Griselda Carrington in Emma Marshall's *Laurel Crowns* needs to learn 'Self culture . . . is a bounden duty and service, when the aim is not merely the achievement of success for the sake of success'. Since 'knowledge is a gift, a power, entrusted to you for the benefit of others', higher education for women unless properly directed could easily become a temptation to selfishness.[39] This is one reason why relatively few didactic novels spend much time describing life at such institutions or eulogizing the independent academic communities there, such as Martha Vicinus describes in *Independent Women*. As Alice Stronach in *A Newnham Friendship* insisted college and degree examinations were valuable for the lessons they could teach about a wider life, and for the capacity for supportive friendship that, like school, it could develop. However, 'To be a useful woman . . . is the real aim of a higher education'.[40] Thus college life was, or should be, a passing and rather dreamlike, if enjoyable period in life, and study thereat was directed towards fitting female students for futures within the accepted, gender-separated spheres. The role models the reading public for this genre were reminded of, were all women who had dedicated themselves to a life of wider service, even if for their own sex. Names like Miss Buss and Miss Beale were well known, and known for their self-abnegation also.[41]

Two other areas which conferred professional status and a womanly glow on some good girls during this period were art and music. It came to be considered that, particularly since success and competence in both realms entailed a certain emotional input, it was both suitable and desirable that a

[39] Mrs Emma Marshall, *Laurel Crowns*, p. 264; Raymond Jacberns, *Four Every-Day Girls*, p. 117.

[40] Martha Vicinus, *Independent Women*, Alice Stronach, *A Newnham Friendship*; Mrs Emma Marshall, *Laurel Crowns*, p. 265.

[41] See, for instance, L.T. Meade, 'Girls' Schools of Today', *The Strand Magazine*, X, Jan.–June 1895, p. 283.

woman with decided (to say nothing of God-given) talent for one or other should be able respectably to earn a living through exercising her abilities in the field. Both these areas could be seen as eminently womanly in certain aspects. High standards required long and sustained dedication over a lifetime to reach and maintain recognized technical levels. Achievements in both fields could also fulfill the womanly requirement of inspiring others with a vision of a higher and purer life. At a less inspired level, both art and music could be used to ornament the home, something which was always the duty of a good woman. As Mary E. Gellie wrote in *Stephen the Schoolmaster*, 'The study of God's works in any way ought to be ennobling, and it is no mean work to add to the pleasure of other people's lives, and help them to see and understand more of the beauty of this world in which they live'. Such an exercise could be 'eminently religious' even though self-indulgent men too often made it 'quite the reverse'. This was where a self-sacrificing woman could do good, by bringing 'beautiful feeling', if not the absolute genius of men, to a work of art or a performance.[42]

The question of artistic genius was certainly assessed on relative gender grounds in an increasing number of didactic tales that dealt with feminine ambitions in the field of art. A woman's capacity for art was always presumed to be less than that of the greatest men, and it could only be maximized by a total dedication to the achievement. Edith Melville in *Stephen the Schoolmaster* is described as 'a born artist', having 'no common talent'. In her uncle's opinion 'it almost amounts to genius'. In addition, she is a younger sister and so less needed at home. It is thus her family's duty to 'do all we can to help her to develop her talent, and make the very most of it' as 'God so evidently intended that she should be – an artist'. Her mother is reassured by the thought that 'She is not likely to be led astray by vanities or frivolity – her talent will save her from that'. Her art mentor agrees that she seems to have the artistic vocation: 'If she will only keep free of matrimony she will make herself a name'. Marriage, however, would see her absorbed in other things and 'then good-bye to painting'. By the end of the novel

---

[42] Mary E. Gellie, *Stephen the School-master: A Story without a Plot* (Griffith & Farran, London, 1879), p. 62.

it is plain that God has given her 'the talent in which she could lose herself' as a compensation for her lack of matrimonial prospects. However it is plain that though she exhibits charming paintings of inspirational subjects such as a girl feeding doves, neither her dedication nor her ability will lift her to the realms of absolute genius.[43]

Edith Melville does not need to earn a living by her art, unlike Madge Charrington in *The Daughters of a Genius* by Mrs George de Horne Vaizey and the vast majority of fictional girls who look to art as a source of income. This genre of fiction was scrupulous in making it plain to readers that an ability to draw pleasingly was by no means equal to genius. Didactic fiction was careful again to warn of the problems and encourage the suitable by indicating methods of assessment and places of training like the Slade School and 'the Royal Female School of Art in Queen Square', or even a private studio with a reputable teacher.[44] Mrs George de Horne Vaizey's Charrington sisters are 'very poor, and must work for ourselves' but they are acknowledged by competent adult judges to have talents worth cultivating as a way of earning a living. On this basis they move to London and the sister with a talent for drawing goes to the Slade to acquire the necessary training to fit her for taking up art as a profession. Madge longs 'to create great subjects on great canvases' but instead her gift lies in the lesser realms of 'caricature and bright original design' and so 'her mission [is] to design pretty leaflets and comic pictures for the nursery'. It is a blow to her but Madge has 'the good sense to realize that it is better to excel in humble work than to struggle painfully after the unattainable' and she has the satisfaction of knowing that her work is appreciated for its professional execution. It had to be pointed out, however, that there were certain drawbacks to working as an artist. If was difficult for the professional female artist to retain the private element considered so important to standards of ladylike womanhood. Madge Charrington has to trudge around to shops and commercial studios to seek a

[43] Mary E. Gellie, *Stephen the School-master*, pp. 187–9; pp. 222–3; pp. 278–9; p. 310.

[44] Mrs George de Horne Vaizey, *The Daughters of a Genius: A Story of Brave Endeavour* (Chambers, Edinburgh, 1903), p. 27; L.T. Meade, *Engaged to be Married*, pp. 87–8.

market and must consult public taste rather than her own feelings in her products.[45]

Still, the artist was better off than the musician in this respect. It was only the fruits of her work and not her person that needed to be on public show. This meant that the artist could produce works of inspiration or decoration without exposing herself too much to the public gaze. The singer or player, no matter how innately modest, had to make a personal appearance. Again, the emotional nature of a good woman leant itself to inspirational performance. Mrs George de Horne Vaizey's Ralph Merrilies in *The Daughters of a Genius* comments of the singer-composer sister Hope Charrington that 'her mind is as lovely as her face. She could not have composed . . . she could not have sung . . . as she did – if she were not everything that is sweet and good.'[46] It is noticeable, however, that fictional performers who also qualify for the accolade of good women or girls, like Hope Charrington, usually have a considerable shrinking from the publicity that accompanies their work, and frequently try to restrict their appearances to semi-private occasions rather than full public concerts. However, they do overcome their shrinking in view of their consciousness of a divinely bestowed talent and a professional dedication.

Full public performance, though, is only permissible when financial exigency means that an essentially private talent, even if amounting to as near genius as a woman can attain, needs to be rewarded with money. The vocalist Hertha Norreys in Mrs Molesworth's *White Turrets* is 'an "artist" . . . of the modern school, retaining all the privileges that are hers by birth, except . . . that she is, or would be if she did nothing, very poor'. It is agreed that in addition Hertha Norreys has 'an undoubted gift' and that in her circumstances 'she was bound to cultivate it. . . . In her case there was no choice'. But as Hertha herself says, she wonders if circumstances and home ties had been different 'how far it would have been right to give up time to cultivating' her voice, particularly as she would have been 'very content' to be a domestic paragon. In such a case she hopes she should 'have had the energy to cultivate my voice and to use it to give

[45] Mrs George de Horne Vaizey, *The Daughters of a Genius*, p. 104; pp. 277–8.
[46] Ibid., p. 128.

pleasure to others, to poor folk above all; but oh, how joyfully I should have hurried home'. It is this consciousness that makes her so admirable as both artist and woman. Moreover, both Hertha Norreys and Hope Charrington retire eagerly from public performance, except as a matter of philanthropy, as soon as they receive offers of marriage from men they love.[47]

There were, in the realms of both art and music, respectable role models such as Fanny Corbeaux, and Miss Henrietta Ray, painters of charming pictures, and Madame Albani, inspiring musician, whose lives were also publicly impeccable. It should be noted, however, that despite the existence of respectable actresses, this tolerance had yet to spread to the acting profession so far as didactic fiction is concerned. Amateur performance in a drawing room setting was one thing, as Mrs George de Horne Vaizey's Peggy Saville showed, but there were still too many overtones of immorality and vulgarity about the stage as a whole and too many plays in particular for any conscientious woman to look to acting as a means of earning a living.[48] It was not until after 1905 that fictional good girls can seek the stage, with all the contaminating possibilities of playing in 'that Norwegian dramatist's works!'[49]

Almost certainly the existence by the 1880s of another, well-established as well as respected 'profession' for women, within the 'artistic' field and with a public aspect, played a considerable role in overcoming prejudice about the social acceptability of women whose talents involve some kind of public display. The first female profession that enabled practitioners to earn money and still retain or even advance a respectable status within middle-class society was that of the authoress, particularly of the didactic fiction intended to per-

[47] Mrs Mary Molesworth, *White Turrets* (Chambers, Edinburgh, 1896), p. 19; p. 53; pp. 106–7; pp. 229–30; Mrs George de Horne Vaizey, *The Daughters of a Genius*, p. 292.
[48] See, for instance, Joseph Johnson, *Clever Girls of Our Time, and How they became Famous Women* (Gall & Inglis, Edinburgh, 1863); 'Portraits of Celebrities at Different Times of Their Lives', *The Strand Magazine*, XIV, July–Dec. 1899, p. 52; 'Illustrated Interviews: Miss Marie Hall, The Girl Violinist: A Romance of Real Life', *The Strand Magazine*, XXV, Jan.–June, 1903, pp. 656–63; Mrs George de Horne Vaizey, *About Peggy Saville* (RTS, London, 1900), pp. 79–92.
[49] Ellen Louisa Davis, *Asceline's Ladder*, p. 32.

petuate the values of that society. The popularity and social recognition accorded to authoresess in this genre can also be seen as a measure of the respectability and even the importance accorded to the messages they attempted to pass on to a new generation. Early writers like Elizabeth Sewell were extremely reluctant to make themselves known as writers outside their family circle. Miss Sewell's first works appeared anonymously. But the wide social approval of the message evoked an interest in the purveyors thereof, and authoresses began to emerge from their domestic closet and, like Charlotte Yonge, to become accepted as part of society in their own right, not just in that of husband or family.[50]

Lady writers from the mid-nineteenth century on were particular fortunate also in the existence of a beloved and much-quoted predecessor in the shape of Jane Austen, who had written her books and achieved greatness, if not the masculine heights of genius, without neglect of home duties. Her example could be used to soothe the qualms of those who feared that time spent writing would be time taken from domestic responsibilities, to the detriment of the family circle.[51] Moreover, the nature of didactic fiction meant a recognition that an essential qualification for writing the realistic type of story required was experience of life and the practical importance of their message to the stability of family life and society as whole. Once known, it soon became apparent that the home lives of women like Charlotte Yonge and Mrs Emma Marshall were, in their respective spheres, irreproachable. Miss Yonge was primarily the interested and dutiful family-orientated spinster daughter and sister, and next the woman dedicated to furthering and strengthening the tenets of the Anglican Church. It was known that much of the profits of her literary work went to endow missionary projects, for instance. Mrs Emma Marshall was first and foremost the busy, dedicated and successful wife and mother, relegating her love of writing to a

[50] Eleanor L. Sewell, (ed.), *The Autobiography of Elizabeth Sewell* (Longman, London, 1907).

[51] Such aspects were much dwelt on in contemporary biographies of Jane Austen, e.g.: Lord Brabourne (ed.), *Letters of Jane Austen, edited with an introduction and critical remarks*, 2 vols (Bentley, London, 1882).

secondary role in the face of 'greater' claims.[52]

The model pattern of their private lives, combined with the undoubted value of their social message, meant that they were welcomed and respected in a professional light in the social circles to which they already had entree by virtue of their family position.[53] Later entrants to the professional writing field continued this pattern of private lives apparently mirroring the standards reviewed in their writing. Problems, yes, including less than perfect marriages at times, but all to be overcome by exercise of the womanly qualities of self-sacrifice, forbearance and compassion, whether in marriage or in a profession.[54]

Hints were even given by these role models on becoming a writer within the genre, and on the necessity for regarding writing as a craft requiring a period of learning and sustained practice and even on the type of initial financial return that might be expected. But the L. T. Meades and Evelyn Everett Greens also emphasized the need for accepting that those who genuinely had the talent to impart a message formed a 'limited class'. The advice was 'Never write merely for the sake of writing!' Not everybody could write: 'One must have a sort of natural bent or gift – God's gift, – and then one has to use that gift, and to make the most of it by hard work' as does Gladys Hepburn, whose efforts to join this select band form the subsidiary plot-line of Agnes Giberne's *Miss Con.* Gladys is a good girl, already with the essentials of womanly humility. In addition, she is willing to treat the writing of fiction professionally. To 'write a five-shilling book' has been her 'dream for years', and much of her adolescence is shown to have been spent writing stories for practice and persevering in spite of criticism. She does not expect success overnight if ever, accepts advice and is willing to discover from the reactions of others

---

[52] Georgina Battiscombe, *Charlotte Mary Yonge: The Story of an Uneventful Life* (Constable, London, 1943); B. Marshall, *Emma Marshall: A Biographical Sketch* (Seeley, London, 1900).

[53] Charlotte Yonge appeared, for instance, in the 'Portraits of Celebrities', *The Strand Magazine*, VII, July–Dec. 1891, p. 479.

[54] Mrs Molesworth's marriage, for example, was unhappy but though her husband's violent temper (result of an injury) resulted in a separation she refused to condemn either husband or the institution of marriage. Mrs Emma Marshall insisted that no marriage could be happy all the time.

whether or not she has a genuine vocation in authorship. Above all, she takes care in sending in carefully written manuscripts to publishers with correct grammar and spelling![55]

By contrast her friend Maggie Romilly, who only wishes to write out of a sense of jealousy of Glady's deserved success, refuses to approach authorship in a proper manner and fails dismally. Maggie's product 'read like a rough copy' and is full of errors, and she refuses to make any attempt to 'improve and polish it a little' because it 'would be a bother'. Few worse things could be said. Maggie is one of those seeking worldly praise and not divine satisfaction, and it is hardly surprising that her manuscript is returned promptly.[56] Tales like this also serve to make it plain that most of the later writers, at least, served their apprenticeship for their ultimate aim of writing fiction for the adolescent middle-class girl by trying their hand, like Gladys, at stories for a working-class, usually urban, market. Certainly the vast majority of later authors, including L.T. Meade, Evelyn Everett Green, Mrs Moleworth and Agnes Giberne herself, started their careers by writing prize books for the Sunday School circuit at the cheaper end of the range. After all, most girls qualified to write didactic fiction by the nobility of their characters would also be experienced in teaching Sunday School classes and might thus be expected to have an idea of the market they were catering for, as well as the necessary messages that had to be included. In addition, the standards for this market were generally less exacting, and essentially, the message needed to be less complex.[57]

In all these artistic fields, however, fiction emphasized that the success rate was comparatively low, and depended as much as nursing or teaching on a true sense of vocation and the consequent willingness to treat the affair as a lifetime commitment. The message was, very firmly, that without genuine, God-given talent, lasting and professional success could not be achieved, and therefore, should not be attempted. It was

[55] Agnes Giberne, *Miss Con, or All those Girls* (Nisbet, Welwyn, 1887), p. 145; p. 66; pp. 94–6; pp. 138–9.

[56] Ibid., p. 97; p. 140.

[57] They also continued writing for this market on occasions, partly for financial reasons, but also out of a conviction of the worthiness of the cause. See J.S. Bratton, *The Impact of Victorian Children's Fiction* (Croom Helm, London, 1981) for further discussion of novels of this type.

necessary to have the womanly and professional humility to accept the verdict of others. Mr Loftus in *The Daughters of a Genius* warned that 'Brain work is uncertain, trying and badly-paid'; that:

'Music and pictures are at a discount in these hard times, and half the artists, by their own account, are starving. . . . . As for story-writing, there are half-a-dozen stars who make a fortune in literature, but the vast majority of authors have a hard fight to earn a living.'

It was hard enough for men, and even worse for women who were not 'made to fight their way' in the public sphere, and could not do so without damage.[58] The books pointed out also that even success in these fields had its dangers. It could lead, for instance, to a woman forgetting to remember that her gift came from God and that worldly success was fleeting and hollow, as sweet voiced Dulce Carruthers discovered. The heroine of C.E.G. Weighall's tale *The Temptation of Dulce Carruthers* succumbs to the lure of popularity and as her mother is told, success has 'rubbed the bloom' off her child so she must 'never expect to see the same little girl again'.[59]

Most middle-class young women workers, however, ran little risk of losing their moral and physical girlish bloom by dint of over-success. Their need to earn a living meant that hard and unremitting toil and a fight with the briars of a workaday world was more likely to rob them of that bloom, one reason, perhaps, why it was expected that few who dedicated their lives, voluntarily or otherwise, to some profession would marry. Many girls who had to work found that 'poverty often interposes between a talent and its subsequent development', and were forced to settle for an alternative and more mundane career. Many more girls had no particular discoverable bent to be given up before settling for less exciting employment prospects.

In certain ways girls were, by the last decades of the century, more fortunate than their predecessors. Paid employment for women had become more acceptable even if it was by no means desirable, and considerably more opportunities existed. Yet at the same time, the established middle-class emphasis on 'professionalism' meant that for women as for men, the most

[58] Mrs George de Horne Vaizey, *Daughers of a Genius*, p. 85; p. 28.
[59] C.E.C. Weighall, *The Temptation of Dulce Carruthers* (Cassell, London, 1893), p. 290.

desirable and respectable of these jobs required the investment of money and patronage. Girls were inevitably at a disadvantage here, in that it was more likely that any available spare funds would be spent first on any boys needing a start in life. Most of the authors in this genre by the turn of the century regretted this, but saw the solution not in a change of attitude within the family, but in an increased benevolence on the part of better-off women such as Mrs Stanhope in *Four Every-Day Girls*, who 'knew how difficult it was for some [girls] to gather the necessary training to equip them for a battle with the world, and . . . determined to use her money, her sympathy, and her experience of life for their benefit'.[60]

In addition, it was necessary to warn girls that while a comely mien was an asset within the domestic sphere, 'in the battle for daily bread good looks are sometimes more a hindrance than a help'. It was always necessary to retain the neat and refined modes of dressing considered so much part of being a lady, but girls like Joan Elliot and Gillian Stretton, who were just 'ordinary, healthy, good-looking English girls' were likely to find the public sphere easier than the beautiful Cherry Hesketh in the tale of *Four Every-Day Girls*.[61] Great caution had to be exercised in finding a safe harbour for such a girl in the wide world.

There were, however, such safe harbours, and 'Openings for women [were] arising on all hands'. Most authors considered that the arrival of the typewriting machine, for instance, offered a useful and secure, if prosaic, opening for the otherwise untalented girl in need of a wage, because 'authors, and statesmen and promoters want such a lot of copying done for them'. The development of typewriting bureaux and large company offices, where women could go and work in company with others of their sex, to say nothing of the possibilities of being able to hire a machine to work at home, instead of being exposed to the perils of being a lone woman somewhere gave typewriting a great boost, and also more or less confirmed it as an essentially 'female' profession. It carried the recommendation of being 'not very difficult' to learn and so not too taxing

---

[60] See P. Levine, *Victorian Feminism*; Raymond Jacberns, *Four Every-Day Girls*, p. 89.

[61] Raymond Jacberns, *Four Every-Day Girls*, pp. 9–10.

for the female frame of mind. The more intelligent and educated lady in the field could add shorthand to her skills as 'a most invaluable accomplishment for the professional type-writer'. L.T. Meade's Emmy Thorn finds that 'a girl who understands shorthand and type-writing is almost always in requisition and can earn as much as three pounds in a week'. Other lady-like accomplishments like languages could also be 'very useful'.[62]

As L.T. Meade commented it was a profession in that it required training and skill. Also it was one which 'a girl who is brought up as a lady can undertake with advantage', and without the considerable outlay required for training that both lady nursing and certificated teaching entailed. Readers were told that six weeks instruction 'from 9.30 to 5 daily' could be obtained for around two guineas. Painstaking application to the task should then result in 'a certain amount of dexterity', which would then improve with practice but which carried with it the immediate prospect of remuneration at around a guinea a week. Out of London, rates were more likely to be around 3d per thousand words for a skilled operator in a bureaux or at home.[63]

Other occupations which could be classed as professions were becoming open. Some ranks of the civil service were taking in ladies in small numbers. Lady journalists began to increase in number, at least in certain aspects of the profession, encouraged by the spread of periodical publications, particularly those designed for women. Philippa in Evelyn Everett Green's *Half-A-Dozen Sisters*, for instance, has ambitions in this area. Armed with a notebook and self-taught shorthand, she intrepidly sets out to observe and write up functions such as local charity functions, socially important events like weddings of prominent citizens and the displays of gifts associated with them. Philippa realizes that for all her quick wits and intelligence, she has neither the knowledge nor the mental resource to compete with male journalists, but believes that women can bring a needed feminine touch to certain areas of her profession.[64]

[62] L.T. Meade, *Engaged to be Married*, pp. 78–80; pp. 85–6.
[63] L.T. Meade, *Engaged to be Married*, pp. 85–6; Evelyn Everett Green, *The Mystery of Alton Grange* (Nelson, Walton-on-Thames, 1899), pp. 79–81.
[64] Evelyn Everett Green, *Half-A-Dozen Sisters* (RTS, London, 1910), 1st edn (1905).

Even shop-work, especially in large and respectable stores or in small and recherché shops selling to women, such as milliners, was another area of expanding middle-class feminine employment. It suffered by comparison to other occupations in being less obviously a candidate for professionalization, yet it was at least relatively secure. Jessica Colvin in Evelyn Everett Green's *The Mystery of Alton Grange*, forced to find work on the death of her father, realizes that she has neither the aptitude nor the education for 'writing, painting or teaching'. She is, however, 'an exceedingly good needle-woman' and being given an introduction to 'the principals of a really good business house' she was accepted as a saleswoman. The employees live on the premises and there are already 'several . . . well-born ladies' employed there, so her reputation and safety are assured.[65] The enterprising heroine of *Cynthia's Bonnet Shop* turns her Irish wits and feminine dexterity and taste to good advantage, and again without losing caste.[66]

Yet while there was an undoubted need for such openings, and while a significant number of girls themselves may have welcomed such advances, didactic fiction reveals a certain disquiet. It was difficult for contemporary opinion to see how employment in these areas fitted into conventional ideas about even the advanced ideals of stereotypical femininity. It was difficult to call typing or selling a vocation, and they had little direct relation to the 'traditional' areas of lady-like domestic responsibility. It was accepted that those women who had to earn a living might have to take such jobs, and in 'honest and honourable work there is no touch of disgrace', but it was seen as better if more established womanly alternatives could be found.[67] Certainly there was considerable resistance to any voluntary seeking out of work in fields that might lead to a too independent spirit, from office work to journalism. Fiction was thus used, for instance, to further the argument that it was unfair and unChristian of girls who did not need such employment to take work away from the needy girls who did.[68]

Didactic fiction from the 1880s increasingly was also re-

---

[65] Evelyn Everett Green, *The Mystery of Alton Grange*, pp. 140–1.
[66] Rosa Mulholland, *Cynthia's Bonnet Shop* (Blackie, Glasgow, 1901).
[67] Evelyn Everett Green, *The Mystery of Alton Grange*, p. 171.
[68] Mrs Mary Molesworth, *White Turrets*, p. 198.

cruited to help advertise the fields of opportunity for feminine talents and energy that existed within the extended private sphere. Growing urban problems and the success of women in earlier decades in working with the poor in both urban and rural conditions led to increasing acceptance of a large-scale middle-class feminine input in coping with the dilemmas. Frank Prochaska's comprehensive study of women and nineteenth-century philanthropy has indicated the enormous reliance of male philanthropists on female legwork.[69] Properly supervised, and reminded not to let emotions get out of hand, ladies were presumed to be able to apply their personal experience of running a house and servants efficiently to the questions of social justice and the correct levels of financial relief amongst the poor. In addition, the women's role as the moral guardians of the race meant that ladies would be particularly effective in improving the condition of the most worrying cases, those who were morally as well as financially poor, by giving them suitable religious messages to relieve at least one element of their poverty. Philanthropy could thus act as an outlet for the energies of girls and women, single and married, who wished for responsibilities outside their homes even when there was no financial imperative. The existence of a genuine need for such services and a female determination to find a more widely useful role in society combined to confer on philanthropy by the 1880s the status of a profession, to satisfy aspirations as well as to ensure charitable efficiency.

By the turn of the century it is difficult to find an author in this genre who had not written at least one novel concentrating on this aspect of contemporary femininity and emphasizing the professionalization of the sphere. Some, including the perennially popular L.T. Meade and Evelyn Everett Green, used considerable ingenuity to bring it into most of their fictional reflections of daily reality. The former's heroines, from Bel-Marjory to Helen Holworthy in *A Knight of Today*, are all to some extent workers in this respect. They set aside carefully calculated periods to be spent succouring the urban poor and wretched in specified districts, usually in London, regarding it as both a trust and a duty. Most of Evelyn Everett Green's heroines occupy themselves in similar ways though many of her

[69] F.K. Prochaska, *Women and Philanthropy in Nineteenth-Century England.*

good girls have a rural as well as, or instead of, an urban background for their efforts. Also, being a firm Anglican with high Church tendencies, Evelyn Everett Green ensures that her girls always work under the supervision of the local clergy or failing that the local medical practitioners, being given 'districts' within a parish to visit.[70]

In the town or in the country, the good girl set aside time that would otherwise be given over to personal pursuits to dedicate it to feeding and educating, spiritually and physically, those less fortunate than themselves. Such model maidens go about their work amongst the 'sad sights' of the working classes with 'a quiet self-possession and a business-like comprehension of their affairs and wants', offering 'practical suggestions' where appropriate. If the 'cases under [their] care want extra help' the method was 'to report them, and leave the matter in the hands of higher authority', usually though not always male.[71] Not all the objects of philanthropy were abjectly poor, many were more in need of lessons in managing all aspects of their lives to the fullest extent than of the more obvious forms of charity such as food distribution. In Evelyn Everett Green's *Olive Roscoe* the Roscoe family's miners got 'very good wages', but their womenfolk needed 'a few ideas of practical economy' from middle-class professionals like Olive to teach them not to throw away cold meat because they did not like it.[72]

Even the investment of a relatively small amount of time could be useful in contributing to the enjoyment and increasing the 'refinement' of the poor. Properly organized evening concerts for 'working men and their wives' were always well attended and 'could not fail to do good'. Such exercises could 'provide them with an evening's amusement in which they would hear nothing but what was free from all taint of sin, and . . . . raise and elevate their moral nature' while keeping them out of public houses etc. It was agreed that far from being offended by patronage a carefully arranged evening of being

[70] L.T. Meade, *Bel-Marjory*, pp. 165–7; L.T. Meade, *A Knight of Today* (Shaw, London, 1877), pp. 84–5; Evelyn Everett Green, *Heiress of Wylmington*, pp. 118–29.

[71] Evelyn Everett Green, *Heiress of Wylmington*, pp. 115–17.

[72] Evelyn Everett Green, *Olive Roscoe, or The New Sister* (Nelson, Walton-on-Thames, 1896), p. 150.

entertained 'by people socially far above them' would make the workers feel the true 'holy tie of universal brotherhood which makes the whole world kin' instead of the false levelling tendency of socialism. Involvement in these concerts could also provide girls with a regular form of voluntary work even if they had talent rather than time at their disposal.[73]

These fictional experiences also provided a useful lesson for girls worried about the possession of overmuch personal wealth in face of acute human misery. It was emphasized that time and concerned Christianity were the first requirements for philanthropic work and that girls with little or nothing to spare financially were contributing their 'widow's mite' by the expenditure of effort. However, as L.T. Meade's Helen Holworthy and her mentor find that 'Kind words went far; kind deeds farther; but money also, to effect any permanent result was indispensable'. Concerned readers were assured that 'in helping the poor to help themselves . . . money could [be] put to a noble use'. Wealth could, and should, be shared but at the same time, this had to be done in practical ways to ensure its best long-term effect. Extravagance of giving was as bad as extravagance of spending. Practical philanthropic experience taught that 'it never answers to do . . . things for nothing. It teaches people to be importunate and discontented'. When people felt they were 'paying for their privilege' they valued them 'accordingly'.[74]

As has been said, not all women with a wish to work in this area were in a financial position to indulge their preferences. Acceptance of the valuable feminine input and of the increasing need for women to seek paid employment came at a time when there was a perceived need for dedicated professional philanthropists. While some wealthy women were single and without family ties to occupy much of their time, too many of them, like Frances Power Cobbe were rather too radical in outlook for conventional opinion to be entirely happy about

[73] Evelyn Everett Green, *Heiress of Wylmington*, pp. 369–70; Mrs Mary Molesworth, *White Turrets*, p. 88.

[74] L.T. Meade, *A Knight of Today*, p. 74; p. 84; Evelyn Everett Green, *The Percivals, or A Houseful of Girls* (RTS, London, 1903), 1st edn (1890), pp. 128–30.

their input into the field.[75] Various large charitable bodies thus began to employ practical and reliable ladies to carry out the philanthropic work in which they interested themselves on a full-time professional basis. Mr Montague in Mrs Molesworth's *White Turrets* arranges for 'the offer of a post in the Reasonable Help Society' to Winifred Maryon, 'provided, of course, you can pass a certain examination'. Such charitable societies tried 'to kill two birds with one stone by engaging to do the ... charitable work', women who qualified for the description of 'penniless girls of a better class', charitably giving them an apprenticeship in the field *gratis* and paying them also. Winifred is employed at a salary of 50 pounds per annum to help organize the efforts and financial inputs of the wealthier patrons, with the expectation of being able to develop a career in the field.[76]

That career might, as in the case of the worthy Miss Mackenzie in Evelyn Everett Green's collaborative tale, *Priscilla*, lead to additional work in local government, though more often such opportunities fell to wealthier women with philanthropic tendencies. On the whole, conventional opinion was reasonably happy, or at least acquiescent, in the participation of women in politics. Their efforts could be very satisfactorily interpreted, like philanthropy, in the light of a logical extension of the domestic sphere. On the whole, however, feminine involvement in local politics made comparatively little impact on didactic fiction. This was partly because few of the authors involved had themselves any practical experience to draw on, and partly because numbers were still small in the period up to 1905. Female involvement in national politics did, however, begin to assume a higher profile by the turn of the century.[77]

As work like that of Philippa Levine and the contributors to Jane Rendall's volume on women's politics in the nineteenth century has shown, the non-possession of the franchise had

[75] But see, for instance, 'Portraits of Celebrities', Lady Henry Somerset, *The Strand Magazine*, VIII, July–Dec. 1894, p. 483; 'Illustrated Interviews': Baroness Burdett Coutts, *The Strand Magazine*, IV, July–Dec. 1892, p. 348, describing the Baroness as 'a truly noble woman'.

[76] Mrs Mary Molesworth, *White Turrets*, p. 115; p. 139; p. 198.

[77] Evelyn Everett Green and H. Louisa Bedford, *Priscilla: A Story for Girls* (Nelson, Walton-on-Thames, 1900), p. 38; p. 330.

never meant that middle-class women at least were debarred from participation in national politics.[78] However, the nature of that participation for the majority was, as fiction stresses, based on accepted presumptions about the separate spheres of men and women. Throughout the period didactic authors stressed that some degree of interest and involvement was considered part of the womanly duty. One reason for this was that given by Lady Basset in Annie Swan's *Across Her Path* when she rebukes Barbara Dale for her lack of knowledge. 'Every woman ought to be well-informed on such a theme', because 'when you get a husband . . . you ought to be able to talk to him about such things. Politics is an absorbingly interesting topic to most men'. The other equally important factor was woman's role as the moral guardian of society. A good woman was always interested in the condition of the community as a whole, and this, naturally and inevitably, gave her the right to essentially political convictions about how to improve the lot of those around her. It was, however, a question of 'political creed' arising from an 'earnest interest in the social condition of the people', which had then to be expressed in 'proper ways'. No true woman would 'mix herself up in noisy political agitations'. That was reserved for the more boisterous male. The good woman exerted political influence by exhortation and precept from within her proper sphere.[79]

Hence Charlotte Yonge's Flora May in *The Daisy Chain* takes the lead in persuading her husband to enter politics. When she is criticized for her actions it is on the basis that her husband is not truly suited to that sphere and she is thus fulfilling personal ambition rather than working as a true woman for the good of her family and her country. Otherwise her background work as a political counsellor, coadjutor and hostess meets with nothing but authoral approval. Miss Yonge plainly saw nothing incongruous in a woman having a grasp of certain aspects at least of political affairs. The point was that a woman was not fitted to the harsh realities of the parliament and the enormous scope of

[78] P. Levine, *Victorian Feminism*; Jane Rendall (ed.), *Equal or Different: Women's Politics 1800–1914* (Basil Blackwell, Oxford, 1987).

[79] E. Conder Gray, *Wise Words and Loving Deeds: A Book of Biographies for Girls*, Lives Worth Living Series, (Marshall Japp, London, 1880), pp. 27–8; Annie S. Swan, *Across Her Path* (Oliphant, Edinburgh, 2nd edn 1902), p. 62.

responsibility and knowledge that fell to the leading politicians of the day. However, when a male member of the family unit was involved in national politics it was an obvious part of the womanly duty to help support his efforts, and it was accepted without question that a suitable feminine input could be highly efficacious. Indeed, the bachelor politician without a mother or sister to deputize for the non-existent wife was in a most unhappy position. As Freda Rutland in Evelyn Everett Green's *The Percivals* understands, it was their engagement which opened up the path to a political career for Julian Hamilton. She expects, in particular, to fill the essential, if supporting, position of his hostess at necessary entertainments.[80]

The political hostess was a well-known phenomenon, but a restricted one, useful simply for the example of how effective a woman could be in a political sense acting within her 'natural' sphere. It was accepted that relatively few middle-class readers of didactic fiction were likely to find themselves placed in a situation where they would have to undertake such responsibilities. Increasing numbers of middle-class girls and women, though still quite small in total however, were likely to be involved in other aspects of party politics such as canvassing and fund-raising during the last two decades of the nineteenth century. In the earlier period, indeed up to the 1884 Reform Act, the efforts of the womenfolk of a family in canvassing were usually limited to talking to members of an immediate social circle whose vote might have a bearing on the outcome of the election. The May sisters exert their efforts on all their friends, for instance, in the cause of getting their brother-in-law returned. The extension of the franchise in elections after 1884, combined with the ending of the system whereby canvassers were paid, provided women with both an excuse and an imperative to increase the numbers of those involved and to widen their efforts in national politics.

The involvement of women in both the Conservative Party's Primrose League and the Women's Liberal Federation provided a base for a variety of work. Women members of the former used their weight to organize fêtes and other entertainments to raise Party funds, for instance. They made little effort

---

[80] Charlotte M. Yonge, *The Daisy Chain*, p. 435; p. 499; Evelyn Everett Green, *The Percivals*, p. 22.

to try to direct the overall path of Party policy, and most women members of the League were following in the paths of family political belief in their allegiance to the Conservative Party.[81] Evelyn Everett Green most strongly represents that tradition in didactic fiction. Many of her stories were set against the rural or small-town background in which the League flourished and saw itself as having most effect. Her tales also indicate the growing acceptance by those who held political beliefs of this nature, of the involvement of the middle- and working-class element in political affairs.

In *In Pursuit of a Phantom* the *nouveau riche* Mr Crossthwaite decides to stand for the local seat and the old-established gentry, lacking a candidate themselves, agree to 'join together to keep out the Radical monster!' This was an important asset, for 'The Squire's influence was strong over a large section of voters who looked slightly askance' at the newcomers. The wives and daughters of the gentry and wealthier tradesmen alike go out canvassing. Lady Amy Conroy, for instance, made great headway with the local agricultural voters with her 'pretty face and arch, persuasive arguments', to say nothing of her love for children 'which went far with the mothers'. In addition, Mr Crossthwaite's daughters gather the youth of their local circle to get up entertainments for the local voters in order to 'make the running for dad amongst . . . those we hope will prove his constituents at the bye-election'. The result is a resounding success, with Mr Crossthwaite 'returned at the head of the poll, and with a substantial majority'.[82] Interestingly enough, these authors also reflect a certain amount of disquiet about the new methods of electioneering: 'I sometimes wonder whether the old overt bribing of voters was not a lesser evil than what one sees now. It is only bribery dressed up'.[83]

In contrast to the Primrose League, the Women's Liberal Federation attracted a more urban, more radical, even a feminist following that was much more inspired by personal

[81] Linda Walker, 'Party Political Women: A Comparative Study of Liberal Women and the Primrose League, 1890–1914', in Jane Rendall (ed.), *Equal or Different*, pp. 165–91.
[82] Evelyn Everett Green, *In Pursuit of a Phantom* (RTS, London, 1906) 1st edn (1905), p. 9; p. 185; p. 45; pp. 214–15.
[83] Evelyn Everett Green, *In Pursuit of a Phantom*, p. 215.

conviction regardless of family political loyalties. It made far less impact, therefore, on didactic fiction even though significant numbers of authors belonged to backgrounds of a distinct liberal persuasion. L.T. Meade, for instance, who was married to Toulmin Smith, made little mention of political affairs in her fiction, but it is plain from what she did say that her political leanings were if anything Liberal. However, she had equally little sympathy for the militant feminist stance that was increasingly associated with the Federation. Certainly she did not think that women were suited to public speaking on such affairs.[84] It seems likely, therefore, that her relative silence, and that of other didactic authors of similar persuasion, was more a matter of a lack of any outlet through which they could happily make a contribution to national politics beyond the established fundamentals. It is thus difficult to gain a representative picture of national politics in genre fiction, but it is still possible to point out the general antipathy that existed towards an extension of the franchise to women. While the newer feminine stereotype was encouraged to be more independent than the earlier version, none of these writers encouraged the idea that women were not primarily linked to the dependent domestic sphere.

There was a general feeling that became reflected in didactic fiction around the mid 1890s. The efforts of some women to break out from the traditional restrictions on their behaviour and occupations, and the publicity that they received in the growing number of periodical publications started a certain counter-reaction against professionalization of women's work, at least outside the home. It began to be feared that the emphasis on 'vocation' as a criterion for ideal feminine employment was having unexpected and unfortunate side effects which had serious implications for social stability as a whole. There were a number of worrying trends that made conventional opinion believe that girls were regarding the 'traditional' majority career of marriage and motherhood as less inviting than an independent life of work. L.T. Meade's Helen Channing declares that she and her sister will never marry, preferring to stay in the 'noble paths of independence' because

[84] See, for instance, 'Illustrated Interviews': L.T. Meade, *The Strand Magazine*, XX, p. 465.

'women are better off' without 'this all-absorbing affection' of romantic love. The Maryon sisters in *White Turrets* agree. Talking of the philanthropic Lady Campion Winifred exclaims '*What* a pity she married. . . . She might have been really great at something, if she had not thrown herself into trammels'. While these fictional girls see the error of their ways, the frequent appearance in the genre of such characters and opinions indicates that society believed that such ideas needed combatting as forcibly and realistically as possible.[85]

Another trend, identified by Martha Vicinus in *Independent Women*, that worried conventional opinion was the growth of celibate sisterhoods or settlements. As has already been seen in chapter 4, dedication to a single life on religious or quasi-religious grounds was regarded by conventional middle-class opinion with considerable suspicion. The existence of sisterhoods was seen by some, despite the good and philanthropic motives behind their foundation, as essentially radical and striking at that foundation of society, the family unit. While celibacy was in itself no bad thing, and considerable efforts were put into encouraging women to accept potential spinsterhood gracefully and positively, wilfully to put the possibility of marriage beyond reach was another, and far more serious matter. Didactic fiction is thus careful to point out, while admitting the worthy work that could be done by such women, that overindulgence in philanthropy or any vocation, at the expense of 'normal' social usage was as much selfishness as sheer idle pleasure, and certainly could not count as a 'profession'.[86]

Gwendolyn Maltby in *The Heiress of Wylmington* is one of those who, without the pressure of financial exigency, had been pressured into the belief that if she is not to waste her life she must seek a 'vocation'. Her spiritual guide gently corrects her. God has placed her 'in [her] present situation' and 'the work that's nearest', her domestic responsibilities, were her true vocation, though they could be expanded to include some philanthropic work. Mr Carlingford argued that:

---

[85] L.T. Meade, *Engaged to be Married*, p. 114; Mrs Mary Molesworth, *White Turrets*, p. 22.

[86] See Martha Vicinus, *Independent Women*.

every now and then men, and women too, ... feel urged and impelled by a strong power from within to abandon the life to which they are born and adopt one of earnest, laborious work and self-sacrifice for the benefit of their fellow men. Thank God that there do exist such spirits ... [but they are] few in proportion to the number of those who go about seeking for a vocation ... A calling such as that must be well-pleasing in our Father's sight; but then it must always have been adopted in obedience to a call which is not given to us all.

Only careful prayer and advice from others in a position to judge could decide how far an individual was 'justified in leaving that state of life to which God has called us, to look out for work which lies out of our path'.[87]

While such arguments might answer for the fortunate middle-class good girl who did not need to bring in an income in order to live, it left unsolved the problem of the numbers of girls from the financially pressed families. Didactic fiction indicates a further change in attitude towards women working for pay. Those good girls who either did not wish, or could not, leave home but needed to use their own resources to find an income were encouraged to utilize their domestic skills. M. M. Pollard's Dorothy Tresilis and the four sisters in Ethel Dawson's *A Happy Failure* agree that they could not leave their mother. As Dorothy exclaims, their problem is 'How money could be honestly earned without diminishing one's self-respect and integrity' or compromising the comfort of their mother. All these girls are, in the words of the Lenthall girls, 'hopelessly ordinary', with no prospect of 'electrifying the world' by their talents. But they have 'health ... and youth, and a fair amount of brains' to face the world with, and the solution of both sets of characters is to apply these to set up a small, respectable boarding house instead of going out as companions or nursery governesses, leaving their mothers in poor lodgings.[88] The Lenthall girls, determined to do things 'professionally', rent a house in rural Cornwall and invest in cookery lessons at the School of Cookery in South Kensington for one, while the rest

[87] Evelyn Everett Green, *Heiress of Wylmington*, p. 354; pp. 356–8.
[88] M.M. Pollard, *Dorothy Tresilis, or Down at Polwin* (RTS, London, 1888), pp. 20–1; Ethel Dawson, *A Happy Failure: A Story for Girls* (Nelson, Walton-on-Thames, 1903), pp. 9–10.

are to act as 'lady-helps'. Under such circumstances, there was nothing 'derogatory' in acting the part of servants to bring in an income. The advertisement in *The Times* is couched in repellingly respectable terms: 'Board and residence offered by a lady to a few ladies and gentlemen. . . . Quiet family life, with every comfort'. The Tresilis family already own a house in such 'pure, fresh and healthy' surroundings.[89]

This course of taking in paying guests, usually in rural surroundings where living was cheaper, with 'applicants' suitably refereed by clergymen or others of unimpeachable respectability, was a course followed by an increasing number of fictional heroines, as numbers of authors saw it as an ideal solution to the problem of maintaining the feminine presence in the domestic sphere and enabling needy women to obtain an income at the same time. The impoverished Irish gentryfolk in Katherine Tynan's *Three Fair Maids* follow a similar pattern, if on a grander scale than either the Tresilis family or the Lenthall girls.[90] Another departure from a previous fictional 'norm' is that these girls are still considered marriageable. Indeed, their courage in taking such a course, combined with their unquestionably ladylike demeanour at all times, is usually an endearing factor in the eyes of their suitors. The Lenthall daughters are 'something like girls! Splendid, by Jove! What pluck, too!'[91]

Genre fiction also indicates the extent to which the idea of a lifelong vocation in employment outside the home was modified by the mid-1890s. It was not considered productive or desirable to present impressionable girls with an 'either' marriage 'or' paid vocation choice. It was better to encourage girls to work, if financially necessary as in the case of L.T. Meade's Emmy Thorn whose fiancé is in India, and then to give up that employment for the greater joys as well as greater sorrows and frustrations of married life.[92] Even those with a vocation for nursing were permitted to leave that calling for the greater one

[89] Ethel Dawson, *A Happy Failure*, pp. 19–20; M.M. Pollard, *Dorothy Tresilis*, p. 20.

[90] Katherine Tynan, *Three Fair Maids, or The Burkes of Derrymore* (Blackie, Glasgow, 1901); Ethel Dawson, *A Happy Failure*.

[91] Ethel Dawson, *A Happy Failure*, p. 137.

[92] L.T. Meade, *Engaged to be Married*, p. 20.

of marriage if opportunity and love offered themselves. Miss Lucas in Evelyn Everett Green's *Sister* is a case in point. She did not expect to wed, but while recuperating from overwork found an earlier romance in the shape of the heroic Colonel Clarence. When he proposed she gladly abandoned the intermittent care of a greater community for the constant care of a smaller one in the knowledge that her experience as a nurse had better fitted her to be a wife than her girlhood training. Experience in a 'hard school', that of the outside world, had taught the value of the domestic sphere – the lesson that every model maiden needed to learn for the good of the country at large, and for her own happiness. As one girl in Alice Stronach's *A Newnham Friendship* sighs:

> 'It's not use shirking it, my friend: our work, our latch-keys, our independence, our comradeships even, are all very well for a time, but not for always. And they cannot compensate us. . . . Take . . . happiness. . . . Marry, have children, know the highest happiness that life can give a woman.'

It was not necessary to give up all work: philanthropy always remained a sphere of activity for the married woman. Ultimately, however, sacrifice of the transient joys of independence was necessary if she was ever to reach true happiness.[93]

Paid employment for significant numbers of women had become an inescapable part of the feminine sphere by the end of the nineteenth century, for a variety of reasons, including economic need and female ambitions. As a result, a much wider range of work options was open to girls seeking waged work by the 1890s. Yet that expansion did not mean that women were no longer limited by gender expectations of their capabilities and social role. Attempts were increasingly made to present employment opportunities as a secondary choice for all but the most unusual of girls, those called by God to a particular lifetime vocation. Marriage and motherhood remained the ideal for the good girl.

[93] Evelyn Everett Green, *Sister*, p. 375; Alice Stronach, *A Newnham Friendship*, pp. 286–8.

Conclusion: Self-sacrifice and Social Control

> Curved is the line of beauty
> Straight is the path of duty
> Walk the straight path and you shall see
> The other ever follow thee.
> *Anon*

Didactic fiction for middle-class girls aimed to put this message across to a wide audience, which would accept the underlying message of self-sacrifice and resulting reward as the control on their lives in all things, whether large or small. In ideal theory, their pleasure came from making the pleasure of others, or at least attempting it. Most authors accepted that the majority of their readership could only hold such a goal before them as a practically unattainable ideal, but it was widely agreed that such a theory represented Christianity for women in its best and most English form.

It is difficult to substantiate any claim that these books had the impact that they were intended to have. The likelihood remains that where these books were read and enjoyed, it was on a basis of the successful creation of a world divorced from everyday reality, especially when stories were set against income levels and styles of living distant from that of middle-class girls of varying levels of affluence. However, this does not alter the fact that contemporaries, particularly the authors, had a considerable faith in the impact of this didactic genre, and took considerable care to reflect the events as well as the attitudes of the period for which they were writing. Reference to affairs such as the Zulu War or the Boer War, for instance, abound in books published shortly after these conflicts made the headlines in England in the interest of ensuring the topicality of the message. It is also necessary to do the authors of these novels, mainly women, the justice of believing that they themselves accepted the opinions and attitudes they promulgated in their fiction, particularly as their lives, so far as current research can tell, shows that they tried to live up to the standards they held out to their readers for emulation.

Study of this genre reveals that many of the contradictions seen as inherent in the role of women in nineteenth-century England by modern scholars were not viewed in that light by contemporaries. The research of women like Felicity Hunt, Jane Lewis and many others, has shown that there were few among even the most radical pioneers of the women's movement in this period who did not continue to view society in terms of separate spheres for men and women. These pioneers saw the essential contribution that women could make to that society as stemming from the inborn differences between feminine and masculine nature. This fiction equally reveals little consciousness, by the turn of the century of a sense of that feminine sphere being in any way inferior to the masculine one. The two areas were, rather, put as complementary in fictional terms also. The *Household Fairy* stereotype that had dominated the thinking of women like Charlotte Yonge had given way only to the more robust version of the domestic ideal, in the shape of the *Home Goddess* put forward by popular authors like L.T. Meade, Evelyn Everett Green and Mrs George de Horne Vaizey.

Yet it must be emphasized that throughout, the good woman, either as *Household Fairy* or *Home Goddess*, was seen as a professional in her own sphere. The problems for the good girl, and for the author, came when she stepped outside her natural sphere, whether voluntarily or involuntarily. In the earlier period, such women were placed outside the bounds of normal middle-class society, forfeiting their right to marriage and motherhood as a result of their need or desire to earn a living in some fashion other than as a *Household Fairy*. The impracticality of continuing such an attitude forced society, as reflected in a new generation of authors, to rethink their dismissal of the growing numbers of women who had to seek remuneration outside their 'traditional' sphere. The continuing concern that becomes ever more prominent as the twentieth century approached was that women would cease to put their

PLATE 10   'I NOW PLACE ON HER HEAD THE WREATH OF BAY, AND
ROUND HER NECK THE CHAIN OF GOLD.'

A moral crown for a rose of virtue. From *The Beresford Prize*
by L.T. Meade (1890; 1907 edn)

domestic responsibilities first, by rejecting self-sacrifice as the greatest feminine attribute.

To this end, while accepting the expansion of the feminine sphere to include a wider range of responsibilities in areas outside the home, fiction stressed the established middle-class view that a degree of social control was necessary to ensure continuation of the essential domestic core to the feminine role. A number of elements with a tradition of use for such attempts was called into play, notably religion. The strong undercurrent of Christianity that runs through all these novels is a reflection of the importance accorded to it in life. Even when personal belief as reflected, for instance, by regular Church or Chapel attendance was not strong, most members of the middle classes found it wise if not absolutely necessary to pay lip-service to the established tenets, as in the case of Lady Allardyce in Evelyn Everett Green's *The Heiress of Wylmington*.[1]

Appeal was also made to the supposed capacity of a good girl or woman to influence those around her, particularly men, in the attempt to add to the importance of the traditional private role of women. L.T. Meade's heroines like *Bel-Marjory*, and those of Mrs George de Horne Vaizey like Nan Rendall in *A Houseful of Girls* are unquestioningly convinced of the effect they can have on the men with whom they come into contact. They are also supremely conscious of the responsibility that this power brings with it. As Nan said 'It was beautiful, inspiring – but, oh, what a responsibility ... To feel that another ... life depended on her for happiness – was this not a reflection to sober the most careless and light-hearted of natures?'[2]

The ultimate sanction, however, was the core of professionalism that ran through the period for both men and women. Amateurs of all kinds, regardless of sex, were not well regarded in their attempts to fulfil a role in life. It is not surprising, therefore, that established society attempted to use professionalism as a sanction on the activities of women from around the 1890s. A hierarchy of desirable professions was established, with the traditional career of *Home Goddess* heading the list.

---

[1] Evelyn Everett Green, *The Heiress of Wylmington* (Nelson, Walton-on-Thames, 1886).

[2] L.T. Meade, *Bel-Marjory: A Story of Conquest* (Shaw, London, 1878); Mrs George de Horne Vaizey, *A Houseful of Girls* (RTS, London, 1902), p. 245.

Following that were vocations which were regarded as still entailing exercise of the traditional feminine virtues, primarily self-sacrifice and caring for the sick or the young. Effectively this gave a high status to women who opted for careers as either nurses or teachers, and a lesser one to the more apparently self-indulgent options of being, say, a journalist or a clerk. Didactic fiction increasingly acted from that period as a guide to suitable careers for model maidens, advising on ways to judge personal suitability and ways to get the requisite training that any profession was presumed to require.

Fiction reflects, however, a swiftly growing concern that even so, women were becoming less inclined to opt for the most important and most demanding role, that of the *Home Goddess*. In reaction, society promulgated the idea that life-long dedication to a vocation outside the home was not automatically necessary. It became more and more common for fictional heroines such as Sister Molly Hepworth in L.T. Meade's *A Sister of the Red Cross* to be rewarded for professionalism and dedication in their work by being given the chance to marry and become a good woman in the most traditional sense. Molly's main desire is 'to benefit her fellow creatures', and after sterling service in a wider sphere in Africa, she returns home to act even more effectively as the wife of Captain Gavon Keith, who has himself deserved such a paragon by winning a Victoria Cross.[3]

The inevitable if unanticipated effect, though it was only beginning to make itself felt in the fiction of this period, was a devaluation of the professional status of women's work. Increasingly, it became seen not as a matter of life-long dedication to a particular calling, as in the case of most middle-class men, but as a temporary experience before the good girl returned to take up her duties as a wife and mother. It remained only for the ideal of the professional housewife to be devalued to rob women of the professional status that so many nineteenth-century authors viewed as being the greatest justification for the existence of separate spheres.

[3] L.T. Meade, *A Sister of the Red Cross: A Tale of the South African War* (Nelson, Walton-on-Thames, 1901), p. 10.

Bibliography

With the didactic fiction, whether directly quoted in the text or not, as far as possible reference is made to editions that are in the British Library. Where this has not been possible, as the British Library's holding in this respect is incomplete for a variety of reasons, the references are to editions in the author's own collection. As a result, the editions quoted are not always the first editions of the work in question, and where this occurs the first date of publication is also given in parentheses if known. Also it has not been possible to cite all the works of contemporary fiction perused, and the bibliography has been largely confined to works intended for the middle-class adolescent market, and largely to most representative works of the best-known authors. The prolific output of such writers means that a comprehensive bibliography would take up nearly a volume in its own right.

Works Published to 1914

ALOE (Charlotte M. Tucker), *Flora, or Self-Deception* (Nelson, Walton-on-Thames, 1911), 1st edn (1866).

Alford, Elizabeth M., *The Fair Maid of Taunton: A Tale of the Siege* (Shaw, London, 1878).

Armstrong, Annie E., *Three Bright Girls: A Story of Chance and Mischance* (Blackie, Glasgow, 1892).

——*Violet Vereker's Vanity* (Blackie, Glasgow, 1897).

Austen-Leigh, J., *Memoir of Jane Austen. By her nephew* (R. Bentley & Son, London, 1882).

Author of a Woman's Secret, *Woman's Work, or How She Can Help the Sick* (Longman, London, 1860).

Aylmer, Mrs J.E., *Distant Homes, or the Graham Family in New Zealand* (Griffith and Farras, London, 1881), 1st edn (1862).

Baldwin, May, *A Plucky Girl, or The Adventures of 'Miss Nell'* (Chambers, Edinburgh, 1902).

Bedford, H. Louisa, *The Twins that Did Not Pair* (RTS, London, 1898).

Bickersteth, Miss E., *Frances Leslie, or The Prayer Divinely Taught* (RTS, London, 1867).

Blaquiere, Dora de, 'How to Help in the House', *Girls' Own Annual,* XIII, Oct. 1891–Sept. 1892).

Boultwood, Harriett, *Martin's Mistake* (RTS, London, 1890).

Brodie, Emily, *Jean Lindsay, the Vicar's Daughter* (Shaw, London, 1878).

Burnett, Frances Hodgson, *A Little Princess: The Story of Sara Crewe* (Warne, London, 1905).

——*The Secret Garden* (Heinemann, London, 1911).

Burstall, Sara, *English High Schools for Girls: Their aims, organisation, and management* (Longman, London, 1907).

——*Frances Mary Buss, an Educational Pioneer* (SPCK, London, 1938).

Callcott, Lady Maria, *Little Arthur's History of England* (John Murray, London, 1860).

Callwell, J.M., *One Summer by the Sea* (Nelson, Walton-on-Thames, 1893).

Caulfeild, S.A., 'Some Types of Girlhood or Our Juvenile Spinsters', *Girls' Own Annual,* XII, Oct. 1890–Sept. 1891.

Chappell, Jennie, *For Honour's Sake* (Partridge., London, 1890).

——*Four Noble Women* (Partridge, London, 1898).

——*Madeleine, or The Tale of a Haunted House* (Partridge, London, 1894).

——*Noble Work by Noble Women: Sketches of the Lives of Baroness Burdett Coutts, Lady Henry Somerset, Miss Sarah Robinson, Mrs. Fawcett, Mrs. Gladstone* (Partridge, London, 1900).

——*Too Dearly Bought* (Partridge, London, 1901).

Coleridge, Christabel (ed.), *Charlotte Mary Yonge: Her Life and Letters* (Macmillan, London, 1903).

Corkran, Alice, *Down the Snow Stairs, or Between Good Night and Good Morning* (Blackie, Glasgow, 1887).

——*Marjory Merton's Girlhood* (Blackie, Glasgow, 1888).

——*The Romance of Women's Influence* (Blackie, Glasgow, 1906).

Craik, Mrs Dinah Mulock, *Agatha's Husband: A Novel* (Ward Lock & Co., London, 1853).

——*John Halifax, Gentleman* (Nisbet, Welwyn, 1898), 1st edn (1856).

——*A Woman's Thoughts About Women* (Hurst & Blackett, London, 1858).

Davis, Ellen Louisa, *Asceline's Ladder* (RTS, London, 1892).

——*Yoked Together: A Tale of Three Sisters* (Nisbet, Welwyn, 1885).

Dawson, Ethel, *A Happy Failure: A Story for Girls* (Nelson, Walton-on-Thames, 1903).

Doudney, Sarah, *Monksbury College: A Tale of Schoolgirl Life* (Sunday School Union, London, 1878).

Ellis, Havelock, *Man and Woman: A Study of Human Secondary Sexual Characters*, Contemporary Science Series (Walter Scott, London, 1894).

Ewing, Mrs Juliana H., *Jackanapes* (Christian Knowledge Society, London, 1884).

——*Six to Sixteen: A Story for Girls*, Queen's Treasure Series (Bell, London, 1908), 1st edn (1876).

Geddes, Patrick and Thompson, J. Arthur, *The Evolution of Sex*, Contemporary Science Series, (Walter Scott, London, 1889).

Gellie, Mary E., *Stephen the School-Master: A Story without a Plot* (Griffith & Farran, London, 1879).

Giberne, Agnes, *A Lady of England: The Life and Letters of Charlotte Maria Tucker* (Hodder & Stoughton, London, 1895).

——*The Dalrymples* (Nisbet, Welwyn, 1891).

——*Decima's Promise* (Nisbet, Welwyn, 1882).

——*Kathleen: The Story of a Home* (Nisbet, Welwyn, 1883).

——*Miss Con, or All Those Girls* (Nisbet, Welwyn, 1887).

Girls and Their Ways, by One who Knows Them: A book for and about Girls (John Hogg, London, 1881).

Gray, E. Conder, *Wise Words and Loving Deeds: A Book of Biographies for Girls*, Lives Worth Living Series (Marshall Japp, London, 1880).

Green, Edith M., *The Cape Cousins* (Wells, Gardner & Darton, London, 1902).

Green, Evelyn Everett, *Arnold Inglehurst, the Preacher: A Story of the Fen Country* (Shaw, London, 1896).

——*Barbara's Brothers* (RTS, London, 1888).

——*The Church and the King: A Tale of the Days of England in the Henry VIII* (Nelson, Walton-on-Thames, 1892).

——*A Clerk of Oxford, and His Adventures in the Barons' War*

(Nelson, Walton-on-Thames, 1898).

——*The Cossart Cousins* (Leisure Hour Monthly Library, London, 1908), 1st edn (1903).

——*Dare Lorimer's Heritage* (Hutchinson, London, 1891).

——*Dickie and Dorrie: A Tale of Hallowdene Hall* (Wells, Gardner & Co., London, 1906).

——*A Difficult Daughter* (Sunday School Union, London, 1895).

——*Dorothy's Vocation* (Oliphant, Edinburgh, 1890).

——*For the Queen's Sake* (Nelson, Walton-on-Thames, 1898).

——*Greyfriars: A Story for Girls* (Leisure Hour Monthly Library, London, 1905), 1st edn (1890).

——*Half-A-Dozen Sisters* (RTS, London, 1910), 1st edn (1905).

——*The Head of the House: The Story of a Victory over Passion and Pride* (RTS, London, 1886).

——*The Heiress of Wylmington* (Nelson, Walton-on-Thames, 1886).

——*Her Husband's Home, or The Durleys of Linley Castle* (Shaw, London, 1887).

——*In Pursuit of a Phantom* (RTS, London, 1906) 1st edn (1905).

——*In the Days of Chivalry: A Tale of the Times of the Black Prince* (Nelson, Walton-on-Thames, 1893).

——*The Jilting of Bruce Heriot* (RTS, London, 1904).

——*Joint Guardians* (RTS, London, 1887).

——*The Lord of Dynevor: A Tale of the Time of Edward the First* (Nelson, Walton-on-Thames, 1982).

——*Maud Melville's Marriage* (Nelson, Walton-on-Thames, 1893).

——*Miriam's Ambition* (Blackie, Glasgow, 1889).

——*Miss Greyshoot's Girls* (Melrose, Ely, 1905).

——*Miss Marjorie of Silvermead* (Hutchinson, London, 1899).

——*My Cousin from Australia* (Hutchinson, London, 1894).

——*My Lady Joanna. Being a Chronicle concering the King's Children. Rendered into Modern English from the Records left by the Lady Edeline* (Nisbet, Welwyn, 1902).

——*The Mystery of Alton Grange* (Nelson, Walton-on-Thames, 1899).

——*Olive Roscoe, or The New Sister* (Nelson, Walton-on-Thames, 1896).

——*The Percivals, or A Houseful of Girls* (RTS, London, 1903) 1st edn (1890).

——*Ruth Ravelstan, the Puritan's Daughter* (Nelson, Walton-on-Thames, 1907), 1st edn (1901).

——*The Sign of the Red Cross: A Tale of Old London* (Nelson, Walton-on-Thames, 1897).

——*Sister: A Chronicle of Fair Haven* (Nelson, Walton-on-Thames, 1898).

——*The Squire's Heir* (Melrose, Ely, 1903).

——*The Sunny Side of the Street* (RTS, London, 1895).

——*Temple's Trial, or For Life or Death* (Nelson, Walton-on-Thames, 1887).

——*Two Enthusiasts* (RTS, London, 1888).

——*Vera's Trust* (Nelson, Walton-on-Thames, 1889).

——*Winning The Victory, or Di Pennington's Reward* (Nelson, Walton-on-Thames, 1886).

——and Bedford, H. Louisa, *Priscilla: A Story for Girls* (Nelson, Walton-on-Thames, 1900).

Greene, Hon. Mrs E., *On Angels' Wings* (Nelson, Walton-on-Thames, 1885).

Grey, Maria G., 'Education of Women'. Letter to the Editor of *The Times*, London, 1871.

——*Old Maids: A Lecture* (William Ridgeway, London, 1875).

Guernsey, Lucy Ellen, *The Foster Sisters: A Story of the Days of Wesley and Whitfield* (Shaw, London, 1882).

——*Lady Betty's Governess, or The Corbet Chronicles* (Shaw, London, 1878).

——*The Orphan Nieces, or Duty and Inclination* (Anson D. Randolph, New York, 1857).

——*Winifred, or An English Maiden in the Seventeenth Century* (Shaw, London, 1878).

Haverfield, E.L., *Blind Loyalty. A Sequel to Our Vow*, (Nelson, Walton-on-Thames, 1900).

——*Our Vow* (Nelson, Walton-on-Thames, 1899).

——*Queensland Cousins* (Nelson, Walton-on-Thames, 1903).

——*Rhoda. A Tale for Girls* (Nelson, Walton-on-Thames, 1901).

Heddle, Ethel F., *An Original Girl* (Blackie, Glasgow, 1901).

Henty, G.A., *Saint George for England. A Tale of Cressy and Poitiers* (Blackie, Glasgow, 1885).

Holt, Emily S., *Ashcliffe Hall: A Tale of the Last Century* (Shaw, London, 1870).

——*Clare Avery: A Story of the Spanish Armada* (Shaw, London, 1876).

——*Earl Hubert's Daughter, or The Polishing of the Pearl* (Shaw, London, 1880).

——*Imogen: A Tale of the Early British Church* (Shaw, London, 1886).

——*The King's Daughters, or How Two Girls Kept the Faith* (Shaw, London, 1888).

——*Lady Sybil's Choice: A Tale of the Crusades* (Shaw, London, 1879).

——*Mistress Margery. A Tale of the Lollards* (Shaw, London, 1868).

——*One Snowy Night, or Long Ago at Oxford* (Shaw, London, 1893).

——*Out in the '45; or, Duncan Keith's Vow. A Tale* (Shaw, London, 1888).

——*Red and White: A Tale of the Wars of the Roses* (Shaw, London, 1882).

——*Sister Rose, or The Eve of St. Bartholomew* (Shaw, London, 1870).

——*A Tangled Web. A Tale of the Fifteenth Century* (Shaw, London, 1885).

Jacberns, Raymond, *Four Every-Day Girls* (SPCK, London, 1900).

Johnson, Joseph, *Clever Girls of Our Time, and How they became Famous Women* (Gall & Inglis, London, 1863).

Kipling, Rudyard, *Kim* (Macmillan, London, 1901).

——*Puck of Pook's Hill* (Macmillan, London, 1906).

Lee, M. and Lee, C., *The Family Coach. Who Filled It, Who Drove It, and Who Seized the Reins* (National Society's Depository, London, 1891).

Le Feuvre, Amy, *Odd* (RTS, London, 1910), 1st edn (1894).

——*Olive Tracy* (RTS, London, 1902).

Lowndes, Cecilia Selby, *Miss Hope's Niece, or Esmee's Choice. A Story for Girls* (Seeley, London, 1889).

MacIntosh, Robert, *From Comte to Benjamin Kidd: The Appeal to Biology, or Evolution for Human Guidance* (Macmillan, London, 1899).

Marchant, Bessie, *A Brave Little Cousin* (SPCK, London, 1902).

——*Cicely Frome: The Captain's Daughter* (Nimmo, Hay & Mitchell, London, 1900).

——*A Girl of the Fortunate Isles* (Blackie, Glasgow, 1907).

——*A Heroine of the Sea* (Blackie, Glasgow, 1904).

——*No Ordinary Girl* (Blackie, Glasgow, 1905).

——*Three Girls on a Ranch: A Story of New Mexico* (Blackie, Glasgow, 1901).

Markham, Mrs, *A History of England* (John Murray, London, 1859).

Marryat, Captain F., *The Children of the New Forest* (Hurst, London, 1847).

Marshall, B., *Emma Marshall: A Biographical Sketch* (Seeley, London, 1900).

Marshall, Mrs Emma, *The Birth of the Century, or Eighty Years Ago* Nisbet, Welwyn, 1881).

——*Constantia Carew: An Autobiography* (Seeley, London, 1883).

——*Eastward Ho!* (Nisbet, Welwyn, 1890).

——*Grace Buxton, or The Light of Home* (Nisbet, Welwyn, 1869).

——*A Good-Hearted Girl, Or, A Present-Day Heroine* (Chambers, Edinburgh, 1899).

——*Her Season in Bath. A Story of By-Gone Days* (Seeley, London, 1889).

——*Houses on Wheels* Nisbet, Welwyn, 1888).

——*Laurel Crowns, or Griselda's Aim: A Story for Brothers and Sisters* (Nisbet, Welwyn, 1889).

——*Over the Down, or A Chapter of Accidents* (Nelson, Walton-on-Thames, 1885).

——*Violet Douglas, or The Problems of Life* (Seeley, London, 1868).

Maudsley, Henry, *The Physiology of the Mind* (Macmillan, London, 3rd edn, 1876).

Meade, L.T., *Bel-Marjory: A Story of Conquest* (Shaw, London, 1878).

——*The Beresford Prize* (Longman, London, 1890).

——*Betty: A School Girl* (Chambers, Edinburgh, 1895).

——*Dorothy's Story, or Great St. Benedicts* ((Shaw, London, 1879).

——*Engaged to be Married: A Tale of Today* (Simpkin, Marshall, Hamilton, Kent & Co., London, 1890).

——*Four on an Island: A Story of Adventure* (Chambers, Edinburgh, 1892).

——*A Gay Charmer: A Story for Girls* (Chambers, Edinburgh, 1903).

——*Girls of Mrs. Pritchard's School* (Chambers, Edinburgh, 1904).

——*A Knight of Today* (Shaw, London, 1877).

——*A Madcap* (Cassell, London, 1904).

——*The Manor School* (Chambers, Edinburgh, 1904).

——*Miss Nonentity* (Chambers, Edinburgh, 1900).

——*Nurse Charlotte, A Story for Girls* (Nelson, Walton-on-Thames, 1904).

——*The Palace Beautiful. A Story for Girls* (Cassell, London, 1887).

——*Red Rose and Tiger Lily* (Cassell, London, 1894).

——*Ring of Rubies* (Innes, London, 1892).

——*The School Queens* (Chambers, Edinburgh, 1903).

——*A Sister of the Red Cross: A Tale of the South African War* (Nelson, Walton-on-Thames, 1901).

——*A Sweet Girl Graduate* (Cassell, London, 1891).

——*A World of Girls: The Story of a School* (Cassell, London, 1886).

Molesworth, Mrs Mary, *The Carved Lions* (Macmillan, London, 1895).

——*The Laurel Walk* (Isbister, London, 1898).

——*Little Mother Bunch* (Cassell, London, 1890).

——*Robin Redbreast: A Story for Girls* (Chambers, Edinburgh, 1892).

——*White Turrets* (Chambers, Edinburgh, 1896).

Mulholland, Rosa, (Lady Gilbert), *Cynthia's Bonnet Shop* (Blackie, Glasgow, 1901).

——*A Girl's Ideal* (Blackie, Glasgow, 1905).

——*Hetty Gray, or Nobody's Bairn* (Blackie, Glasgow, 1884).

Norgate, Kate, *England Under the Angevin Kings*, 2 vols (Macmillan, London, 1877).

Normanby, Lord, *The Contrast* (H. Colbum & R. Bentley, London, 1832).

Oliphant, Linton, Alexander et al., *Women Novelists of Queen Victoria's Reign* (Hurst and Blackett, London, 1897).

Parkes-Belloc, Mrs Bessie, *Peoples of the World* (Cassell, London, 1870).

Phipps, C.M.K., *Douglas Archdale: A Tale of Lucknow* (London Literary Society, London, 1885).

Pitman, Mrs Emma R., *Lady Missionaries in Foreign Lands* (Partridge, London, 1889).

——*Indian Zenana Missions*, Outline Missionary Series (John Snow, London, 1881).

——*Missionary Heroines In Eastern Lands. Woman's Work in Mis-

sion Fields (Partridge, London, 1895).

——*My Governess Life; or, Using My One Talent* (Blackie, Glasgow, 1883).

Pollard, Eliza F., *Florence Nightingale, the Wounded Soldier's Friend* (Partridge, London, 1891).

——*The Lady Isobel. A Story for Girls* (Blackie, Glasgow, 1899).

——*My Lady Marcia. A Story of the French Revolution* (Nelson, Walton-on-Thames, 1901).

——*The White Dove of Amritsar. A Romance of Anglo-Indian Life* (Partridge, London, 1896).

Pollard, M.M., *Cora, or Three Years of a Girl's Life* (The Girls' Own Paper' Office, London, 1882).

——*Dorothy Tresilis, or Down at Polwin* (RTS, London, 1888).

Ruskin, John, *Sesame and Lilies* (Smith Elder & Co., London, 1865).

Sewell, Eleanor L. (ed.), *The Autobiography of Elizabeth Sewell* (Longman, London, 1907).

Sewell, Elizabeth M., *Amy Herbert*, 2 vols (Longman, London, 1844).

——*The Experience of Life* (Longman, London, 1853).

——*Principles of Education Drawn from Nature and Revelation, and Applied to Female Education in the Upper Classes* (Longman, London, 1886).

——*Ursula, A Tale of Country Life* (Longman, London, 1858).

Snow, Laura Barter, *Honour's Quest, or How They Came Home* (RTS, London, 1903).

Spencer, Herbert, *The Principles of Ethics*, 2 vols (Williams & Norgate, London, 1892).

Stickney Ellis, Sarah, *The Daughters of England* (Fisher, Son and Co., London, 1845).

——*The Education of Character, with Hints on Moral Training* (John Murray, London, 1856).

Strickland, Agnes, *Lives of the Queens of England* (Colburn, London, 1851–2).

Stronach, Alice, *A Newnham Friendship* (Blackie, Glasgow, 1901).

Swan, Annie S., *Across Her Path* (Oliphant, Edinburgh, 2nd edn, 1902).

Taylor, Ann and Taylor, Jane, *The Poetical Works* (Ward Lock and Tyler, London, 1877).

Tennyson, Alfred, Lord, *Idylls of the King* (Moxon, London, 1859).

Thomas, Evelyn L., *Ruth's Path to Victory* (RTS, London, 1898).
Turner, Ethel S., *The Family at Misrule* (Ward Lock, London, 1895).
——*Seven Little Australians* (Ward Lock, London, 1894).
Tynan, Katherine, *Three Fair Maids, or The Burkes of Derrymore* (Blackie, Glasgow, 1901).
Tytler, Sarah, *Girl Neighbours, or The Old Fashion and the New* (RTS, London, 1888).
——*A Lonely Lassie. A Tale* (RTS, London, 1893).
——*Papers for Thoughtful Girls: With Sketches of some Girls' Lives* (Daldy, Isbister & Co., Edinburgh, 1862).
Vaizey, Mrs George de Horne, *About Peggy Saville* (RTS, London, 1900).
——*Betty Trevor* (RTS, London, 1907), 1st edn (1905).
——*The Daughters of a Genius. A Story of Brave Endeavour* (Chambers, Edinburgh, 1903).
——*A Houseful of Girls* (RTS, London, 1902).
——*More About Peggy* (RTS, London, 1901).
——*Pixie O'Shaughnessy* (RTS, London, 1903).
——*Sisters Three* (Cassell, London, 1900).
——*Tom and Some Other Girls: A Public School Story* (Cassell, London, 1901).
Warner, Anna B., *Susan Warner ('Elizabeth Wetherell')* (G.B. Putnam's Sons, New York, 1909).
Watson, Lily, *A Fortunate Exile: A Story of Swiss School Life* (RTS, London, 1896).
——*The Mountain Path* (RTS, London, 1888).
——*What Shall I Read?* (RTS, London, 1887).
Weighall, C.E.C., *The Temptation of Dulce Carruthers* (Cassell, London, 1893).
Wetherell, Elizabeth (Susan Warner), *Ellen Montgomery's Bookcase* (Nisbet, Welwyn, 1853).
——*Nobody* (Nisbet, Welwyn, 1882).
——*Queechy* (Warne, London, 1877).
——*The Wide, Wide World* (Bliss, Sands & Co., London, 1896), 1st edn (1852).
Witts, Florence, *In the Day of His Power: A Story of Christian Endeavour* (Sunday School Union, London, 1902).
Wood, Mary Anne, *Letters of Royal and Illustrious Ladies of Great Britain, from the commencement of the twelfth century to the close of the reign of Queen Mary. Edited chiefly from the originals*, 3 vols

(H. Colburn, London, 1846).

——*Lives of the Princesses of England, from the Norman Conquest*, 6 vols (H. Colburn, London, 1849–55).

——*The Sisters of Trenton Manse* (Sunday School Union, London, 1902).

Yonge, Charlotte M., *Aunt Charlotte's Stories from English History for the Little Ones* (Marcus Ward & Co., London, 1873).

——*Beechcroft at Rockstone*, 2 vols (Macmillan, London, 1888).

——*A Book of Golden Deeds* (Macmillan, London, 1888).

——*The Chaplet of Pearls* (Macmillan, London, 1871), 1st edn (1868).

——'Children's Literature in the Last Century', *Macmillan's Magazine*, XX, May–Oct. 1869.

——*The Clever Woman of the Family* (Virago Press, London, 1983), 1st edn (1865).

——*Countess Kate* (Macmillan, London, 1863).

——*The Daisy Chain* (Macmillan, London, 1856).

——*English Church History* (National Society's Depository, London, 1883).

——*Heartsease, or The Brother's Wife* (Macmillan, London, 1865).

——*The Little Duke, or Richard the Fearless* (Macmillan, London, 1854).

——*The Making of a Missionary, or Daydreams in Earnest* (National Society's Depository, London, 1900).

——*Practical Work in Sunday Schools, by Charlotte Mary Yonge, a Teacher of Many Years' Standing*, Religious Knowledge Manuals (National Society's Depository, London, 1881).

——*Scenes and Characters, or Eighteen Months at Beechcroft* (Macmillan, London, 1886).

——*Stray Pearls* (Macmillan, London, 1888).

——*The Trial: More Links of the Daisy Chain* (Macmillan, London, 1883).

——*The Two Sides of the Shield* (Macmillan, London, 1885).

——*Unknown to History: A Story of the Captivity of Mary of Scotland* (Macmillan, London, 1882).

——*The Young Stepmother* (Macmillan, London, 1865).

——(ed.), *Biographies of Good Women: 'More Precious than Rubies'* (J. & C. Mozley, London, 1862).

A large number of newspapers and periodicals were consulted for reviews and publishers' notices, of the books and their message. Both newspapers and periodicals, but chiefly the latter, were consulted for interviews with authors. The most useful in these respects are given below.

Aunt Judy's Annual Volume
The Bookseller
Cassells' Magazine
The Christian
The Contemporary Review
Girls' Own Paper
Macmillan's Magazine
The Manchester Guardian
The Morning Post
The Monthly Packet
Pearson's Magazine
Publishers' Circular
The Strand Magazine
The Times
The Windsor Magazine

Secondary Sources

Abel-Smith, Brian, *A History of the Nursing Profession* (Heinemann, London, 1960).

Adburgham, Alison, *Silver Fork Society: Fashionable Life and Literature from 1814 to 1840* (Constable, London, 1983).

Alexander, Sally, 'Women, Class and Sexual Difference in the 1830s and 1840s: Some Reflections on the Writing of a Feminist History', *History Workshop Journal*, 17, 1984, pp. 125–49.

Ariès, Philippe, *Centuries of Childhood* (Jonathan Cape, London, 1962).

Arnold, Guy, *Held Fast for England: G.A. Henty, Imperialist Boys' Writer* (Hamish Hamilton, London, 1980).

Arnstein, Walter L., *Protestant versus Catholic in Mid-Victorian England: Mr. Newdegate and the Nuns* (University of Missouri Press, Columbia, 1982).

Avery, Gillian, *Childhood's Pattern: A Study of the Heroes and*

Heroines of Children's Fiction, 1770–1950 (Hodder & Stoughton, London, 1975).

——*Mrs. Ewing* (Bodley Head, London, 1961).

——*Victorian People in Life and Literature* (Collins, London, 1970).

Basch, Françoise, *Relative Creatures: Victorian Women in Society and the Novel, 1837–67* (Allen Lane, London, 1974).

Battiscombe, Georgina, *Charlotte May Yonge: The Story of an Uneventful Life* (Constable, London, 1943).

Blackie, Agnes, *Blackie and Son: A Short History of the Firm 1809–1959* (Blackie, Glasgow, 1959).

Branca, Patricia, *Silent Sisterhood: Middle Class Women in the Victorian Home* (Croom Helm, London, 1975).

Bratton, J.S., *The Impact of Victorian Children's Fiction* (Croom Helm, London, 1981).

Briggs, H.Y. John and Sellers, Ian (eds), *Victorian Nonconformity* (Edward Arnold, London, 1973).

Burman, S. (ed.), *Fit Work for Women* (Croom Helm, London, 1979).

Burstyn, Joan, *Victorian Education and the Ideal of Womanhood* (Croom Helm, London, 1980).

Cadogan, Mary and Craig, Patricia, *You're A Brick, Angela! The Girls' Story 1839–1985* (Victor Gollancz, London, 1986).

Calder, Jenni, *Women and Marriage in Victorian Fiction* (Thames & Hudson, London, 1976).

Coveney, P., *The Image of Childhood* (Penguin, Harmondsworth, 1967).

Crawford, Patricia (ed.), *Exploring Women's Past: Essays in Social History* (George Allen & Unwin, Sydney, 1983).

Davidoff, Leonore, *The Best Circles: Society, Etiquette and the Season* (Hutchinson, London, 1986).

——and Hall, Catherine, *Family Fortunes: Men and Women of the English Middle Class, 1780–1850* (Hutchinson, London, 1987).

Davin, Anna, 'Imperialism and Motherhood', *History Workshop*, 5, 1978, pp. 9–65.

Delamount, Sara and Duffin, Lorna (eds), *The Nineteenth-Century Woman: Her Cultural and Physical World* (Croom Helm, London, 1978).

Dempster, J.A., 'Thomas Nelson and Sons in the Late Nineteenth Century: A Study in Motivation', *Publishing His-*

tory, Part I, 13, 1983, pp. 41–87; Part II, 14, 1984, pp. 5–63.

Dyhouse, Carol, *Girls Growing Up in Late Victorian and Edwardian England* (Routledge & Kegan Paul, London, 1981).

Eastlea, Brian, *Science and Sexual Oppression* (Weidenfeld & Nicolson, London, 1981).

Eldridge, C.C., *England's Mission: The Imperial Idea in the Age of Gladstone and Disraeli* (Macmillan, London, 1973).

——(ed.), *British Imperialism in the Nineteenth Century* (Macmillan, London, 1984).

Elshtain, Jean Bethke, *Public Man, Private Woman: Women in Social and Political Thought* (Martin Robertson, Oxford, 1981).

Gilbert, A.D., *Religion and Society in Industrial England: Church, Chapel and Social Change 1740–1914* (Longman, London, 1976).

Girouard, Mark, *The Return to Camelot: Chivalry and the English Gentleman* (Yale University Press, New Haven, 1981).

Golby, J.M. and Purdue, A.W., *The Civilisation of the Crowd: Popular Culture in England 1750–1900* (Batsford, London, 1984).

Gorham, Deborah, *The Victorian Girl and the Feminine Ideal* (Croom Helm, London, 1982).

Harrison, Brian, *Separate Spheres: The Opposition to Women's Suffrage in Britain* (Croom Helm, London, 1978).

Hobsbawm, E.J. and Ranger, Terence (eds), *The Invention of Tradition* (Cambridge University Press, Cambridge, 1983).

Holcombe, Lee, *Victorian Ladies at Work: Middle-Class Working Women in England and Wales, 1850–1914* (David & Charles, Newton Abbot, 1973).

——*Wives and Property: Reform of the Married Women's Property Law in Nineteenth-Century England* (Martin Robertson, Oxford, 1983).

Hollis, Patricia, *Ladies Elect: Women in English Local Government 1865–1914* (Oxford University Press, Oxford, 1987).

Hunt, Felicity (ed.), *Lessons for Life: The Schooling of Girls and Women 1850–1950* (Basil Blackwell, Oxford, 1987).

Hyam, R., *Britain's Imperial Century 1815–1914: A Study of Empire and Expansion* (Methuen, London, 1976).

——and Martin, G.W., *Reappraisals In British Imperial History* (Macmillan, London, 1975).

John, Angela V.(ed.), *Unequal Opportunities: Women's Employment in England 1800–1918* (Basil Blackwell, Oxford, 1987).

Kamm, Josephine, *Hope Deferred: Girls' Education in English History* (Methuen, London, 1965).

——*How Different from Us: A Biography of Miss Buss and Miss Béale* (Bodley Head, London, 1958).

Levine, Philippa, *Victorian Feminism 1850–1900* (Hutchinson, London, 1987).

Lewis, Jane, *Women in England 1870–1950: Sexual Divisions and Social Change* (Wheatsheaf Books, Brighton, 1986).

——(ed.), *Labour and Love: Women's Experience of Home and Family, 1850–1940* (Basil Blackwell, Oxford, 1987).

MacKenzie, John M. (ed.), *Imperialism and Popular Culture* (Manchester University Press, Manchester, 1986).

Manton, Jo, *Sister Dora: The Life of Dorothy Pattison* (Methuen, London, 1971).

Moore, Katherine, *Victorian Wives* (Allison & Busby, London, 1985).

Pedersen, Joyce, S., 'Schoolmistresses and Headmistresses: Elites and Education in Nineteenth Century England', *Journal of British Studies* XV, 1975, 1, pp. 135–62.

——'Some Victorian Headmistreses: A Conservative Tradition of Social Reform', *Victorian Studies*, 24, summer 1981, pp. 463–88.

Pinchbeck, Ivy and Hewitt, Margaret, *Children in English Society*, 2 vols (Routledge & Kegan Paul, London, 1973).

Prochaska, F.K., *Women and Philanthropy in Nineteenth-Century England* (Oxford University Press, Oxford, 1980).

Pugh, Martin, *The Tories and the People 1880–1935* (Basil Blackwell, Oxford, 1985).

Quigly, Isobel, *The Heirs of Tom Brown: The English School Story* (Chatto & Windus, London, 1982).

Radford, Jean, (ed.), *The Progress of Romance: The Politics of Popular Fiction*, History Workshop Series (Routledge & Kegan Paul, London, 1986).

Reader, W.J., *Professional Men: The Rise of the Professional Classes in Nineteenth-Century England* (Weidenfeld & Nicolson, London, 1966).

Rendall, Jane (ed.), *Equal or Different: Women's Politics 1800–1914* (Basil Blackwell, Oxford, 1987).

Rosaldo, Michelle Zimbalist and Lamphere, Louise (eds), *Woman, Culture and Society* (Stanford University Press, Stanford, 1974).

Rubenstein, D., *Before the Suffragettes: Women's Emancipation in the 1890s* (Harvester Press, Brighton, 1986).

Showalter, Elaine, *A Literature of Their Own: British Women Novelists from Bronte to Lessing* (Virago Press, London, 1984).

Sutherland, J.A., *Victorian Novelists and Publishers* (University of Chicago Press, Chicago, 1976).

Thompson, F.M.L., *English Landed Society in the Nineteenth Century* (Routledge & Kegan Paul, London, 1963).

Vicinus, Martha, *Independent Women: Work and Community for Single Women 1850–1920* (Virago Press, London, 1985).

——(ed.), *A Widening Sphere: Changing Roles of Victorian Women* (Methuen, London, 1980).

——(ed.), *Suffer and Be Still: Women in the Victorian Age* (Methuen, London, 1980).

Index

Works cited are by title, for lists under author see bibliography